INDOMITABLE
SACRAMENTANS

INDOMITABLE SACRAMENTANS

A Social History of Catholics
in the State Capital

STEVEN M. AVELLA

AMERICA
THROUGH TIME®
ADDING COLOR TO AMERICAN HISTORY

America Through Time is an imprint of Fonthill Media LLC
www.through-time.com
office@through-time.com

Published by Arcadia Publishing by arrangement with Fonthill Media LLC
For all general information, please contact Arcadia Publishing:
Telephone: 843-853-2070
Fax: 843-853-0044
E-mail: sales@arcadiapublishing.com
For customer service and orders:
Toll-Free 1-888-313-2665

www.arcadiapublishing.com

First published 2023

ISBN 978-1-63499-453-8

Typeset in 10.5pt on13pt Sabon
Printed and bound in England

Acknowledgments

I am grateful to those who helped me produce this book.

Dr. Joseph M. White and Dr. Angelyn Dries read the initial drafts and offered helpful comments.

I found many of the pictures I used in this book at the Center for Sacramento History, which houses the photo morgues of the *Sacramento Bee* and the *Catholic Herald*. I thank Kim Hayden, Nicholas Piontek, and my friend, director Marcia Eymann, for their help.

The Nevada Historical Society in Reno provided some of the photos. I thank Dr. Catherine Magee for her kindness.

The picture of Dr. Gregory Phelan is from the California Room of the California State Library. Mr. Michael Dolgushkin located it. The microfilm and library collections of this library were invaluable. My thanks to all the staff.

The Archives of the Sisters of the Cenacle, North American Province, gave me access to their records and sent me some of the photos used in the book. I thank Archivist Jerice Barrios and the Sisters for their help.

The indefatigable and patient Ms. Jean Iacino offered critical production assistance. I thank the people at Fonthill Media for their good work.

I dedicate this book in gratitude to the countless Sacramento Catholics who toiled in anonymity to build the local church and to implement the value of their faith in the public sphere. Their names are often forgotten, except by the God who inspired them. May their memory be a blessing.

Steven M. Avella
March 19, 2022

Contents

Introduction

Pope Francis notes: "the decisive events of history" were always marked by people "whom no history book ever mentions." This is a book about some of mostly unknown people whose religious values contributed to the development of Sacramento—a place that had many such citizens. They are mostly locked in old books, newspaper accounts, and photographs. Some have been freed from obscurity by new historical perspectives.

Religious beliefs, religious leaders, ordinary believers, and institutions have played a critical role in global history and in the formation of national and especially city life. Sacramento's religious institutions provided critical services to the city (health care and education). Religious buildings occupied important urban space. Faith communities helped the city adjust to various waves of immigrants who came to settle in the Californian capital. Religion also provided an outlet for public philanthropy, charitable action, and ethnic leadership. Sacramento's history is incomplete without some understanding the contributions of its variety of religious bodies and individuals. People do things because they believe. This book uses the Catholic Church in Sacramento as a case study to examine the role of hitherto unexamined men and women in important areas of urban life. Hopefully, it will reveal a hidden sub-stratum of human "agency" in public life.

Catholicism is a belief system of great antiquity, brought to the Americas by Europeans. Catholicism is a set of beliefs, but also a way of life, a religious culture, and a powerful shaper of imagination. The Catholic Church provides an agenda for moral and ethical behavior. One could say this of all the religious bodies in Sacramento, but few had the physical presence and institutional breadth of the Catholic Church.

I have written on this theme in other works and mostly focused on the role of Catholic elites: bishops, priests, and religious sisters. Indeed, one could not write a historically accurate account of Catholicism in Sacramento without referring to them. However, the emphasis on these elites has traditionally overshadowed the agency of "ordinary" men and women who were not only the cooperators in this task, but in some instances, the initiators and always the primary economic resources for Catholic works. This book will advance a sharper picture of the role of lay Catholics (*i.e.*, those not ordained or taking religious vows).

This is not a new direction in historical writing. For nearly a generation, social and cultural historians have focused on a history "from the bottom up." It has provided students of history with a fuller, richer, and more complete account of the past. Thanks to many local historians, we know more about the "agency" of heretofore hidden actors in Sacramento history: women, African Americans, and "ordinary" citizens. We can better appreciate the impact of ideas, ideologies, and popular movements when we see them in action in the lives of people.

This book reveals a new set of characters who believed and acted with significant implications for the institutional and spiritual lives of their co-religionists and the city. For faith communities like the Catholic Church that are hierarchical and heavily invested in institutional development, this study provides an important insight into the reality of lived religion. "Lived religion" is hard to quantify and poses a challenge to researchers searching for reliable sources. However, the social and cultural realities of religious communities require some appreciation of the religious beliefs and cultural values of ordinary believers. The "faithful" are mostly anonymous, but never invisible. The monuments of Catholic life in Sacramento are often the result of the efforts of nameless people who took the initiative apart from the clergy. They raised funds, contributed labor, and provided materials and organizers that transformed the local environment. Catholics believe in a "communion of saints." These invisible figures are an important part of that touching church doctrine.

Sacramento has been the subject of several studies—both professional and popular—over the years.[1] Sacramento's development reflected the geographic and demographic trends of the Central Valley.[2] Stretching for 450 miles north to south between Redding and Bakersfield, this broad, watered, and rich farmland became the agricultural heartland of the state and supplier to the nation. Spanish and Mexican outposts were scarce in this broad valley (there were no missions), but nonetheless, large land grants and the forces of the gold rush and the railroad enabled the growth of communities such as Redding, Red Bluff, Oroville, Marysville, Stockton, Fresno, Modesto, and Bakersfield. Sacramento itself traced its origins to the contested boundaries of the land grant to Johan Sutter and even more to the gold rush and the advent of the Central Pacific Railroad. Chosen as the state capital in 1854 and repeatedly surmounting natural and human-made disaster, Sacramento has a fascinating history that stretches the full length of California's Euro-American history.

This book offers a new perspective on local religious history. Among other things, it challenges some long-held myths about the origins of Catholic life, underscores the importance of women in church-building (a must for a patriarchal Catholic Church), points to hidden Catholic benefactors whose resources and organizational skills are easily forgotten, and surfaces the role of lay leadership in establishing immigrant space in the city. Catholic men and women, motivated by the tenets of their faith, played an important role in Sacramento's public life. As in other parts of the United States, they endured their share of discrimination based on their faith. Catholics also maintained their own "tribal" culture by occasionally demonstrating their faith in public. These celebrations often spilled into the streets, winning press attention and manifesting the visibility of Catholic numbers. Catholic celebrations were often the chosen vehicles of ethnic pride.

Equally important is the extent to which the Catholic citizens of Sacramento absorbed and identified with Sacramento's "indomitability." Although built on a precarious location, Sacramento refused to succumb to floods, fires, and the threats of a sometimes-bullying railroad for more land. They built higher levees, raised up the streets, fought back against business exploitation, improved their city services, and developed their surrounding lands. Sacramento Catholics were also fighters—erecting over and over again an earlier church at Seventh and K Streets (St. Rose), and then building a magnificent cathedral just one block north of the state capitol buildings. They managed ethnic growth, developed health care facilities and shelters for dependent children. Catholics were among the city's leadership and refused to accept second-class status whether it was imposed by nativist organizations such as the Ku Klux Klan. Wherever the people went, the Catholic Church was there. Sacramento Catholics were indomitable—in fact, they may have been the only ones to understand the early city motto written in Latin: "*urbs indomita.*"

Writing this sort of history has its rewards and pitfalls. Positively, we can appreciate more accurately the extent to which lay men and women—often working behind the scenes—made possible providing for the sick, demonstrated effective community leadership, and contributed to the beautification of the city. However, historical resources about some of these men and women had to be eked out of newspaper accounts, obituaries, probate records, and other historical documents.

"Ordinary" people do not leave a lot of documents behind, and those that do often have their materials destroyed by relatives, executors, and others. The search for these sources is much easier now with digital technology, but still requires considerable digging. Whatever the challenges, the story of those "hidden voices" deserves to be told.

The Beginnings:
The Untold Story of
Dr. Gregory Phelan

Historical works often gravitate to foundings and pivotal moments. Sometimes, these can be accurately pinpointed. Other times, the story is not so precise. Who began the Catholic Church in Sacramento? Clerical historians, such as the author and others before him, for a long time attributed this to a fellow cleric: Dominican Father Peter Augustine Anderson. He is often cited in popular literature—and repeated uncritically from one account to another—as the "founder" of the Catholic Church in Sacramento. In 1950, the centenary of the first Mass by Anderson in Sacramento was commemorated by a three-day Eucharistic Congress—an extravaganza with religious services and presided over by Cardinal Samuel A. Stitch of Chicago.[1] This version of the truth even extended to the 2005 renovation of the Cathedral of the Blessed Sacrament, where a fanciful cartoon of him in blue jeans has been drawn into the vestibule wall.

However, Anderson's role as the "founder" of Sacramento Catholic life needs revision. Sharing this honor was a medical doctor, Dr. Gregory Phelan, who was moved by his concern for the dead and dying in early Sacramento—a very unhealthy place. Phelan may have done more to gather together members of the local church and pressed the hardest to bring clergy and other Catholic settlers to the city. Phelan is an unrecognized hero of early Sacramento Catholicism.

Origins

Sacramento began as a chancy proposition. Its Euro-American origins date back to 1839 with the efforts of Swiss-German entrepreneur John

Sutter.[2] A roving soldier of fortune, Sutter secured a massive land grant from the Mexican government that he dubbed New Helvetia. On these lands, he ranched, as well as raised crops and flocks. With the assistance of the local indigenous people, he built a comfortable existence. He erected a fort that became a handy trade and hospitality center for people traveling through the region. New Helvetia existed as a sleepy outpost of the Mexican frontier, and Sutter evidenced little interest in city-building. But in 1846, after his fortunes began to decline, Sutter surveyed a piece of high ground south of his fort and named it Sutterville. Local entrepreneur and western pioneer Lansford Hastings tried to make a go of the new community, but the discovery of gold at the American River changed everything.

Anxious miners, eager to "skedaddle" to the gold fields, bypassed Sutterville and landed their barges and sloops at a site where the American and Sacramento rivers met. The new *entrepôt* had been claimed by Samuel Brannan, a Mormon adventurer who had already opened a successful store at the fort. Brannan had allegedly been the first to spill the news of the gold strike in San Francisco and then deftly positioned himself at a frame store on Front and J Streets to take maximum advantage of the miners who needed supplies as they headed for the American El Dorado. Brannan and other entrepreneurs (such as Samuel J. Hensley, Pierson B. Reading, and Jacob Snyder) hastily created a commercial entrepôt on the banks of the Sacramento. By late 1848, thousands of miners were already making their way to the embarcadero as boats and ships of various sizes put in at the docks and disgorged their passengers. Before passing on to the mines, the Argonauts spent liberally for the commodities that Brannan and his rivals provided.

Fortune smiled again on Brannan when John Sutter, anxious to pay-off debts he had accumulated over the years, turned over the financial affairs of his land holding to his son John Sutter, Jr., in 1848. Sutter, Jr., turned to Brannan for help and also a lawyer from Oregon (and California's first governor), Peter Burnett, who specialized in the legalities of land sales. Sutter, Jr., had the lands adjoining the fort surveyed in early 1849 and began to market the lots to eager buyers. Brannan and Burnett, as well as other large land speculators gobbled up huge amounts of this prime city land near the river front and "Sacramento City" as Sutter, Jr., agreed to call it, soon began to take shape. Sacramento grew, surmounting the perils of flood, fire, and disease. Its success was in part due to the location of the state capital in 1854 and later its designation as the western terminus of the Central Pacific Railroad.

Sacramento Catholics: History, Demography, and Identity

Every major religious denomination settled in Sacramento and began worship services. Although we have no accurate count, there were Catholic men and women in early Sacramento. Before clergy arrived "to save the day" self-identified and devout lay Catholics provided leadership, financial resources, and organizational life to Sacramento. Most importantly, they gathered a fledgling community which prayed together likely using prayer books brought with them from the east. These same Catholics claimed a portion of the city and built their first church. Lay Catholics like their fellow Sacramentans had to weather the early instability of the community and endure the crises of fire, flood and pestilence that threatened the city's existence. Like all religious bodies, the church adopted the spirit of an early city motto: "*urbs indomita*" (indomitable city).

Sacramento's Catholics were not an insular or ghettoized community. They mixed freely and openly with people of other denominations, and the rate of intermarriage between Catholics and non-Catholics was amazingly high when compared with other cities of the Midwest and the East. As a result, Catholics and non-Catholics in Sacramento lived for the most part a rather peaceable existence—a not unusual reality in a city that did not place a high premium on religious identity. In Sacramento, as in other western cities, a particularly irenic relationship existed between churches and the city negotiated by lay leaders who kept a foot in the worlds of church and public life. Throughout its history, some of Sacramento's most important Catholic leaders where lay men and women who combined active careers in politics, land speculation, the professions, and city development with an active and visible Catholic identity. In fact, these easy boundaries between public life and private faith seemed common.

Phelan

The traditional story of Catholic beginnings in Sacramento begins in late 1849 or 1850 when Catholic laymen first united the city's scattered Catholic populace and lobbied church officials for a permanent ministry. One of the most important was a New York-born physician, Gregory J. Phelan (1822–1903). Phelan took the lead in arranging church affairs.

Dr. Gregory Phelan, a native of New York City, was born December 23, 1822.[3] After attending medical schools in Massachusetts and New York, he answered a call for physicians to come west. Sailing round the

Horn, he arrived in San Francisco on July 22, 1849, and soon decamped for Sacramento. He was also deeply devout.

Phelan was one of the leading citizens of Sacramento and a pillar of its fledgling medical establishment. He served in the 1850s on the city's first school board, was a founder of the city's first medical association, and in the 1860s was the city and county physician of Sacramento as well as the superintendent of the Sacramento County Hospital. Phelan owned large swaths of land on the city's eastern extremities. He was its most prominent Catholic layman and one of the first to boost the city's image in eastern Catholic newspapers by stressing the presence of a stable Catholic Church as an incentive for settlement. In 1855, he married Cecilia Blanchet, the sister of two Catholic bishops, Augustin and Francis, the heads of two northwestern dioceses in Washington and Oregon.

In his first year in Sacramento, Phelan worked closely with Sacramento's sick and dying citizens. Sacramento, perched on flatlands near the rivers, was frequently overrun by flood waters and unsanitary living conditions. It was a petri dish for a number of communicable diseases: cholera, dysentery, and various fevers. Phelan sat at the bedside of these dying souls and his concern for their wellbeing pressed on him. A diary fragment reveals what was likely a traumatic experience for him in early Sacramento. In January 1850, he tended to a man named George Lawrence, who had contracted dysentery and quickly succumbed to this illness. Phelan and three others volunteered to bury him. He wrote to friends back in New York:

> Only four of us were present. How melancholy and lonely it appeared ... No minister of religion, no burial service, no weeping and mourning not a relative present. Only four of us here present to perform this work of Mercy and none of us had ever seen or heard of him three months previously.

He described the burial of the dead with grisly details such as coyotes opening the grave and devouring the deceased. "I hope I shall not die in this miserable place ... No minister or priest have I seen to visit the sick or read the funeral service."[4] He especially felt the lack of organized religion in Sacramento and lamented that many had to die without the comforts of religion. It was this concern for the dead and dying, and especially his fear that unrepentant souls might face a terrible eternal punishment, that motivated him to press for a stable ministry in Sacramento. Phelan was quite evidently a serious Catholic and wished he could have provided the ministry of a priest or minister to help the dying in their final moments.

That same year he began writing articles for eastern Catholic newspapers about conditions in California. His writings appeared most frequently in the New York-based Catholic newspaper *The Freeman's Journal*. Using the *nom de plume* "Philos," Phelan provides us with the little we know about Catholic life in first-generation Sacramento. Phelan continued these occasional articles until 1858 when the "Irish and Catholic" *San Francisco Monitor* provided more than enough news about Sacramento for eastern sources.

Building a Catholic Church: A New Perspective

It is certain that Phelan gathered local Catholics together to pray and plan for a permanent church foothold in the developing city. It was through his contacts with his clerical brothers-in-law and Catholics in the east that a priest was sent to Sacramento—not to live there, but to include it as part of a wide-ranging itinerant ministry. In 1850, Father Peter Augustine Anderson, a convert and a native of Ohio, arrived in California from St. Joseph Priory in Somerset, Ohio. He reported to Father Anthony Langlois of San Francisco, who dispatched the young Dominican to conduct an itinerant ministry to Sacramento and to the gold country.[5] With Anderson, he sent a grandiloquent letter done in formal pontifical style, with large letters addressed: "TO THE CATHOLICS OF SACRAMENTO CITY." The letter urged the Catholic faithful of the city and its environs to accept Anderson as their new pastor, empowering him to collect funds for a new church.[6]

Phelan placed an ad in the local press announcing Anderson's arrival and the holding of Mass. He also rented quarters at Fifth and L Street for a first Catholic center and also a modest house for the new pastor. When he arrived, they escorted the new priest to the hastily assembled chapel located a few blocks from the city's thriving embarcadero, writing back to eastern newspapers, Phelan detailed early Catholic developments in Sacramento:

> At length a priest has arrived and primary steps have been taken towards building a church in this city. On the seventh of August the Rev. A. [*sic.*] Anderson, O.S.D. came here from San Francisco. His object was to administer spiritual aid to such as required it, to collect the scattered Catholics into a congregation and build a church.

On August 11, 1850, Anderson celebrated his first Sunday Mass in Sacramento, probably the first many had attended in a long time. Phelan sent an account of it to the *Freeman's Journal*:

On Sunday August 11, (notice having been inserted in the papers), our little church was filled by a very respectable assemblage principally Catholics. There were from 70 to 80 persons present of whom about a dozen were ladies. Before commencing Mass, Rev. Mr. Anderson delivered a short address. He stated that it had been so long since many of them had been to Church that they probably had almost forgotten many things; and as for those who differed in religion, he assured them that there was nothing of the mummery or show in the forms and ceremonies and dress but on the contrary, that they all tend to attract the mind and keep it fixed on the great sacrifice of Mount Calvary, which was here being renewed. He reminded the hearers of the awful solemnity of the Mass and of the necessity of attentive and respectful deportment during its celebration. After reading the Gospel, Rev. Mr. Anderson delivered a very eloquent and appropriate discourse taking for his text the parable of the Good Samaritan.[7]

Phelan further noted, "On Sunday afternoon, Rev. Mr. Anderson baptized three children. One of these was born at the foot of the great Sierra Nevada Mountains and is named after our Illustrious Pontiff; for this one, I was asked to assume the responsible office of "Compadre."[8] Phelan concluded his report, "In the evening Re. [*sic*.] Mr. Anderson delivered an excellent discourse on Confession." Afterward, a meeting to determine a permanent location for the Sacramento flock took place. Phelan reported, "A committee of 13 was appointed to act in the matter and to report progress to the pastor who is vested with veto power."[9] This "Committee of 13" was chaired by Phelan. They set to work making plans for the permanent establishment of Catholicism in Sacramento.

Although the celebration of Mass is one of the pivotal moments in the foundation of a Catholic Church, Anderson was hardly in Sacramento long enough to make a lasting impression on the city's Catholic populace. He departed a mere six days after his arrival and traveled to San Francisco, promising to return in three or four weeks. "He intends, as soon as possible to visit Sonora, Marysville, and other places where Catholics reside," wrote Phelan.[10] In San Francisco, Anderson began another church building project in Happy Valley in present-day Shasta County.[11] Moreover, Anderson was not the only priest serving in the city. Phelan reported in the *Freeman's Journal* in October 1850 that "a Spanish clergyman" was in the city "busily engaged in administering the consolations of religion to the sick and dying."[12] Anderson never stayed long in Sacramento nor was the city high on his list of pastoral priorities. Anderson simply built on what others had done. The Committee of 13 then took the initiative. Future California governor, convert Peter Burnett, stepped forward and donated a permanent site for a new church at Tenth and I Streets.[13] However, this site was caught up in Sacramento's "squatter" dispute. Phelan reported that "a shantee" had been built by a squatter couple who "claimed ownership of possession." Anderson was consulted and was anxious to avoid trouble; he offered to pay for the land's improvements "if the lot would be given up." The husband was willing to agree to this but not his wife. Phelan noted with disdain that the woman, "no doubt a supporter of the 'Woman's Rights convention' claimed half the lot and refused absolutely to part with the property." Unwilling to get the new church off on the wrong foot, the Catholic committee refused to take legal action to eject the squatters.

Anderson only returned in October and by this time Burnett donated another lot (lot 8), at Seventh and K Streets, "a more central location than the other."[14] Here, was the first permanent site of Sacramento's first Catholic church. It was named to honor the patroness of Anderson's Dominican Order, St. Rose of Lima.[15] A small wooden church was hastily erected on the spot. Later, in the 1860s, Burnett would deed the adjacent lot seven to the Catholic Church.

Anderson baptized four babies before the cholera epidemic that ravaged Sacramento in the fall of 1850 felled him. Heroically, he worked among the sick and dying for a brief time and contracted the dread disease, dying on November 29, 1850. "After two weeks illness," Phelan wrote sadly, "he surrendered to his Maker and Redeemer that life which had been devoted to His service on earth." His mortal remains were waked and eulogized in the temporary chapel on Fifth and L and were interred at Seventh and K Streets where the new chapel was being erected.[16] His remains were later transferred to a Dominican cemetery in Benicia.

Sadness at Anderson's untimely demise was intensified when the small frame church he had begun was blown down by a windstorm. Despite his heroic service in the cholera plague (earning him the sobriquet "Martyr of charity"), however, Anderson's ministrations to the city were short, lasting only from August until November 1850. It is hard to imagine that many Catholics of Sacramento really knew him.[17] Without Anderson's supervision, plans went forward for the creation of a permanent Catholic church.

Going Forward

Despite the tragic loss of Anderson, Phelan and his committee forged ahead. In May 1851, "We in Sacramento have concluded to enlarge our little church as it has become too small for the rapidly increasing congregation." At length the first resident pastor, John Ingoldsby, was sent in late 1851. But, before plans for a bigger and better St. Rose Church could be realized, another disaster struck. Fire erupted in Madame Lanos's millinery shop on November 4, 1851, and ravaged the city. Some 12,000 people were left homeless and many of the city's buildings, including the newly dedicated St. Rose Church, were destroyed. Efforts to rebuild were stymied that winter when nature's floodgates opened, and the swelling banks of the Sacramento River submerged the streets in the first of a series of disastrous inundations. A disconsolate Ingoldsby and his parishioners transferred services to the city courthouse. Priest and people set to work again and erected another wooden church on the site, which was not ready until the following September 1852.[18]

Sacramentans had little chance to enjoy a respite from fire and flood. To the horror of disaster-weary citizens, another fire roared through the downtown, destroying twelve city blocks.[19] This time, St. Rose again came perilously close to destruction—as the flames came within 100 yards—but miraculously escaped as courageous Sacramentans covered the roof with wet blankets." Phelan records their determination: "[they] acted as though they intended to save the church at all hazards."[20] Wooden structures were just not going to work in disaster-prone Sacramento. Brick buildings were now the order of the day in Sacramento's growing downtown.

On May 1, 1853, Archbishop Joseph S. Alemany appointed a new pastor, Father John Quinn, to replace Ingoldsby, who had been summoned back to San Francisco. The new pastor wasted no time.[21] Quinn took matters into his own hands, and little was heard of lay cooperation and the Committee of 13. On September 13, 1854, the *Sacramento Daily Union* announced: "We are informed that the Roman Catholic society in this city is contemplating the erection of a brick church edifice, sixty feet front by one hundred fifteen feet deep on their vacant lot at the corner of K and Seventh Street."[22]

The new, larger, and hopefully permanent church began with a modest basement church designed by architect James Magill and was completed by Christmas 1854. Quinn recruited the experienced architectural team of William Craine and Thomas England to finish the building. Craine, an Englishman from the Isle of Man, had come to San Francisco in 1849. Quinn spent a fantastic $50,000 on the new structure, determined to use the best materials available to make sure the church was sturdy and visually elegant. The inscription over the main portal, taken from the Epistle of James, read "Be ye doers of the word, and not hearers only."

With the appointment of a permanent pastor, Phelan retired to his practice and helped build up the medical profession in the city. Between 1862 until 1870, he had charge of the city and county hospital. He married in 1855 and sired six children, one of whom followed him in the medical profession, another in mining, and a third became vice-consul in Brussels, Belgium. In 1870, he departed Sacramento and lived abroad until 1876, when he moved to San Francisco, where he died in November 1903. One account of the dedication of the cathedral in 1889 had Phelan returning to the capital to be part of a celebration the people hosted for Bishop Patrick Manogue. For thirty-six years, St. Rose was the center of Catholic life in the city. Scenes of the unpaved K Street show the unsightly tower perched atop the church and surrounded by saloons and eateries, like the Golden Eagle Hotel, and one block east of the horse market at Sixth and K, both of which boomed with business. Among the church's illustrious visitors were figures like Leland Stanford and Horace Greeley.[23] Journalist and social critic Henry George had his marriage blessed at St. Rose. The erection of a permanent church was an important breakthrough for Catholics.[24]

Phelan disappears from the story of Sacramento Catholicism in part because his family life and his work as a physician probably occupied much of his time. He reappears briefly in 1862 during the brief pastorate of Father John Cassin, where he urged the priest's removal because he was not caring for the city's sick and dying.[25] Quinn and other clergy and religious dominate the city's Catholic narrative. Phelan may have been disinvited to help any longer and this may have severed a tie with the growing number of Catholic laity who had been his backers. Quinn and his successors soon discovered the limits of clerical direction of Catholic affairs in a city where Catholics were a minority. His lavish spending on the new church was more than the parishioners were able to afford and they were content to let things remain unfinished or unrepaired. Quinn and other clerics had to rely on continual fundraising projects to fund their dreams: teas, socials, and fairs, hosted primarily by church women, and even outreach to non-Catholics and many citizens "without regard to creed."[26] In one of his last reports, Phelan noted that Bishop Joseph Sadoc Alemany had come for the dedication and that the prelate "was waited upon by a number of gentlemen of different denominations."[27]

Phelan's role has been overlooked for many years as popular accounts credit Anderson for "founding" the Catholic Church in Sacramento. Phelan himself, occupied with family and career, quietly left the city. But a fresh look at Dr. Phelan suggests a re-thinking of Catholic origins. Planning this first church began with the initiative of lay persons who were "doers of the word." St. Rose was his monument, but later, as the church began to literally sink beneath the upraised portion of K Street, Sacramento Catholics were content to leave it as it was. Only a forceful bishop, backed by hundreds of thousands of dollars from rich benefactors, could change that.

2

Who Built
the Sacramento Cathedral?

Today, the Cathedral of the Blessed Sacrament is a city treasure—and a church whose congregation mirrors the spectrum of age, race, gender, and ethnicity that is the pride of the city. Until the COVID-19 crisis of 2020–2022, its masses were full and its parishioners enthusiastic and engaged. It was a venue for concerts and offered docent-guided tours that attract hundreds. It is even today one of the most architecturally elegant structures in downtown Sacramento. Its historical origins, both in writing and in tours, are covered in the typical nostalgia used to describe the origins of local churches. The popular literature always elevated the central role played by Bishop Patrick Manogue. This tall and robust Irish-born priest of the Nevada frontier was indeed a builder, an organizer, and a dreamer. His successor memorialized him in a funerary relief plaque and a handsome portrait of him is visible to people who enter the cathedral by its majestic front doors. He was a major force behind what local journalists referred to as "Sacramento's Cathedral." Yet when all is said and done, we really do not know who contributed the funds to build this mighty temple. As Catholic journalist Eleanor Doyle noted, "There are no bills, no records of bills or receipts."[1]

But Manogue cannot claim the sole responsibility for this impressive building. Sharing (mostly anonymously) in the glory were those who contributed to it. These too are important and often unrecognized players in this Sacramento drama. As he found out to his chagrin, Manogue could not rely for much financial support from the mostly working-class Sacramento Catholics. The narrative of the indomitable will and vision of Bishop Patrick Manogue has to be nuanced by and recognition that he was heavily reliant on the wealthy people and benefactors who supported the project. The reality of indifferent financial support from Sacramento Catholics haunted his successor.

Patrick Manogue was born in 1831 in Desart, County Kilkenny, Ireland, and immigrated to the United States. His plans to pursue priestly studies in Chicago were interrupted by a brief stint as a hard-rock miner in Moore's Flat in Northern California. When he resumed studies for the priesthood, the local bishop, Joseph Sadoc Alemany of San Francisco, sent him to St. Sulpice in Paris, where he learned the austere piety of his teachers. Here he acquired a love for the majestic churches of the city.

When he returned to the United States in late May 1862, he was assigned to Virginia City, Nevada, as community that had become the center of one of the mining booms of the nineteenth-century West.[2] It had a small Catholic church, St. Mary of the Mountains, founded by Father Hugh Gallagher in 1860. In 1862, Virginia City included some 4,000 denizens, among them Samuel Langhorne Clemens (Mark Twain), who worked as a reporter on the city's newspaper, the *Territorial Enterprise*. The town was just on the cusp of a major growth arc, and the next year, a mining boom lifted the population to about 15,000. Virginia City witnessed an explosion of construction—homes, business buildings, and gas and sewer lines crisscrossing the mining city. Nearby stamping mills provided work for many. The development of rail links gave Virginia City a renewed burst of energy in the late 1860s and set the stage for its next revival in 1873 and 1874 with the discovery of the Big Bonanza, a fabulous silver strike that lifted Virginia City's population to a record 25,000 people.

In Virginia City, the 6-foot 6-inch Manogue was a person of prominence—well-respected in the community. One of his admirers, journalist Arthur McEwen, wrote that he was a man "imbued with the hearty masculine spirit of the place."[3] Due to destructive fires and the stress of rapid growth, Manogue was confronted with the need to build and re-build the church. A series of improvements took place between 1852 and 1877. The last of these rebuildings (in 1877) won the notice of the *Territorial Enterprise*, which described it as "the finest in Nevada." Redwood arches, fine paintings, and elaborate sanctuary furnishings adorned the interior. Atop it was a high steeple equipped with an early fire-extinguishing apparatus—a necessity in the dry climate of the desert.[4] All of this drew on the funds of local millionaires.

The church was his signal accomplishment, but not his only one. Manogue created charitable and educational institutions that supplemented the work of the parish. Summarizing his years in Virginia City, Manogue wrote to a priest in Rome: "When having charge for 20 years of Virginia City, I put up two churches at a cost of over $160,000, a hospital at $40,000, an orphan asylum for $30,000 and schools averaging $20,000." He concluded with an understatement: "I have been now thirty years on this Pacific Coast and I may lawfully say I have not been idle." In the letter, he also alluded to the cadre of wealthy friends he had accumulated over the years: "The friends made during that time [the Virginia City years] are scattered far and wide and are encountered everywhere on this coast."[5]

Compassion Pays Off

Manogue's effectiveness was based in part on his physical brawn, but also his willingness to go wherever he was called. He was a manly man, and he got on well in the rough male culture of the mining community. After all he had been a miner himself on Moore's Flat. But he had no illusions about the sometimes-abusive way they treated their spouses. In times of crisis, these women turned to him, and he listened sympathetically. This accumulated a reservoir of gratitude. In response, women were his most generous benefactors. Two women in particular became close friends: Theresa Rooney Fair and Marie Louise Hungerford Bryant (Mackay)— both of whose fortunes would be placed at his disposal in Sacramento.

Transition to Sacramento

In 1881, Manogue was made coadjutor (assistant) bishop of the Diocese of Grass Valley. In 1884, Bishop Eugene O'Connell finally retired, and Manogue was appointed the first bishop of Sacramento (replacing Grass Valley as the Catholic center of Northern California and western Nevada). Manogue had already planned to replace the deteriorating St. Rose of Lima Church and to build a new and more prestigious cathedral. Through the instrumentality of local shipping merchant Captain Thomas Dwyer, he purchased several lots a block north of the state capitol building and across the street from the Christian Brother's school, which had been on that site since 1876. This property between 11th and 12th and J and K on the Sacramento grid became the prime location for the growing Catholic community. The building of the cathedral commenced in 1886, and three years later, it was ready for dedication. It was a huge Gilded Age building, replete with a towering spire, an elegant façade, and a seating capacity of nearly 1,500. The interior décor was unfinished, and the altars were likely temporary, but the great cathedral was dedicated in the presence of a great throng on June 30, 1889.

Who paid for this? The sale of the old St. Rose Church at Seventh and K Streets to the federal government brought some funds, but more were needed and the prospect of collections from city Catholics or even around the diocese was unpromising. On the day of the dedication of the cathedral, tables were set up to collect money from men and women—a gift of $5 would merit a mention from the pulpit. However, Sacramento Catholics gave little. As veteran journalist Eleanor Doyle remembered:

> Old timers in Sacramento, whose families date back to the Manogue era, recall his chief disappointment while Bishop of Sacramento, was the lack of response from the laity towards helping build the Cathedral. He often commented upon the lack of financial support.

Indeed, Manogue's hard-driving ways had not cultivated enough good will at least with rank-and-file Catholics in the city to provide the needed funds. But, as Doyle notes, "it was an open secret in those times that he was being given sufficient help from the Bonanza Kings of the Comstock, and there was really not an actual need for their contributions."[6] Absent a groundswell of local support, Manogue then turned to his benefactors, Theresa Fair and John W. Mackay, husband of his dear friend Marie Louise Mackay, Big Bonanza multi-millionaires. These two women and their families contributed substantially to the Catholic cathedral.

Manogue's Generous Women

Theresa Rooney Fair (1836–1891) was the wife of Mackay's partner James Fair. She was born in New York in 1838 of Irish parents. At age four, her parents brought her to California where her father briefly tried mining. But, like many others, he found greater profit in "mining the miners." Setting up boarding houses and retail outlets for miners in Virginia City, the Rooneys lived a comfortable life. They also opened up their parlor to visiting priests for the celebration of Mass, and that is likely where they met young Father Patrick Manogue. Theresa was educated in New York boarding schools, but dutifully returned to the West to help her parents with their business. Apparently, she had been married and widowed, but was willing to try marriage again.

On December 31, 1861, at the age of twenty-four, she married James Fair (1831–1894). Of Irish birth (at Clogher in County Tyrone), Fair was a fireplug of a man, with a big black beard and a genius for mining. He had come to America in 1843 at age twelve and moved to California in 1850 where he undertook quartz mining in the Feather River country and even farming in Petaluma. Fair was not a Catholic, but certainly respected the religious faith of his wife. Theresa Rooney was already a good friend of Manogue, who presided at their nuptials. Theresa bore four children—two girls, Theresa (Tessie) and Virginia (Birdie); and two sons, James, Jr., and Charles. All were baptized and reared as Catholics. When they struck it rich, Theresa made sure that the Fairs donated generously to Father Manogue's renovations of the Virginia City church. She also showed an active interest in the schools and hospital that Manogue had helped found in Virginia City.

But the Fair marriage suffered under the strains of great wealth. In 1883, Theresa Fair divorced her husband who had apparently been philandering for years. When Theresa ejected her husband from the San Francisco mansion he had built, Manogue came to San Francisco to try to reconcile the two.[7] This effort failed, and Theresa sued for divorce in the Nevada courts. The case—which involved public accusations of adultery and named the women involved—played out through the month of May 1883. James Fair counter accused his wife of adultery with the family attorney. Among Mrs. Fair's defenders was Manogue, who gallantly defended Theresa, vigorously rebutting James Fair's insistence that the infidelity had been mutual. Manogue also urged that she demand a just portion of the Fair's $12 million silver fortune for herself and her children. The court agreed, and in the end, she received nearly $5 million and was assigned custody of the daughters Therese and Virginia while the sons went to James.[8] Therese repaid the kindness abundantly.

Fair donated generously to the Sacramento Cathedral project, but apart from a few paintings in the cathedral, the public would not remember her role. Her major gift was the erection of a now-demolished three-story mansard-style mansion directly to the east of the new cathedral all the way to 12th Street—where it faced the German Lutheran church. She wrote to Manogue, "Erect a suitable and fitting mansion for yourself and send me the bill of expenses." The home, which served as the residence for Sacramento's first three bishops as well as the priests of the cathedral until the 1920s, cost $25,000 ($591,000 in 2010 dollars).[9] In the parlor of this house was a portrait of Theresa Fair. She also directed Manogue to purchase three oil paintings, *The Holy Family*, *Death of a Martyr Bishop*, and *Deposition from the Cross*, which hang in the cathedral to this day. Theresa's two daughters, Theresa and Birdie also contributed generously.

Sadly, in 1923 wrecking balls demolished the residence. Bishop Patrick Keane built a new structure to the north of the cathedral (the present Presbytery) to house resident priests. For many years, it was also the office of the bishop and his small staff. The furniture and paintings of the old residence were transferred to a new home on 21st and M (Capitol) and then lost or discarded when the episcopal mansion moved again to the suburbs in the 1940s. By 1923, likely few remembered the generosity of Theresa Fair, except her daughters, Theresa and Virginia (Birdie) who left their own windows in the cathedral. Without her money and the possible pledge of more, the cathedral and the episcopal residence would never have been a reality. Fair donated handsomely to the San Francisco cathedral as well and to a myriad of charities that she kept to herself. Just before her death, Fair supposedly attempted to rewrite her will in order to provide an additional $50,000 to further decorate the interior of the cathedral, but she died suddenly of Bright's Disease (kidney failure) on September 13, 1891, and was unable to complete the change in time.[10] Her elaborate funeral was held in the San Francisco Cathedral. She was attended by local San Francisco clergy to the moment of death.[11] In her final will, she left everything to her children.

Fair was also the connection with another major benefactor, John W. Mackay, whose wife Marie Louise Hungerford Bryant, a Virginia City widow (and victim of an abusive marriage), had been the object of Manogue's kindness in time of need. Many know about Mackay, who had a distinguished career as a miner and an early communications tycoon, but few acknowledge the bond between Mackay's wife, Marie Louise, and Manogue.

Marie Louise and John Mackay

Marie Louise Hungerford Bryant was born in Brooklyn in 1843, the daughter of a Mexican War veteran. Her family went west, and she began her life in the mountain town of Downieville, California. Eventually, her family moved to Virginia City, and she married at a young age to a local doctor, Dr. Edmund G. Bryant—a popular local physician and also a mining speculator. The couple had two girls. It was a happy marriage at first, but as time went on, Dr. Bryant became an alcoholic and user of opium, growing increasingly abusive to his wife and children. He even allowed one of his daughters, Marie, to die of a throat ailment by refusing to treat her and allegedly battered his second daughter, Eva, who thereafter walked with a limp all her life. Marie joined her parents, who had moved to Virginia City, and came to know the popular Father Manogue, who had come to Marie Louise's assistance—comforting her after the death of her daughter and arranging for the little tyke to be buried in the rough Virginia City cemetery. Historian Gregory Crouch wrote, "After the death of her baby, Louse Bryant leaned hard on the priest's shoulders." Bryant himself died painfully of tetanus in 1866 and left the twenty-two-year-old

Marie alone to support her daughter. With Manogue's help, Marie found work teaching conversational French and sewing for the camp's well-to-do ladies.[12] One account had her running a boarding house.[13]

Playing the matchmaker, Mackay was formally introduced to Marie Louise by Theresa Fair, who had invited the young widow to dinner, and the two met on occasion in the Fair parlor. John Mackay (1831–1902) was born in Dublin, Ireland, in 1831 to a Catholic family, but rarely practiced his faith. He came to the United States with his parents. Mackay's was a rags-to-riches story. He supported his family by working as a "Newsie" for the New York Herald and later as a shipbuilder in New York. Drifting steadily westward, he landed for a time in Louisville, Kentucky where he owned a saloon. In 1851, he joined the hordes migrating to California, taking the perilous journey around Cape Horn to San Francisco. At first, he worked the placer mines in Sierra County. In 1859, he migrated to Virginia City, Nevada, in the wake of the fabled Comstock Lode silver strikes. Doing day labor, he saved up enough to buy his own claims. He struck it rich in "Kentuck" mine and invested his profits together with those of some fellow Irishmen, James C. Flood, William S. O'Brien, and James G. Fair (husband of Theresa), and in 1873, they struck one of the largest veins of silver in the Consolidated Virginia Mine, the so-called "Big Bonanza." This mine produced more than $400 million ($9.9 billion in 2022) in four years. Mackay and his associates were now fantastically wealthy.

Due to a stutter, Mackay was a man of few words, but he and Fair were mining geniuses. Unlike the rakish Fair, Mackay was utterly upright in his personal behavior. The Fairs entertained Mackay regularly and one Christmas invited him to dinner where he met the widow Bryant. He was quite smitten with her, and, after a courtship, Manogue married them in November 1866.[14]

No doubt, Marie Louise had told her new husband of the kindness of the priest who helped her through her darkest hours. One of the first things Marie did after her marriage was erect a tombstone over the barren grave of her daughter. Mackay then became a willing benefactor of Manogue. When a fire ravaged the city, Mackay generously offered to help through a fund Manogue administered. He told Manogue that he could always call on him for money. The couple had two children, both boys, and Mackay became a father to little Eva and paid for a surgery to correct her hip. No doubt at Marie Louise's urging, Mackay donated generously to Manogue's projects in Virginia City, but he also liked and respected the pastor. When a fire destroyed Manogue's church, Mackay donated handsomely to construct a bigger and more beautiful gothic church. He also underwrote the Catholic school and an orphanage in the city. A local hospital, named for the patron saint of his wife St. Marie Louise, was also erected in the town.

By 1877, the Big Bonanza was exhausted and at the urging of Marie Louise, Mackay reluctantly left Virginia City and took up residence in San Francisco. Marie Louise adapted rapidly to the new wealth, remaking her image from a struggling miner's wife to a *nouveau riche* "baroness." They lived for a time in San Francisco and New York, but she later took up residence in Paris and London and tried to shake off the grime and dust of Virginia City. Eventually, she settled at a large estate on Long Island where she ruled the social circle until her death in 1928. Mackay helped to found banks and established the Commercial Cable Company (later International Telegraph and Telephone) to capitalize on the emerging transatlantic "communications industry." Mackay contended with no less than the legendary monopolist Jay Gould for supremacy in this field and, besting his rival, he made similar plans to lay cable across the Pacific Ocean. Mackay invested in mines in other parts of the country, timber lands, and even a sugar and elevator company. He served on the board of two railroad companies. Manogue's kindness to his wife would redound to the benefit of Manogue's cathedral building.

Fair and Mackay are reputed to have been the single largest benefactors of the Cathedral of the Blessed Sacrament, reportedly giving as much as $100,000 in 1887 ($3.1 million in 2022). There is no monument to Mackay in the cathedral, nor even a paper trail of his generosity. The total cost of the Cathedral of the Blessed Sacrament was never revealed.

What is underappreciated was the role Manogue's sincere concern for the wellbeing of the women involved—Theresa Fair and Maria Louise Mackay—played in fulfilling his dream of building a great cathedral. His advocacy of them and tender service at times of real need in their lives was the deciding factor in their generosity. John Mackay, a man of few words and hardly a Catholic, must have been very grateful for Manogue's care for the abused Marie Louise. Theresa Fair certainly remembered his efforts to reconcile her marriage and his defense of her virtue. After her husband's death in 1902, she continued his benefactions to the church, donating the princely sum of $1,000 to Father Thomas Tubman who built St. Thomas Aquinas Cathedral in Reno.[15] Other people's money also included generous donations from within and even more remarkably outside the Catholic fold.

Reclusive Millionaire: Anthony Coolot

The Fairs and the Mackays were well-known tycoons. Another less visible but still highly active force in Sacramento Catholic life was August Coolot (1821–1900). His was the most lavish benefaction of the cathedral at its opening and even today: a beautiful row of elegant custom-made stained-glass windows, imported from the Tyrolean region of Austria, depicting the Last Supper and designed to refract the radiance of the morning sun. Coolot's gift cost $1,500 ($48,600 in 2022). This glorious window embodied the central mystery of the cathedral's name.[16]

Coolot lived near the cathedral on J Street between Eighth and Ninth. He was born in Austria on November 19, 1821. His wanderings began at an early age, but he spent some time in the French colony of Algeria and developed a facility in French and love for its culture. At the age of twenty, he migrated to the United States, living first in New York, and then relocating to New Orleans where he found work and an outlet for his Francophile tastes while working at a large glass and crockery operation. In 1854, he set out for California and attempted mining in Nevada County near Moore's Flat, where earlier young Patrick Manogue had worked. Within six months, he gave it up and came to Sacramento, where he found work in a crockery and glass store. It would be no coincidence that his most significant gift to the cathedral would be stained glass. He struck out into his own retail business and eventually operated a wholesale cigar and tobacco business.

Coolot was one of the civic middlemen who fought hard to keep Sacramento on its sometimes-perilous location, pushing back against floods and fire with street-raising and brick buildings. He hailed the advance of the Central Pacific and purchased bonds and supported other civic betterment associations. In 1861, he married Margaretha Sommer, a native of Bavaria, who had come to California the year before. The couple had three children: Maria Antoinetta, Clara, and a son, Augustin. Staunch German-speaking Catholics, the Coolots remained faithful parishioners first of St. Rose Church on Seventh and L and later of the cathedral. Coolot's wealth and generosity soon began to be whispered throughout Sacramento and many claimed he was a millionaire. Indeed, he engaged in real estate speculation, owning eighty-six "fine pieces of paying property" within Sacramento and some "best class" property in San Francisco. He formed the American Tobacco Company to manage his retail business, and at the time of his death, the company was worth $175,000 ($6.2 million in 2022). His holdings in government bonds were reportedly in six figures. "His income from all sources was inevitably enormous," reported the press at the time of his death, estimated at $2 million ($71 million in 2022).[17] Coolot died without a will. His son-in-law, Melchior Diepenbrock, would carry on his tradition as a major participant in Sacramento Catholic life, as would his daughter-in-law Rebecca Coolot, who also gave generously of her time and treasure for Catholic causes and the care of the poor in the capital city.

Although a member of the cathedral building committee and known by many cathedral parishioners, Coolot was a reclusive man, living above his tobacco store for fifty years and only becoming a naturalized citizen a few years before his death at the age of seventy-nine on November 30, 1900. He was rarely seen in on the street "and perhaps never at a place of public amusement."[18] At his funeral Mass, celebrated by Bishop Grace and attended by a number of clergy to whom Coolot had likely been generous, the press reported that "The sermon was short and not laudatory, because Mr. Coolot as in life, wanted to be in death noticed as little as possible." His funeral prayer card read: "This only do I ask of you. That you remember me at God's altar.–St. Monica." Coolot's name on the inscribed dedicatory panel on the lower part of the center panel is not visible to the naked eye. He likely would have wanted it that way.

The Dapper Colonel: James McNasser

Some gifts to the cathedral were made by local merchants and entrepreneurs who had a deep stake in the success of Sacramento and who viewed the cathedral as "a fitting ornament" to a city on the rise. Such was the identity of the man who donated one of the northern clerestory windows in the sanctuary Colonel James McNasser (1827–1896). Born in Ireland on April 27, 1827, in County Tyrone, he was brought to the United States at the age of two, settling first in Burlington, Vermont.[19]

As a young man, he joined the westward move to California arriving in 1852 and taking up the beef-cattle business. McNasser and his associates drove herds from Los Angeles and San Diego County to the mines in Grass Valley. He purchased a large stock ranch at Benson's Ferry on the Mokelumne River and another ranch in Davis where he bred and prepared beef-cattle. McNasser was also "great admirer of horse flesh and followed the occupation as much for pleasure as for business." His interest in horse-breeding and sales took him to Kentucky where he received the honorary title of "Colonel." McNasser lived and worked out of Denver for a time, marrying there and beginning his family. His commercial linkage with Denver would continue even after he moved to California. He procured and sold horses, bringing back several carloads from Denver and other points and selling them in Virginia City and San Francisco.

In the early 1880s, he moved from Denver to Sacramento where he built a home at 10th and L Street and leased the Golden Eagle Hotel, which was located adjacent to St. Rose Church at Seventh and K Streets. In 1886, he purchased a ranch of 1,046 acres about 4 miles south of Sacramento on Riverside Road. He also bought up large tracts in the "Pocket" area, where he cultivated fruit and also alfalfa. His hopes to reclaim much of the land were dashed when a city drainage canal failed and the excess water and sewage from the city overspread his acres and made it impossible to cultivate. McNasser then took a lead in water control affairs in the lands between Sacramento and Freeport and helped create a reclamation district. However, when he felt the needs of his Pocket property were not covered adequately, he led a secession and helped create another district. The entire matter was mired in litigation at the time of his death in 1896.

McNasser was also a speculator in Sacramento properties and owned parcels around the city. At one point, he tried to buy up prime property near the capitol building but withdrew from the bid when owners of the parcels demanded too much money. He was a much-admired public citizen. When conducting the Golden Eagle Hotel, McNasser occasionally dispensed "rare juices of the grape in unlimited quantities" and free lunches. He always appeared in public impeccably dressed. He may have met the first bishop in Virginia City where he traded in horses and perhaps attended Sunday Mass. Likely, they got to know each other through St. Rose. Manogue was an occasional patron at the Golden Eagle where the dinner feting him after the cathedral was built was held. McNasser's name would have been well-known to the Sacramentans who attended the cathedral.

In 1894, his wife died and McNasser grieved her loss deeply. A carriage accident near Routier in Sacramento County left the now seventy-three-year-old capitalist badly injured. He moved to Salt Lake City to be with his daughter where he died in May 1896. His body was brought back to Sacramento for funeral and burial. He lay in state in the cathedral and after a solemn Mass presided over by Father Matthew Walsh and Bishop Thomas Grace was buried in the city cemetery. Among his pallbearers were some of the city's leading professional men, realtor William Turton, lawyer Robert T. Devlin, James O'Neil, and land speculator and Oak Park founder, E. K. Alsip.

The Women of the Windows

The gifts of wealthy men, however flashy they were, were dwarfed by those of Sacramento women, often with their husband's fortunes. Of the twenty-five windows in the apse, side shrines, and transepts, women donated nine of them. When one includes the nave windows and other works of art, women were the cathedral's primary artistic benefactors, as they were in the advancement of art in general in Sacramento. Theresa Fair had been the best of benefactors. No doubt at her urging, her daughters donated windows in both church transepts. Neither of them appeared to persevere in their Catholic faith, nor did they live in Sacramento. Theresa (Tessie) Fair's gift, *The Last Communion of St. Jerome*, is to be found in the south transept. Directly across from it is St. Augustine with his mother St. Monica donated by her sister, Virginia (Birdie) Fair. These two heiresses ascended to the heights of social prominence and occupied a special status in Gilded Age society. As many young *nouveau riche* types of the era, they contracted loveless marriages both of which ended in divorce.

Ellen Flannigan Dwyer, native of Kings County, Ireland, was the wife of Thomas Dwyer, the man who had purchased most of the plots of land on which the cathedral stands today. Captain Dwyer, as he was known, secured his fortune by shipping along the Sacramento River and also opening up a successful cartage business which moved the goods from the harbor to outlying areas. Ellen bore four sons, Francis T., John J., William P. (father of Monsignor Richard Dwyer), and Thomas E. Her one daughter, Mary E. Dwyer, became the wife of Sacramento attorney, legal scholar, and later U.S. attorney Robert T. Devlin. The Dwyer family and their associates also contributed handsomely.[20]

Dwyer partner Daniel McCarthy provided funds for the window of the Ascension. These two windows alone cost about $1,000. In the north clerestory of the sanctuary, a stained-glass grouping of the four evangelists was bestowed in memory of Harley Hooker, a young man who died in a gruesome accident at the railyard yards. To the left of the sanctuary, above the altar dedicated to the Blessed Virgin, Hannah Rose Rigney, the wife of Thomas Dwyer's associate, installed a window to honor the Assumption of the Blessed Virgin Mary. To the right of the altar, in the shrine to St. Joseph, Anna Josephine Kaseberg, wife of a prominent Placer County rancher, donated a window depicting the "Flight of the Holy Family into Egypt."[21] The wealthy Yolo County ranching widow Agnes Bemmerly gave "St. Paul Preaching to the Athenians," also in the south transept.

From Unbelievers

The exterior of the cathedral was enough to impress visitors and local denizens. But the interior too provided a space for civic-minded Sacramentans of all faiths to showcase the city's new found love for art.[22] As Father John Quinn observed in his funeral eulogy of Manogue, "note the names of the donors of these beautiful windows and these works of art on the walls about you and you will find they are the names of the loyal sons of Abraham, the Protestant, the scoffing infidel, and the honest skeptic."[23] Most significant were the gifts of non-Catholics, whose extensive travels abroad made them aware of the role of cathedrals as the repositories of great art and fitting objects for their philanthropic impulses. Margaret Crocker gave the cathedral a series of six stained glass windows with insets of the stations of the cross, which she had purchased from a European church.[24] She also gave the cathedral an elegant depiction of the prodigal son story that crowned the windows of the north transept. Jane Lathrop Stanford, who was deeply impressed by Catholic art and culture, and who drew on the model of the elaborate Roman church of St. Paul outside the Walls for the famous chapel of Stanford University, commissioned a replica of Raphael Sanzio's *Sistine Madonna* to be placed in a prominent location in the new cathedral. Jewish merchant David Lubin donated a copy of Guido Reni's powerful masterwork *St. Michael Defeating Satan*, which hung in Rome's Capuchin Church. The benefactions of Margaret Crocker, David Lubin, and Jane Stanford reflected not only their generosity but their appreciation of churches as places to reflect the elevation of culture in a city by the creation of sites of beauty. Other art works brought the cathedral walls to life.

Bishop Manogue's health began to decline shortly after the dedication of the cathedral. Afflicted by both diabetes and cirrhosis of the liver, he slowly lost all energy.[25] As his energies waned, unfinished parts of the cathedral occupied his mind. With an anonymous donation of $7,000, he began to finish off the expansive underground of the church in hopes of using the remains of old St. Rose (pews, altars, and statuary) to create a chapel for children. He also added meeting rooms for Catholic societies.

In late 1894, he commissioned frescoers under Sacramento artist Thomas L. O'Neil to decorate the sanctuary. He also ordered a bell cast at a Cincinnati foundry to replace the former bell that had been removed from the old St. Rose. Manogue reaped the fruit of his effective ministry, particularly in Virginia City. Most of these benefactors were women. Their role in building this great temple is nowhere memorialized or celebrated.

Bells

Manogue's successor, Bishop Thomas Grace, was thrifty and even penurious by nature, and was not inclined to do much with the cathedral. However, at the urging of Rector John Quinn (1899–1906) benefactors stepped forward. One important woman who did so was Mary Bithell a native of England.

Her husband, James Bithell, was a native of New York, born in 1827. As a young man, he acquired a working knowledge of the publishing business. He arrived as a gold-seeker in California in 1851. Abandoning the gold fields, he became a bookseller (one of the first in northern

California) in a brick store he erected on J Street between Fourth and Fifth Streets. Undaunted by fires in 1852 and again in 1854, he built up a solid business and became an important and supplier to Sacramento County and the state of California. When his first wife died, Bithell (sometimes spelled "Bethel"), briefly returned to New York in 1855, where he married Mary Emma Gray, a native of London, England and the couple had one son, Zachariah. James quit the bookstore in 1874 and devoted the rest of his life to real estate and lending money. With his profits, he invested in the Capital Gas Company and the Bank of Dixon. He also speculated in real estate in Sacramento, Placer, and Solano Counties. By the time he died in July 1896, Bithell was worth nearly $300,000 ($10.6 million in 2022). He left his entire estate to his wife Mary. Bishop Thomas Grace officiated at his service.[26]

With her riches, Mary Bithell, likely urged by Cathedral rector John Quinn, donated the four face Cathedral clock in 1901. The new Seth Thomas "Number 17" hour and quarter strike clock had four illuminated faces. Bells struck a single note for each quarter hour and rang out majestically at the top of the hour and pealed the news of Christ's birth at the Christmas celebrations of 1901.They also announced the new electrical illumination of the sanctuary—always before lighted by gas jets.[27] Mary's other benefactions included funding for the Christian Brothers School, then at 12th and K directly across from the cathedral.

Mary died on July 8, 1912, and Bishop Grace was the executor of her estate.[28] She made numerous bequests to the local Catholic Church including $1,000 for the Sisters of Mercy at the Grass Valley orphanage. She also left a similar amount to the Sacramento Orphanage and Farm Association formerly known as the Protestant Orphan Asylum of Sacramento. She became attached to the work of Father Dennis Crowley, a San Francisco priest who ran the San Francisco Catholic Youth Directory, a receiving home for boys. To him she also left the sum of $1,000 and to Sacramento's Home of the Merciful Savior. She personally gifted Bishop Grace, with $2,000 and gave $500 (a small fortune in those days) each to the pastor and assistants of the Cathedral of the Blessed Sacrament. She even left money for the building of a new YMCA structure.[29] The rest of her estate went to her granddaughter Helen Gray and her sister Helen Feeney. Upon her sister's death, she asked that the remainder of what she had given be handed over to the Diocese of Sacramento for the education of priests. She then directed Bishop Grace to sell the remainder of her property in order to pay his final bills and use the money according to his own discretion.

Bithell's generosity was recognized by the Christian Brothers who praised her generosity, but little has ever been said of her part in the life of the cathedral. Her amazing generosity is nowhere commemorated in the cathedral whose chimes are now electronic. The clock Quinn bought was unceremoniously dumped in the cathedral square when the first round of renovations took place in the 1970s. Interested collectors reassembled the clock works. Currently, it sits in storage vault in the Center for Sacramento History. The memory of the cathedral benefactors does live on in fanciful stories, but documentation is scarce. When a local architect asked Jesuit historian John T. McGloin for the costs of the cathedral, the historian complained that the documents may have perished with Manogue himself. Others speculate that the renovations of cathedral in the 1970s, overseen by priests with little appreciation for local church history may have unceremoniously dumped the precious sanctuary lamp (later recovered), side altars, and the works of the clock. What was lost was priceless and recovering those benefactors is critical for a richer history of this great church buildings—still one of Sacramento's architectural gems.

3

Fighting the Irish Establishment: The New Immigrants and Their Leaders

Catholicism—like all non-indigenous American religions—is a European system of belief and practice that was brought to North America by imperial powers. A large and diverse bibliography exists describing the religious worlds of native Californians and their interaction with European missionaries. The famous mission system is an important facet of religion's impact on Californian history.

In the nineteenth and twentieth centuries, Catholic immigrants came in waves to the shores of the United States—first large numbers of western and northern Europeans (German-speakers and Irish) and later from southern and Eastern Europe. The attraction of America, "pull" factors included the prospect of jobs, land, and property ownership. Developments in Europe and abroad, "push" factors included political upheaval, persecution, and diminishing economic possibilities.

In the American West, immigrants were also lured by gold. Large numbers of single Irish men came to California looking to make their fortune. Other groups found California's agricultural possibilities an enticement, others, the various manufacturing shipping, and service jobs that allowed them to make a decent living for themselves and their families.

Sacramento was a microcosm of this diverse ethnic history—with various groups settling in the state capital—living at close quarters in the compact grid of Sacramento streets. It is easy to romanticize the immigrant heritage. DNA searches, genealogists, and others have made a cottage industry out of exploring ethnic heritage and roots, but immigrant realities are often more complex. Rivalry and dominance were also part of the immigrant story among Sacramento Catholics. So also, was bitter reaction to "furriners"—directed at their origins and sometimes their Catholic religion.

In Sacramento, the largest Catholic immigrant group were the Irish. They dominated the ranks of leadership (bishops, clergy, and sisters) for many years. They brought their own form of Catholic life to the parishes, schools, and health care institutions they founded and staffed. They were the backbone of Sacramento Catholicism for many years. But others came as well—German speakers (Germans, Swiss, and Austrians), Italians, Portuguese, Mexicans, Slavs, and Filipinos. Each of these Catholic groups eventually carved a niche for themselves in the city—creating clubs, fraternal societies, funeral homes, marching bands, and above all their own churches and devotional life. In fact, immigrant Catholic lay leaders played prominent roles in community formation as they fought for a sense of place in the growing Sacramento community. Their role in Sacramento's history needs a greater study.

Immigrant Catholics faced all the obstacles of newcomers, but one, particularly hard to bear, was the hostility of the mostly Irish Catholic clergy and religious to the other ethnic groups in the city. The Irish-dominated church was very slow to welcome diversity in Catholic Sacramento.

Ethnic Sacramento

In the late-nineteenth and early-twentieth centuries, the steady flow of immigration to the United States continued unabated and indeed accelerated with the demands for unskilled industrial labor and urban service providers. The earliest immigrant groups to leave a mark on emerging Sacramento were the Irish, the Germans, and the Chinese. About 1885, the character of this immigrant flood changed from being primarily northern and western European and Asian to southern and eastern European. In Sacramento, labor needs generated by the Southern Pacific Railroad and the canneries drew on the labor of scores of new immigrants to the city: Italians, Portuguese, Slavonians (a generic name for Croatians and Serbians), Japanese, and Mexicans. They also ran the hotels, bakeries, restaurants, laundries, and saloons that expanded to meet part of this new commercial life. The following chart provides data related to the number of foreign-born residents (excluding those of foreign parentage) in Sacramento County:

Year	Number of Foreign-Born	Percentage of Sacramento County Population
1890	13,212	32.75%
1900	12,736	27.74%
1910	19,166	28.27%
1920	14,998	16.48%

Source: U.S. Census Reports 1890–1920.

Sacramento's ethnic groups made their presence felt spatially and culturally. Their neighborhoods tended to cluster in relatively small enclaves near the city's commercial and industrial districts. The city's various nationalities attempted as best they could to maintain some form of community cohesiveness.[1] Within these districts, social clubs, mutual aid societies, and retail outlets for food and clothing reflected their culture and background.

They also built ethnic churches. In 1895, for example, German-speakers opened a church and school. In 1900, the church named for St. Stephen was established in a remodeled carriage house at Third and O streets to minister to the medley of Catholic groups in the ethnically diverse West End. This durable facility served the community until 1969. Indeed, almost every ethnic group that later founded a church of their own began in this former carriage house and their children attended its grammar school. An often-neglected point in parish histories was that these churches were founded not only for purposes of linguistic and cultural preservation, but also as an act of lay autonomy. Lay leaders, often working in tandem with clergy, spearheaded these new institutions with land acquisition, monetary donation, and public action.

Resistance to Immigrant Autonomy

As noted above, Irish Catholics dominated the ranks of the clergy and religious. The first three bishops of Sacramento were natives of Ireland. They held sway over the life of the local church until well into the twentieth century. Since they prided themselves on their ability to adapt to their new circumstances, they expected other Catholic groups to do the same. But just as importantly, Irish Catholic bishops and priests feared that too great a proliferation of parishes and other parallel institutions (e.g. schools and orphanages) would financially cripple the relatively small Catholic community in Sacramento. In particular, the poor response to cathedral fundraising reflected their unwillingness and inability to shell out large sums of money for the church. Money was always a problem for the Sacramento church since there were few huge fortunes to underwrite these endeavors.

However, foreign-born Sacramento Catholics defied Irish resistance to their goals. These groups insisted that their spiritual and cultural needs required separate churches. Lay leaders, sometimes working with sympathetic clergy, played a pivotal role.

German Catholics

The first ethnic group to challenge Irish domination were the city's Catholic German-speaking community. The German contingent, although numerically smaller than the Irish, constituted an important part of nineteenth century Sacramento Catholic life.[2] At one point according to the 1852 census, they even briefly outnumbered the Irish in Sacramento County, numbering 730. By 1860, the number had nearly doubled, reaching its peak in 1890 when 2,182 Sacramentans were of German birth.[3] Although most were skilled laborers (such as barbers, shoemakers, and merchants), there were others in the unskilled fields.[4]

Sacramento German speakers grew prosperous in dairying and brewing with the Swiss-born Inderkum and Ruhstaller families piling up tidy fortunes in both businesses. However, one of the wealthiest German speakers in Sacramento was the Austrian-born merchant Anthony E. Coolot, a local tycoon, whose benefaction to the Cathedral of the Blessed Sacrament we have already seen. The Coolots and their relatives were among the premier German Catholic families of Sacramento.[5]

German Sacramentans had a network of active associations through which they took care of their own social needs and fostered cultural bonds. One of the most important of these groups was the branch of the Turnverein that began in Sacramento in 1854. Although officially hostile to organized religion and Catholicism in particular, they erected a Turner Hall on K and Tenth streets in 1859, which served the wider community. Equally important was the expression of German culture through religious observance. Three major denominations—Lutheran, Methodist, and Catholic—established churches specifically for Germans. Already in 1867, Reverend Matthias Goethe had established a permanent German Evangelical Lutheran congregation.

The earliest ministry to German-speaking Catholics in Sacramento began in the 1850s with the work of Father Florian Schweninger, a missionary Benedictine monk from the Abbey of Fiecht, near Innsbruck, Austria. Schweninger traveled the length and breadth of Northern

California until his death in 1868, establishing communities of Catholics, including St. Joseph in nearby Marysville (where a stained-glass window commemorates his ministry and where he is buried) and in neighboring farming communities. Phelan related the coming of Schweninger to Sacramento in the summer of 1854 and revealed the presence of German Catholics at St. Rose:

> Not long since we were visited by Father Florian who has charge of the northern counties, bordering, Oregon, and on the head waters of the Sacramento ... Being the only German priest in the archdiocese he went to San Francisco to attend such of his countrymen as could not speak English. Returning, he remained here a few weeks on the same mission; and during his time he assisted our worthy pastor in organizing and instructing a choir for our church.[6]

A First Effort

Services for German-speaking Catholics were infrequent, and as time went on, demands for their own "religious space" increased. Above all, they wanted preaching and confessions in their own language. A common fear among church leaders was that disgruntled German Catholics would simply join the Lutheran church where they could hear services in their own tongue. Replicating a similar development in other parts of the country, Germans initiated the formation of their own national parish and desired to control parish life. Already in 1870–71, Sacramento German-speaking Catholics collected funds for a separate church from the approximately 100 German families of St. Rose's. This effort had been endorsed and supported by Anthony Coolot who had even purchased a lot for a new German Catholic church. The *Bee* recorded the purchase:

> NEW CATHOLIC CHURCH—Through the persevering efforts of a few German Catholics of Sacramento a site for another church of this denomination has been purchased and paid for. It is lot No. 3, K and L, between Thirteenth and Twelfth Streets, 80 feet by 160, and the price paid was $1,625. The immediate steps will be taken to provide for the construction of this temple of worship.[7]

To mobilize support for the project, Sacramento German-speaking Catholics invited the famed Austrian Jesuit, Franz Xavier Weninger, to deliver a public address. Weninger was a nationally known apostle of German Catholics. Wherever he went, he urged German Catholics to build their own churches and schools and to take all steps to preserve the German language insisting repeatedly: "Language preserves faith." The igniting spark for this secessionist movement took place in the wake of an unfortunate incident that pitted the Irish and the Germans of Sacramento against each other.[8]

The extent to which conditions in Europe influenced ethnic Sacramentans is reflected in the tensions that erupted between the two groups with the German victory over France in the Franco-Prussian War of 1870–71. Sacramentans avidly followed the battle reports that appeared in both daily papers of the city. When the Prussian armies smashed into Paris in early 1871, Sacramento's Germans spilled joyfully into the streets. Over 1,500 exulting citizens marched in a torchlight parade, igniting bonfires at the intersections of the streets, shooting fireworks, and singing repeatedly "*Die Wacht am Rhein*."[9] Sacramentans of French descent watched glumly as their fellow citizens celebrated the triumph of the Prussians. The Irish in particular, sensitive to the jackboot of foreign occupation on their native soil, quickly came to their support. The city's annual St. Patrick's Day celebration in 1872 showed their solidarity with France. In the celebrations of 1872, Sacramento's Irish Catholics hung French tricolor flags inside St. Rose's Church and invited the French consul general to be a guest of honor during the subsequent banquet. German-speaking Catholics were so incensed at this insult that they decided to move forward with their own parish.

What halted this effort toward a new church were actions of the church hierarchy in San Francisco. Archbishop Joseph Sadoc Alemany of San Francisco refused to give permission for the new church-even though he had allowed the formation of St. Boniface Parish in San Francisco for Germans and had given permission to establish and build a German Catholic church in Marysville. Indeed, as historian James Gaffey notes "an intensive program [of ministry] to this community [Sacramento] had not occupied a high position on Alemany's list of priorities."[10]

Alemany was likely convinced to follow this line by the pastor of St. Rose, Father Patrick Scanlan, who was in the midst of retiring a large debt left over from church renovations of the 1860s and was anxious to build a boy's school. A potential walkout of prosperous Germans would be a financial disaster. Scanlan then promised the angry German-speakers that the church would never again be used for nationalistic purposes. He also procured the services of a German-speaking priest for St. Rose and later to the cathedral and a temporary peace was restored.

This was an uneasy truce. Germans boasted of a long tradition of German religious culture, worship, art, music, literature, and saints. By contrast, Irish Catholicism, in their view, was oppressed and traumatized by the victimization of the church in Ireland. It lacked a solid tradition in the decorative arts of music. By the 1890s, German Catholic's antipathy for the dominant Irish flared again. German Franciscan Clementine Deymann observed of Sacramento's German Catholics, "our German people are only too often very coarse in their expressions about the Irish, about their people, the priests and bishops."[11] The German-speaking priest, Father Leon Haupts, who had served for several years, returned to his native Belgium after the new cathedral was finished in 1889. Germans again pushed for their own worship space. This time, they were wise enough not to appeal solely to their ethnic needs but pitched the idea as a response to the growing Catholic population of the eastern part of the city. They once more faced spirited opposition from the Irish but pushed back with strong lay leadership and the support of German friars.

A New Push for German Space: Melchior Diepenbrock

A new generation of leaders took up the cause. Melchior Diepenbrock, who had married one of Coolot's daughters, rose in prominence. Diepenbrock did not need marriage to enhance his prestige. He was the offspring of a high-ranking lawyer and judge in Germany, who was also related to the Cardinal Prince Archbishop of Breslau. Born in Bochholt, Westphalia, in 1858, Diepenbrock came to the United States in 1879. In 1885, he settled in San Francisco, where he became proprietor of a Catholic bookstore and supply house, as well as editor of the first German Catholic newspaper on the West Coast. In 1888, he married Coolot's daughter, Clara Louisa, and in 1891, he moved to Sacramento when he was invited to become part of his father-in-law's thriving enterprises.[12] By 1902, Diepenbrock's holdings included a 1,600-seat theater on the corner of Twelfth and J Streets (named for him), a 600-acre ranch 9 miles south of Sacramento that produced asparagus, beans, and alfalfa, and also a successful dairy farm that supplied milk to San Francisco. The father of ten children, Diepenbrock was a respected and more visible voice for Catholic affairs than even his father-in-law. His children also rose to become prominent in city professions.[13]

Diepenbrock had the support from other benefactors, including Swiss dairymen Joseph and Salome Inderkum, and John Meister, the owner of the Capitol Dairy across the American River. John Wunder, a native of Germany, was the proprietor of the popular William Tell Hotel on J Street between Eighth and Ninth. Melchior Beeler, who worked at Sacramento's prosperous Buffalo Brewery, was a native of Switzerland whose daughter joined the Franciscan Sisters at the school. By 1890, there were over 2,100 foreign-born Germans, as well as a distant colony in the farming village of Nicolaus. Sacramento Germans looked enviously at San Francisco, where German-speaking Franciscans headquartered in Teutopolis, Illinois, were permitted to open the German church of St. Boniface on Golden Gate Avenue. A new archbishop, Patrick Riordan, allowed the friars to open in sparsely populated Lake and Mendocino counties. In 1892, Riordan, also allowed them to open a parish in Fruitvale, a suburb of Oakland. The next year, the archbishop permitted the formation of St. Anthony's Parish, a second German national community in San Francisco.[14]

German pressure for their own church in Sacramento came to the attention of the Minister Provincial of the German Franciscans, Father Michael Richardt, and his provincial counselor (called a "definitor" in Franciscan nomenclature) Father Clementine Deymann. They traveled west from Illinois to visit Bishop Patrick Manogue in March 1893 with an offer to set up a ministry to the Germans in Sacramento. Manogue greeted them courteously and allowed himself to ruminate aloud on what the Franciscans could do if they were admitted to the Sacramento diocese.

A Case Study of Irish Opposition

Manogue still continued to worry that economic conditions were not robust enough so that Sacramento Catholics could not sustain a second parish—an argument advanced by his own local clergy, especially cathedral rector, Father Thomas Grace. But Manogue must have left the door open a crack because several months later Richardt again pressed Manogue for admission to the diocese. Once again, the prelate discouraged him noting "the dullness of the place and times" precluded such a move, that this was not the "*tempore opportuno*."[15]

Within a year, the tide turned in favor of new parish. A big breakthrough came in 1894, when one of Manogue's consultors, Father Matthew Coleman, the Irish-born pastor of St. Joseph's in Marysville who had successfully accommodated Germans in that community for many years, urged that "something must be done for the Germans."[16] Coleman's intervention apparently broke the Irish logjam over even considering the new parish, but even more pressing was the continued growth and development of Catholic life of Sacramento east of Eighteenth Street and the increasing distance of these Catholics from the cathedral. Without ready access to the Mass and sacraments, German Catholics might fall away.

An added consideration was the spiritual needs of the Sacramento County Institutions, poor house, and hospital on Stockton Boulevard. As

Dr. Phelan had noted many years ago, the needs of the sick and dying required pastoral attention. For the cathedral clergy who were called to these bedsides, the trip was not easy. Why not let the Franciscans take it over? The icing on the cake for the cash-strapped Sacramento diocese was the hope that financing of the new parish be carried mostly by the Franciscan friars who had sources of income that parishes did not have. Manogue also noted that there were many Swiss dairymen living in the country and commented: "You ... have the county poor house in your district and I think four or five breweries." By May 1894, Manogue sent word to Richardt "that I should be pleased to see him on important business on his next visit to the coast."[17] Richardt delegated one of the community's definitors Father Clementine Deymann from Watsonville to negotiate with the diocese.

Deymann finally arrived in September 1894. Manogue was in ill health but was alert enough to go forward with the new parish. In deference to the wishes of his Irish priests, he insisted that the new church be territorial rather than national. Whatever parish that was begun had to include a diverse array of Sacramentans. He informed Deymann that the new parish boundaries would begin at Eighteenth Street and extend northeast as far as the American River or city limits, east to the city limits, then at Thirty-first Street, and "four or five miles into the country and south as far as three miles from Freeport." He preserved a 3-mile limit from Freeport because of the existence of a Portuguese church there. That the parish had growth potential was clear to Deymann, who noted Manogue's observation that "the city is extending toward the East and southeast not towards the north on account of the American river and not towards the south on account of low lands."[18]

In a concession to the sensibilities of the Irish who now lost a lot of their territory, the largely German-born friars chose an Irish-surnamed padre, Father Augustine McClory, to begin the new enterprise. McClory was a proficient German speaker despite his Irish name. Interestingly, Manogue, probably anxious to loosen the purse strings of the well-heeled Sacramento Germans, balked at this at first, noting that "in my estimation it would be better to have a German in name and language starting as I had many conversations with the German people about a German Church."[19] However, on further reflection he acknowledged that a non-German pastor would be a better choice for the purpose of downplaying the "ethnic" character of the new parish and allaying the fears of his Irish brethren.

The new pastor arrived in Sacramento on or near October 16, 1894, in company with Deymann, who signed the final papers creating the parish. McClory took up residence at Manogue's home and began looking for property to plant the new parish.[20] McClory's arrival in Sacramento was noted in the city newspapers, as were his plans to secure property. Deymann reported that despite McClory's lack of administrative experience, "his whole appearance makes a very favorable impression with the people."[21] McClory surveyed the lands along 24th and 25th Streets, settling on a half-block of K Street between 25th and 26th, directly across from the ruins of Sutter's Fort. This property included two houses and sold for $7,000. "The bishop felt this place is best of all and he said 'It is a bargain and we ought to take it,'" wrote Deymann to Richardt. Deymann then urged McClory to close the purchase.[22] McClory felt the undertow of opposition. "I think the sooner we start in the better," he wrote to Richardt, "because I am pretty handicapped here ... In fact, the Bishop is the only one in the house who is enthusiastic over the new congregation—you can guess the rest!"[23] The Germans had their parish, but they had to pay for it.

When McClory informed Manogue that he had very little money, he noted "The Bishop was entirely taken aback at what he called the 'revelation' when I told him of how little I could pay, cash down. He said he didn't know where I could borrow the money." As he had learned when building his majestic cathedral, Sacramentans did not part with their money easily. "Although the mountains are full of gold, the people say money is scarce and it is 'hard to get at it.'" The ailing Manogue made only the concession that allowed the friars to minister to German speakers within the cathedral's territory. This particular concession had been secured almost off-handedly by Deymann in the final negotiations. As things were wrapping up, he asked Manogue, "What about the Germans who live in the cathedral parish—will they have the privilege to come to us?" the prelate "hesitated to answer." Jumping into the silence, Deymann pressed about whom would hear confessions for the Germans outside the parish boundaries, to which Manogue replied, "Oh, yes, I give them all liberty about that." But catching himself, Manogue asserted the primary identity of the new parish as English-speaking when he insisted "as regards other privileges (*i.e.*, fund-raising and school recruitment) I do not like to grant them."[24] In the end, Manogue stuck with his Irish colleagues. He reassured his fellow Hibernians that a new parish would not affect their bottom line.

McClory soon overcame difficulties with financing and shortly after the New Year 1895, Richardt arrived with Brother Adrian Wewer, the order's architect. Wewer set to work designing a church, which would be named in honor of St. Francis of Assisi. In the meantime, the friars rented the Union Hall on 20th and O Streets as a temporary church. They celebrated weekday masses and other sacramental celebrations in a small chapel created in the cottage on the church property. By early February,

Wewer had drawn up plans for a frame church and construction was contracted by Hook and Sons for $5,126. St. Francis Church went up in record time. The first services were held on Palm Sunday April 7, 1895. Manogue as a last token of generosity gave the fledgling parish the bell that originally hung in the tower at St. Rose Church. Work began at once on a school building, and by November 1895, St. Francis School opened. Several Sisters of Mercy reluctantly came daily from St. Joseph's Academy to teach the initial thirty-seven students. In 1896, a new two-story friary replaced the cottage in which the friars resided. The parish grew steadily.

Walking a Fine Line: Being German and American

To make this new parish work and to satisfy the needs of neglected Germans required skills and ingenuity of subsequent pastors. Irish suspicions of the German friars intensified when German-speakers out-paced the English-speaking in parish support. "It's the old story," wrote German-born Pastor Godfrey Hoelters in late 1900, "the Germans and the Irish can't get on, and that it's hard to get the Irish to support the church and school regularly."[25] Ongoing suspicion from the Irish clergy also complicated the efforts of the Franciscans, complained Hoelters, "The Rev. Ph. Brady [a member of the cathedral clergy] ... works against us at every turn, but comes here for confession."[26]

Nonetheless, Hoelters held the parish together and did his best to accommodate both groups. He reported to his superiors at Easter in 1901, "to avoid tension between the Irish and Germans, I have to preach myself in English and German on both feasts, in addition to two sermons every Sunday."[27] Hoelters would go on to build the new St. Francis Church, whose simple external mission-style belied an interior rich in the décor and color of German churches elsewhere. Support for this came from leading city businessmen and members of the Chamber of Commerce, who had pledged to help build the new edifice. But even here, opposition from Bishop Grace and the cathedral clergy reared its head. After Grace had given his permission for a new church building and fundraising began, the friars were informed by local mortician Thomas Gormley, a confidant of Bishop Grace, that the prelate opposed raising money from local businessmen who lived in the cathedral parish—the very group who had urged a new mission style church "that would be an attraction for the Eastern tourists and an advertisement for the city of Sacramento." Grace also accused Hoelters of holding fundraising meetings without his knowledge or approval. Hoelters responded forcefully that everything about the fundraising had been done with Grace's knowledge and consent. No one had contradicted his episcopal right and authority.[28]

At least externally, the friars went along with Manogue's instruction that this was not an ethnic parish. But, in fact, it was—at least for a time. Lay German Catholics aided by the timely intervention of the friars, pushed for this parish. St. Francis's German-speaking parishioners heard German sermons and could confess their sins in their native tongue. The friars perpetuated other German Catholic customs and traditions, particularly in decor and music. The influence of German Catholic laity was felt in 1907 when Sacramento's German Catholic organization sponsored a statewide meeting of the State Federation of German Catholic Societies of California that September. Modeled on the popular Katholikentage of Germany, this gathering featured liturgy, speeches, cultural events, and formal papers on topics of general interest. One of the speakers was Diepenbrock, who lectured on "Catholics as Citizens of the United States."

On Sunday, September 8, 1907, over 1400 German Catholics marched in procession (acclaimed as "the largest street parade of a religious nature ever held in Sacramento") to the Cathedral of the Blessed Sacrament where Bishop Thomas Grace bid them welcome and hosted them at a solemn pontifical Mass.[29] The event brought prominent German Catholic clerics and laity from all over the country to California's capital. The prospect of hosting another gathering of this type no doubt generated enthusiasm for a new St. Francis Church to replace the first wooden structure and, in all likelihood, generous contributions as well.

Accommodating and Surviving the Compromise

St. Francis pastors learned to live with the requirements of dual-language ministry in Sacramento. However, for some, St. Francis was not German enough. One disgruntled friar, Brother Eugenius, complained to his superior about the lack of initiative in recruiting German parishioners:

> That the sheep [the Germans] seek the shepherd instead of the shepherds seeking the lost sheep.... There are supposed to be considerably more than 1000 German Catholics here. And what is to happen to them if we are concerned only with those who come to church while letting the others go, or if we speak to them, only when we are collecting money?[30]

Yet the parish was perceived by the local clergy and community as a German parish. This was painfully clear when United States went to war with Germany in 1917 and anti-German sentiment ran high in

Sacramento. The local friars and some members of the community came under suspicion of disloyalty. Sniping at the "Dutch" church and the "Dutch" friars affected the community creating fear and likely led to a diminishment of its collections So extensive was this perception that in December 1919, after the war was over, Father Humilis Wiese, OFM, the pastor of the parish felt compelled to clarify and actually deny that the church had anything to do with Germans or German culture. In a public statement, he insisted that while the friars were German and bilingual because a Franciscan rule required "that each priest shall be familiar with at least two modern languages besides his own," he firmly rejected the notion that St. Francis was German or "Dutch" Parish, representing Manogue's request that Germans be served pastorally by the friars, but insisting: "Once and for all, St. Francis is not a German parish." He warned that people who referred to it as such did so as "the result of invincible boorish stupidity or cowardly envious malice."[31]

He could get away with this preposterous assertion because by this time, the city's demographics east of Eighteenth Street (the parish's western boundary) were themselves multiethnic and diverse. To the parish belonged the Swiss German Inderkum family, but also the Irish nationalist editor Thomas A. Connelly and the Mitchell family, whose son Brendan was a priest of the Franciscan order were parish members. An examination of the dedications on the church windows for the structure erected in 1910 reveals more "English" names than German names. But German art, music, and spirit continued in the parish choir was directed by Prussian-born Anton Dorndorf, a choirmaster of the old school. For many years, St. Francis' choirs perpetuated the German love for elaborate orchestral music. Later interior of the church included a work by Joseph Mayer, an artist of Munich including the crucifixion group above the main altar and the medallions in the arch above the communion rail depicting Eucharistic" types" of the Old and New Testaments. Although these were donated by a "Miss Brogan," their artistry and spirituality were German.

Taking Care of the West End: Ellen Margaret Bowden

The fancy homes and upscale realities of east Sacramento were an unlikely place to play out the ethnic issues of the city. The true "melting pot" or middle ground of Sacramento's ethnic groups was the neighborhoods of the West End—a stretch of streets moving west from Seventh Street to the banks of the Sacramento River and from the railway yards to the Y Street levee. Essayist Ernesto Galarza describes the medley of people and races living within blocks of one:

Lower Sacramento was the quarter that people who made money moved away from.... The lower quarter was not exclusively a Mexican barrio, but a mix of many nationalities. Between L and N Streets two blocks from us, the Japanese had taken over. Their homes were in alleys behind shops, which they advertised with signs covered with black scribbles. The women walked on the street in kimonos, wooden sandals, and white stockings, carrying neat black, bundles on their backs and wearing their hair in puffs with long ivory needles stuck through them ... Chinatown was on the other side of K Street toward the Southern Pacific Shops. Our houses were old, but those in which the Chinese kept stores, laundries and restaurants were older still ... In the hotels and rooming houses scattered about the barrio where the Filipino farm workers, river boat stewards and houseboys made their homes. Like the Mexicans they had their own pool halls, which they called clubs. Hindus from the rice and fruit country north of the capital staying in the rooming houses when they were in town ... The Portuguese and Italian families fathered their own neighborhoods along Fourth and Fifth Streets southward toward the Y-Street Levee. The Poles, Yugo-Slavs and Koreans, too few to take over any particular part of it, were scattered throughout the barrio. Black men drifted in and out of town ... It was a kaleidoscope of colors and languages and customs that surprised and absorbed me at every turn.[32]

Galarza's somewhat romantic recollections notwithstanding, the West End had a downside—dilapidated housing, poor streets, and brackish water. It was also afflicted with various social pathologies such as prostitution, illegal gambling dens, urban violence, and other kinds of public disorder. Religious institutions continued to abide in the city's oldest, now aging West End district, including the old Congregational church whose square towers still presided over the lower city. But as new foreign-born families arrived and the city spread eastward, declining church memberships nudged the churches to follow their congregations.

Ironically, Catholics had been among the first to abandon the area west of Seventh Street when the St. Rose property was sold to the federal government in 1887. Although St. Joseph's Academy still remained on the fringe of the area, without St. Rose, there was no Catholic church in a neighborhood that had a large number of Catholic citizens. Nor did there appear any great interest in creating a mission station. West End Catholics had to hike the nearly eleven blocks to the cathedral if they went to church at all.

Bishop Manogue died in February 1895, and his successor, Thomas Grace, became one of Sacramento's most beloved citizens. However, as the gentle and accommodating Grace had an abhorrence of debt and showed uncharacteristic "spine" in opposing the proliferation of ethnic parishes.

Even when the sheer growth of the Sacramento ethnic community challenged the idea of "English-only" churches, Grace tried to hold to his convictions. His opposition was only overcome by determined laity. On the West End, the benefactor was a pious woman named Ellen Margaret Bowden who forced his hand by donating a building that could be made into a church and a school; he agreed to allow a worship space for the various peoples gathered on the west end.

Ellen Margaret "Ella" Bowden (1855–1926), another of the often neglected lay "founders" of Sacramento Catholicism, was the youngest of the four children of Irish-born Richard and Margaret Bowden.[33] The couple immigrated to California in the 1850s. Ellen was born in San Francisco, but her family settled in Sacramento. Ellen attended St. Joseph's Academy, and the family belonged to St. Rose and the cathedral parish. Ellen and her three brothers lived with their parents on the west side of the city. Tragedy befell the couple as their three sons—James, Stephen, and Richard—all died before reaching adulthood. As the sole surviving child, Ellen foreswore marriage to remain with her parents until their deaths. Her father lived until the age of eighty-four, dying in 1898; her mother followed two years later at the age of eighty-eight. Encouraged by Father Philip Brady, a recently ordained cleric from County Cavan who had been stationed at the cathedral in the 1890s, young Ellen turned to religious pursuits and charity to fill her days. The death of her parents left her a sizeable inheritance, which she lavishly gave to the Catholic Church. Her priestly friend was one of the chief recipients of her largesse.[34] The charitable Bowden purchased the stable house and servant quarters of the Crocker Mansion, located on Third and O Streets. The structure was a two-story building that had two huge rooms on each level. She renovated the building, transforming the lower portion into a church. In April 1900, she presented this as a "gift" to Bishop Grace, along with a handsome $5,000 endowment for the care and upkeep of the building.[35] She then donated an additional $500 for renovations on the new church. The work lasted throughout the fall, with some of the liturgical furniture coming from the old St. Rose. On December 8, 1900, Grace dedicated the structure named to honor the memory of Bowden's brother Stephen. At her insistence, the altar society of the new church would be named in honor of her mother, Margaret. Later, a school and day care center would be attached to the church.

One woman's philanthropy made the stable house-turned-church the home base for virtually every major Catholic ethnic group in Sacramento: Italians, Portuguese, Croatians, Japanese, Mexicans, and Filipinos. Over the years, hundreds of Catholic Sacramentans received their first formal religious instruction in the upper quarters, which had been transformed into classrooms. St. Stephen's Church was a microcosm of the diversity of Sacramento's West End. No other city institution, with the possible exception of Lincoln Elementary School, reflected this so clearly. As a gathering place for Catholics of many nationalities, St. Stephen's was an instant success. "Every Sunday since the dedication of the Church its capacity has been heavily taxed," wrote a correspondent for the *Monitor*. "The congregation has proved too much for the church and a second Mass has become necessary." Virtually every Catholic ethnic group attended St. Stephen's services—a veritable United Nations of nationalities—listening to the Mass in ancient Latin, while they strained to understand the words of the sermon delivered in the Irish accented English of the visiting priest. In addition to the liturgical celebrations, on the upper level a Sunday school was held for the parish children, providing preparation for the sacraments and proper religious instruction from the catechism. St. Stephen's was the staging ground for churches serving the Italians, the Portuguese, the Japanese, "Slavonians i.e., Croatians, Mexicans, and finally as a center for a lay spirituality group called Cursillo.[36]

One final benefaction of Miss Bowden was the purchase of land and the building of the simple church structure at Thirty-ninth and H Streets in East Sacramento. She was ever loyal and unfailingly generous to her old friend Father Brady, who had founded a new church in the growing neighborhood, originally called St. Stephen's. The old St. Stephen's at Third and O had been abandoned and sold to a Japanese theater in 1930. She asked that the new church be named in memory of her brother, Stephen. Ellen Bowden died on October 28, 1926, leaving an estate of $200,000 (over $3 million in 2022).[37] After all the disbursements had been made, Brady was left with a tidy $10,000, the seed money for a new parish church, priest's residence, and school. Brady's health, however, also began to falter under the strain of organizing and building. Indeed, at the time of the first masses in the new church, the *Bee* noted that he was afflicted with influenza.[38] After three years of declining health, he died in 1929.[39] Bowden's legacy in Sacramento Catholic life is understated. Her lonely burial site in an obscure corner of St. Joseph's Cemetery is the only reminder of this remarkable and generous woman.

Sacramento's Italians

St. Stephen's identity as a multi-ethnic church was a temporary phase of its history. Eventually, largely with lay leadership and some strategic clerical support, independent ethnic churches emerged. It was never easy. The Italians were among the first to break away. Lay leadership was critical.

One of the largest immigrant communities in Sacramento were the Italians, many of whom were attracted to Sacramento by work in the rail yards and other commercial enterprises such as hotels, retail shops, service work, and barbering. They hailed from various regions of Italy, but the largest number were from central and northern Italy. They steadily increased in number from the second half of the nineteenth and into the early twentieth century. In 1852, only forty-one Italians resided in Sacramento County. By 1870, the number had increased to 123; in 1890, 521 foreign-born Italians resided in the county. By 1910, a sharp increase occurred with the census registering 1,820 foreign-born Italians. This number peaked in 1930 when 3,004 Italians were counted. These numbers, however, did not include people who had one Italian parent, or Italians whose parents were both Italian-Americans. In 1910, Italians comprised 4 percent of the total population of the county, only outranked by the Japanese at 6 percent. By 1920, the Italians still held second place, but had slipped to 3 percent of the total population. In 1930, they tied with Mexicans and Portuguese for second rank with 2 percent of the population; in 1940, they remained second but had slid to 2 percent of the total county residents.[40]

Italians lived in close proximity to each other. Italians first lived in an area bounded by Fifth and 26th Streets west to east and C through F Streets north to south. By 1910, they began migrating out of these neighborhoods taking up residence in the southern half of the city—especially in the newly developing area of Oak Park. Later, they would move eastward. Italians played an important role in restaurant and food industries in Sacramento. As their wealth and social prominence increased, their leadership emerged.[41]

Luigi (Louis) Caffaro—Community Leader

Among the cadre of Italian businessmen and local leaders, Luigi Caffaro stood out. Often found in the center of public events celebrating Italian culture and life, he was described as "one of the most prominent members of the local Italian colony."[42] Born in Lessolo, Torino, in the Piedmont region of Italy in 1854, he came to the U.S. in 1882. He married Francesca Perino in 1892 and had two sons. Caffaro was a hotelier, opening the Roma Hotel on Second and I and the popular Commercial Hotel in 1904 at Third and I. He acquired considerable properties in Yolo and El Dorado Counties and also plots in the Chinatown areas of Sacramento near the fetid China Slough. His Commercial Hotel property stood in the way of the expansion of an electric car depot and on one occasion the property was smashed by an errant Southern Pacific box car. Caffaro had the company rebuild the wall and he inserted a cannon in the wall facing any future potential damage.

Caffaro belonged to a number of fraternal societies including the Bersaglieri a marching regiment. He was involved in Italian affairs and because of his wealth and prominence commanded considerable respect. Caffaro helped established a short-lived Italian school in 1908. When it failed, they pressed the school board and the state legislature to permit the teaching of Italian in public schools.[43] In 1907, another prominent Italian businessman, Victor Pannatoni, a native of Via Reggio, began the weekly *La Capitale* newspaper which remained in print until 1945. The paper served as a medium of communication throughout the Italian colony. When the property was purchased for the first Italian church on Eighth Street, the deed was in Caffaro's name.

An Ethnic Church

The growing size of Sacramento's Italian community found an important point of organizational unity at St. Stephen's. In 1888, Pope Leo XIII issued the encyclical *Quam Aerumnosa*, which lamented the poor spiritual care of Italian Catholics abroad and urged bishops to make provisions for them. This encouragement was received by Sacramento Italians who looked to the formation of an Italian church to provide an outlet for Italian culture and social needs.

Caffaro and others were able to work with an Italian-born priest of the Sacramento diocese, Father Michael Gualco.[44] Gualco, an independent minded priest in Chico, was able to press the growing demands of Sacramento's Italian community on a reluctant Bishop Grace. Gualco, a native of Capriata d'Orba, near Genoa, was ordained to the priesthood in Milan in 1864. After a stint in the eastern United States, he came to California in 1868 and held a number of posts in the Bay Area and eventually worked in Placerville and Folsom, where he became the first Catholic chaplain at Folsom prison. He then spent a brief time as pastor of St. Christopher's Parish in the rural burg of Galt in southern Sacramento County. In 1889, Manogue dispatched him to Chico, to lead St. John the Baptist Parish and to tend to missions at the small agricultural communities of Gridley, Oroville, and Cherokee.[45]

Gualco was urbane, articulate, and extremely capable. His visibility as the only Italian-speaking priest in the Sacramento diocese led Caffaro and other individuals and representatives of Italian organizations to approach him regarding specialized ministry to the Italians of Northern California.

Gualco, who feuded with Grace over the need for the Catholic hospital in Chico, willingly conveyed the complaints of the areas Italians to Apostolic Delegate Archbishop Diomede Falconio in Washington, D.C. Grace paid little heed to Gualco's complaints until 1903, when Falconio paid a visit to California. At a meeting with Grace in the spring, Falconio insisted that the bishop do more to accommodate Italian Catholics. With Falconio's not-so-gentle push, Grace moved away from his "English only" policy and began to seek Italian-speaking priests for the people of Sacramento. In 1903, Falconio visited Sacramento and in private conversation urged Grace to do more for local Italians. A grateful Italian community gave the cathedral and beautiful sanctuary lamp, which Falconio blessed with much pomp and ceremony.[46]

In 1905, Bishop Grace visited Rome to report on the state of affairs in his diocese and Gualco accompanied him.[47] On the way to Rome, the two men stopped in Washington, D.C., to visit the apostolic delegate to receive further instructions about the trip. When the two arrived in Italy, Grace placed the selection of the Italian priests in Gualco's hands and, after the visit in Rome, departed for a vacation in Ireland. Gualco returned to his native northern Italy and found two priests, Temistocle Eugenio Mela and Dominic Taverna, and a seminarian, Benso Massimo, willing to come to California. He arranged for their passage to America and reported to the delegate that these three "ought to satisfy our people."[48]

But Grace dragged his feet on carrying out the plans for the new church. Only the two priests arrived in the fall of 1905. Content only with Irish priests from his own All Hallows College in Dublin, Grace abandoned the seminarian recruited to come to America. As a result, the young man affiliated with a Texas diocese instead.[49] It was left now to Mela to get the project off the ground. He was assigned to the cathedral, but first spent some time in Chico with Gualco learning English and acculturating himself to the ways of America. Taverna, originally assigned to Reno, was sent to the town of Sutter Creek in Amador County where he remained until 1918. Ultimately, he succeeded Mela in Sacramento.[50]

Mela was first dispatched on Sundays to say Mass at St. Stephen's and began separating out the Italian members of the polyglot community in order to organize them into their own church. The new Italian church, to be located on another spot, was called St. Mary's. Mela soon met Italian community leaders like Caffaro and other local notables and began to assess the prospects of financing an independent Italian parish.

However, fearful that enough money could not be raised to build a church or to support a clergyman, Grace changed the plans and insisted that Mela form another polyglot community combining Italians and

Portuguese in a common parish. There was some precedent for this in the large Portuguese church of St. Joseph in Oakland, which had combined all the Latin nationalities into one church. By providing masses for each of the ethnic groups (with a sermons and confessions in their native tongue) and some creativity in church decor (allowing distinctive statuary and devotional sites), church leaders hoped a unity in diversity might be possible. It also made sense financially. After all, it had appeared to work at St. Francis. Bishop Grace issued an edict stating that Mela "is the recognized pastor of all the Italian Catholics of Sacramento. Also, of all the Portuguese and Spanish. I hope all those good Catholic people will avail themselves of his ministrations and that they will contribute liberally to help him build a church."[51]

By late December 1906, the committee purchased an 80 × 60-foot lot on Eighth and N Streets, directly next door to the Stanford Mansion. A fundraiser for the building took place in the Catholic meeting lodge, Serra Hall, in January 1907, realizing, according to one source, "a neat sum" that pushed the building plan forward.[52] A small temporary structure was completed by the end of May.[53] On June 9, 1907, Monsignor Thomas Capel dedicated the new structure named in honor of St. Mary.[54] To accommodate his diverse parishioners, Mela scheduled a service at 7 a.m. for the Portuguese and a second at 9 a.m. for the Italians. No services for the Spanish-speaking were planned.

Mela was a good man, but not very skilled with finances or community relations. His polyglot parish was a financial disaster. Even with elaborate plans, the community could only raise enough money to build a relatively small building, and this nearly broke the bank. Grace's indifference to the ethnic church was evident. When bill collectors descended upon the hapless Mela, the embattled pastor attempted to get aid from Bishop Grace, only to discover that the prelate had decamped for his annual vacation and could not be disturbed. Not knowing where else to turn, Mela traveled to San Francisco and poured out his troubles to Archbishop Patrick Riordan:

> I came to Sacramento on Wenesday [*sic*.], I looked right away for His Grace my own Bishop, but I was told that he went to the Springs. So, now I am here in a trouble which really I do not know how to get off. Almost every day some collector call [sic] upon me and this make me sick. Yesterday one of them was insist that I had to promise to pay at least half of a bill of $130 before night. I do so. I was forced to make a debt of 60 dollars with one good French lady and to give away the only ten dollars I had and which were given to me the day before for ten masses. I do not think this fair, so, I recommend my church and myself to your Grace for advice and help.[55]

To add to Mela's problems, internal strife erupted among the Italians when Father Gualco in far-off Chico began to field complaints from disgruntled members of the Sacramento Italian colony who resented the fact that the Eighth and N property and the church were titled in the name of Mela and not the bishop of Sacramento.[56] Gualco reported this impropriety to the apostolic delegate in Washington, D.C.[57]

Eventually, the property of St. Mary's was deeded over to Grace, but Gualco kept up a steady drumbeat of complaints to Falconio regarding Grace's "failure" to minister to Italians in Reno and other parts of the diocese. He also reported the prelate for ignoring the Germans in Woodland. Grace calmly defended himself when confronted by Falconio with another raft of Gualco-generated complaints, Grace declared:

> In reply to your letter concerning the alleged neglect of the Italians and Germans I would say that all is done for those people that can be done and that most conscientiously.... I get two or three new young priests from the old country [Ireland] every summer and the diocese is very well supplied.[58]

Gualco's death in 1912 brought an end to this agitation, and the Italian community continued to grow and steadily improve under Mela's watchful eye. "Little Father Mela," as C. K. McClatchy was wont to call him, earned the respect of his Italian parishioners, primarily through his simple lifestyle. When he died in the influenza pandemic of 1918, McClatchy eulogized him: "Everybody in Sacramento knew Father Mela, and everybody liked him. He was patient, industrious, sincere, generous, and self-sacrificing."[59] McClatchy quoted approvingly a comment by prominent Irish Catholic politician and funeral director, William Gormley:

> Father Mela had done a great deal for his parishioners to come here from Italy for their sake, to learn the English language, which he could not speak on his arrival here and to strive [as] hard as he had done to bring back into the fold the delinquent members of his race.[60]

Italian Growth

St. Mary's continued as a cultural center for the Italian community. Historian Bruce Pierini notes, "St. Mary's served as a spiritual, social and ethnic hub for the Italians of Sacramento."[61] Sacramento's Italian community found a point of unity in the church, despite regional and internal differences that shadowed its establishment. St. Mary's and the nearby city park were an important gathering point for religious events, festivals, picnics, and parades. Both Mela and Taverna encouraged ethnic social activities and lent church facilities to other Italian organizations and causes. Taverna also helped found the popular Dante Club, one of the most important social organizations among Italians in Sacramento. During its first three years, the club met in St. Mary's Hall. St. Mary's would have a rebirth on Sacramento's growing east side after World War II, but the new parish would be a mixture of nationalities that required only a limited Italian identity (festivals and devotionalism) rather than the full-bore ethnic language parish.

The Portuguese

The Portuguese community, a much closer and more financially stable group in Sacramento, also challenged the resistance of the Irish to ethnic parishes

Amid the broad ethnic medley in the West End described earlier was an increasing number of Portuguese, drawn heavily from the Atlantic islands of the Azores, Madeira, and the Republic of Cabo Verde. Nearly 90 percent of all Portuguese immigration to Sacramento came from these islands. The Azores alone accounted for almost 80 percent.[62] A later group would come from the Portuguese mainland between 1906 and 1921, largely to escape political turmoil. Yet another group would arrive after 1957, escaping a natural disaster on the island of Fayal. Portuguese immigrants often remained in clusters representing their native islands. In California, they tended to settle first in rural areas, becoming shepherds and dairymen primarily in the Central Valley but also in other arable lands in the state.[63] Groups of Portuguese immigrants were to be found in all California cities from the 1850s on, commencing first in Oakland. In the 1890s, Portuguese immigrants from rural areas began to move into Sacramento, making it the second largest urban center of Portuguese life in the state.

Sacramento County's Portuguese population had its origins in the agricultural areas that abutted the east bank of the Sacramento River, Freeport, Pocket, and Riverside districts. On both sides of the Sacramento River, a vibrant Portuguese colony developed known as the "Lisbon District." These reclaimed swamplands became rich truck and dairy farms, giving the community a strong economic life. The Portuguese also worked in the Sacramento Brick Company yard, which provided building materials for any number of Sacramento homes and businesses as well as the Cathedral of the Blessed Sacrament.[64] From these areas, Portuguese moved into Sacramento city proper, taking up residence in undeveloped areas on the south side (the portion of the city south of R Street) near the present site of Southside Park. The Portuguese colony staked out land east and north between Third and Fifth Streets and along R, S, and T Streets along the fringes of the Japanese and Chinese neighborhoods. This well-defined urban enclave came to be known as the "Arizona" neighborhood, a corruption of the term "Azores."[65] The number of Portuguese grew steadily in Sacramento, their various businesses providing jobs for the community, especially the canneries, which employed more and more women for seasonal work

Fraternal and mutual aid societies among Sacramento's Portuguese had begun in 1872 and expanded in 1901 with the United States Portuguese Relief Society. Portuguese businesses served the specialized needs of the community: grocers sold special foods, vintners imported wines from the old country, and social gatherings replicated the essential elements of culture, music, dancing, and various types of public celebration. Communication was facilitated by the rise of the Portuguese press in the city. By the latter part of the nineteenth century, Portuguese language newspapers had begun in San Francisco and Oakland. In 1900, Sacramento's first Portuguese newspaper, *A Liberdade,* was launched by a former Catholic priest, Guilherme Silveira da Gloria.[66] One of his earliest collaborators in the Portuguese press was another Sacramentan very much involved in Sacramento's Portuguese community, Manuel S. Quaresma, who in 1903 began a rival paper called *O Imparcial.*[67] These two journals helped to draw the community closer together and certainly provided a good deal of religious news.

In 1893, the number of Portuguese Catholics south of Sacramento in the area of Freeport and Clarksburg grew so steadily that community leaders were able to cajole Manogue to allow them to establish St. Joseph's Church in Freeport, served by Father Seraphino Gabriel Soares. It became a magnet for Sacramento-area Portuguese. Portuguese Catholics had been among the most fervent parishioners of St. Stephen's Church, and Portuguese women, especially those who worked in the canneries, sent their children to the parish school. The forces of ethnic separatism were strong among a people as well organized and devout as the Sacramento Portuguese. Where would they attend Mass and hold their special devotions?

At first, the Portuguese were exhorted by Bishop Grace to join St. Mary's Church. Reluctant to start a separate parish, Grace had insisted that Mela operate a bi- or tri-national parish by providing services for all. But Mela's inability to speak Portuguese and to understand the special needs of his Lusitanian parishioners made it difficult for the experiment to work. Some had already "defected" to the cathedral.[68] Many refused to have their children baptized at St. Mary's and brought their offspring to Portuguese churches in San Jose or Freeport. To help address their needs, Mela hired a

Portuguese priest, Father E. Silvera, to celebrate the earliest Sunday Mass and to deliver the sermon in the Portuguese language. This mollified some parishioners and St. Mary's showed an immediate increase in its Portuguese attendance. Others, however, began to demand a separate church.

Manuel S. Williams was a respected Portuguese grocer. Born in the Azores in 1849, he had come to America and owned a grocery store on the corner of Eleventh and Q Streets. He also bought up properties in the area and took the lead at meetings in his store to press for a separate church.[69] The catalyst for separation received important support in 1907 through the visit by a high-ranking church official, Bishop Enrique DaSilva.[70] The visiting prelate was a native of Lisbon and came to California as a wandering refugee from the East Indies where he had been ejected from the leadership of a Portuguese mission diocese. DaSilva commenced an inspection tour of Portuguese Catholics in diaspora around America. In 1906, he appeared in San Francisco and was there in early 1907 when Coadjutor Archbishop George Montgomery of San Francisco died unexpectedly. Archbishop Patrick Riordan, who was in ill health and now deprived of assistance in his twelve-county archdiocese, appealed to DaSilva for help. He thus began conducting episcopal duties (confirmations, etc.) and also visited the large Portuguese contingent in Oakland, San Jose, and elsewhere, providing episcopal dignity to the annual rounds of festas, confirmations, and other public celebrations.[71]

In August 1908, he came to Sacramento as the ranking prelate at the Grand Convention of the Young Men's Institute (YMI).[72] The cathedral monthly news magazine noted that during his brief stay in the city:

> He met a great many Catholics and non-Catholics ... and everyone ... was charmed by his great affability as well as by the extreme cordiality of his manners. Though belonging to the royal house of Portugal, the Bishop is delightfully Democratic and is approachable to all.[73]

Among those who approached him were Williams and the Sacramento Portuguese, who felt pride in his nationality.[74] In early March 1909, DaSilva visited Sacramento stopping at various churches, visiting with members of the state legislature and with representatives of the growing Portuguese population in the city.[75] Simmering discontent with Father Mela among the Portuguese at St. Mary's was no doubt fanned into flames by DaSilva, who very likely urged the group to press for their own parish. During the early months of 1909, informal meetings among the parishioners, abetted by Father Silvera, led to the drafting of a petition to Bishop Grace for the creation of a separate Portuguese parish, headed by a Portuguese priest.

Rumors of the petition and demands angered Father Mela, who believed he was providing well for his Portuguese parishioners, and desperately depended on their financial support. In retaliation, he discharged the Portuguese priest when the latter showed up for an early morning Mass Sunday in April 1909. The dismissal galvanized the already discontented Portuguese. A number of Portuguese arose *en bloc* during the service and stalked to the cathedral, vowing never to return.[76] Mela added further fuel to the fire by telling a reporter that Silvera's dismissal was necessary "for the good of the congregation."[77]

The enraged Portuguese circulated another petition to Bishop Grace, this one thoroughly condemning Mela (although the language was later toned down) and demanding once again the establishment of a separate Portuguese parish. Signed by Williams and 319 heads of households representing 1,400 Portuguese in Sacramento, the petition began:

We, the undersigned Portuguese Catholics knowing the necessity of erecting a Portuguese church in this city and having a Portuguese priest to preach to us in our native language most humbly petition Your Lordship to grant us permission.[78]

Grace was in Jackson on a confirmation trip during the fracas, but the seriousness of the matter was conveyed to him when the signatories of the petition warned him that they would "appeal to the Pope and submit their cause to him." Apparently, the matter reached Archbishop Falconio, the apostolic delegate. In a letter, to Falconio, Mela blamed the uproar on Grace, noting that Mela had worked with the Portuguese, but that the bishop had allowed a Portuguese (DaSilva) to come from Fall River and they intended to split away taking much needed financial support with them. He further noted that the Portuguese owed the Italian church precisely $2,333.30.[79]

Upon his return to the city, Grace sought to calm passions, urging the Portuguese to return temporarily to St. Stephen's for worship until a decision could be reached on their petition. Some did and Portuguese ministry continued in the old church throughout the remainder of the spring and into the summer. An especially fervent celebration of the Holy Spirit festival took place in late May, preceded by a Mass in St. Stephen's presided over by Father Seraphim Soares of Freeport.[80] Finally, in late summer of 1909, Grace reluctantly approved the establishment of a Portuguese church. He appointed Terceira native John V. Azevedo, then assisting at Sutter Creek, as its first pastor. The parish officially commenced on October 24, 1909.[81] Azevedo formed a committee consisting of Manuel Williams and Manuel Enos, two successful grocers. It was Manuel

Williams who donated land on the corner of Twelfth and S Streets. By 1913, St. Elizabeth Church was dedicated, the *Bee* noting, "The dream of Portuguese Catholics for their own place of worship ... will become an accomplished fact."[82] This church, sitting diagonally on the corner of 12th and S Streets, occupied a unique niche on the grid of Sacramento.

As long as the ethnic neighborhood that surrounded St. Elizabeth persisted, the church was an important symbol of unity and pride for the Sacramento Portuguese community.

The Latinx Presence

Spanish-speaking numbers in Sacramento had been growing since the 1930s forward. Most of them were Catholics. Here too, clerics led the way, but beneath the public reporting of ministry to Spanish speakers were laypersons of the same caliber as Gregory Phelan. Resourceful, hardworking, and capable people did much of the actual work of organizing and encouraging local ministries.

Historians of Spanish-speaking ministry in Sacramento point to the Feast of Our Lady of Guadalupe, celebrated in the community of Broderick's Our Lady of the Blessed Sacrament Church. These celebrations in nearby Yolo County (directly across the Sacramento River) first took place on December 14, 1919. Here, a Latino Catholic Francisco Ortiz and his family organized and hosted the celebration of this important day for Mexican Catholics. Its high attendance merited the celebration of a rare Solemn High Mass.[83] The Ortiz celebration no doubt focused attention on the rapidly growing Hispanic population, so much so that the next year, Bishop Thomas Grace himself traveled to Broderick to celebrate this Mass. In 1923, his successor, Bishop Patrick Keane, did the same.[84]

Focus turned on the presence of Spanish-speaking parents and children on the West End, and the growing dependence of Mexican women on the daycare services offered by the Franciscans at Grace Day Home on the west end. In the late 1920s, Father Stephen Keating a former Salesian Priest who was multi-lingual was recruited to help form a coordinated effort for Spanish speakers, but Keating could not do it himself.

The Work of Stephen "Padre Esteban" Keating and Frederico Falcon

Bishop Robert Armstrong succeeded Keane in early 1929. Prior to coming to California, he had worked with migrant laborers in the fruit orchards of central Washington State. From the start, he directed cathedral rector, Thomas E. Horgan, to study the religious and social conditions within Sacramento's Mexican community, as well as the surrounding region, and to keep track of the volume of ministry taking place with them.

In the report issued at the end of 1930, Horgan noted that about 5,000 Mexicans lived in the Sacramento area, 3,000 of whom were permanent residents. The remainder were agricultural workers who stayed in the city six months or less. At the cathedral, 300 Mexican families registered but more than that came to Mass. In addition to sacramental and catechetical programs for the children of the Mexicans, they also required critical social services. To advance his work, Keating recruited two Spanish-speaking lay people (both natives of Fresnillo, Zacatecas). One was Frederico Falcon, a worker at the Southern Pacific, whose former career before coming north was as a musician and schoolteacher. Falcon had a large extended family who assisted him in his work. The other layperson was a young woman, Magdalena Martinez. She had tried convent life but had frail health and could not manage the rigors of religious life. She lived first with her family in Los Angeles and then came to Sacramento.

Frederico Falcon was born in Fresnillo, a mining city in Zacatecas, Mexico where he worked as teacher and a musician. He entered the United States in May 1919 and lived for a time in El Paso, Texas. After the death of his first wife, he married Maria Cleofas and raised a family. He found work with the Southern Pacific Railroad and in 1926 was transferred to Sacramento. He volunteered to work with Keating to survey the needs of the growing Mexican community in Sacramento and helped arrange the first gathering of the Mexican community. He and Martinez were constantly at the service of the city's growing Mexican cohort. Their tasks were varied. They helped get marriages blessed, served as sponsors for confirmation (later Falcon took his daughters Aurora and Socorro as *madrinas*). He and Martinez replicated Mexican devotions, helped plan and finance funerals, directed dramas in the cathedral basement, prepared Christmas baskets, and translated for people who needed help. Falcon, his daughters remembered, had a beautiful tenor voice and often sang at celebrations in the cathedral. His wife, Maria Cleofas, supported these efforts, supplementing Frederico's income with seasonal work at the Sacramento canneries to help support the family and took in foster children.[85]

Eventually, Falcon quit his job at the Southern Pacific (despite all its benefits) and went to work identifying the needs of the community and helping Spanish-speaking Sacramentans secure necessary social services. Martinez assisted basic catechetical work, instructing scores of children in religious doctrine and preparing them for their first Holy Communion and Confirmation. Keating, Falcon, and Martinez organized a panoply of Catholic social groups to attract Mexicans such as the Holy Name Society, the Christian Mothers, and a Santa Inez group for young women. The Junior Holy Name also welcomed new Mexican members.[86]

Martinez worked alongside the Sisters of Mercy to organize and teach a six-week summer vacation school for Spanish-speaking children at St. Joseph's Academy. She also instructed the young people in certain domestic and practical skills. She reached out to Evelyn Restano of the Catholic Ladies Relief Society, an association of Catholic laywomen who served as teachers to young Mexican girls. Restano noted in her report to the organization: "Our cooperation consisted in helping maintain the interest of the other girls by teaching them to sew and providing material for this work ... many of our women responded and excellent results followed."[87] Every annual report the women of the Relief Society dutifully recorded the numbers of dresses made, napkins and handkerchiefs embroidered, and clothing repaired. In 1932, the recording secretary noted that, "The ladies also remodeled about two dozen dresses and slips for the children who made their First Communion and Confirmation, who could not afford to pay for them."

Seeking financial assistance, Keating reached out to the Catholic Ladies Relief Society in October 1928, informing the women that the Mexicans had come to provide cheap agricultural and industrial labor but noted that of the 500 relief cases in Sacramento County, seventy of them were Mexicans. Poor wages, enforced idleness, illness, and poor religious instruction were the many plights of Mexican immigrants, and they required additional assistance.[88]

Keating, Falcon, and Martinez won the acclaim of city and county social welfare officials. Keating noted: "The value of the work ... is attested by the fact that the local agencies invariably act favorably upon any case that we recommend to them as deserving."[89] In the realm of social work, Falcon and Martinez placed children in orphanages and adults in mental hospitals, provided free burials, jail visitation, distributed clothing and food, and assisted with casework in other agencies. Until the Mexicans acquired their own church, their social gatherings were held at the cathedral. This was no easy task as social conditions among Sacramento's Mexican community worsened in the depressed 1930s. Many laborers had worked in the fields and canneries and were now jobless. Bitter competition for scarce jobs led to concerted efforts by the United States government in 1931 to repatriate Mexicans living in the United States.[90] In Sacramento, as government agents rounded up Mexican nationals and placed them on trains going south. Falcon and Martinez did what they could to intervene, but the Mexican community dwindled. Eventually, as

Falcon and Martinez shouldered more and more of the load. Martinez' health faltered, and she moved to Stockton where she died in 1936. After Father Keating left the city and the priesthood, the work fell on Falcon.

A New Mexican Church

Mexican numbers soared again after 1942, when California began the bracero or farmworker program. Necessitated by wartime agricultural needs, the program allowed large numbers of Mexicans to enter California legally to provide cheap labor. Large numbers of men, women, and children arrived to work during the picking season and then laid low for a number of months until work resumed in the fields. On the West End of Sacramento, Hispanic visibility increased. The student body at St. Joseph's Academy and Holy Angels schools became increasingly Hispanic. More and more Hispanic surnames appeared in cathedral baptismal, marriage, and funeral registers.

As other ethnic groups before them had done, the Mexican community became increasingly insistent on having its own new church. Before he left the priesthood, Keating had begun an ambitious fundraising plan for a new Mexican church.[91] However, their goal of raising $25,000 was stymied by the Great Depression and the attendant decline in the number of Mexicans living in Sacramento. With the renewed job activity and numbers of the 1940s, Keating's successor Father Raymond Renwald took up the task and looked to Falcon for help. Renwald taught himself Spanish and began to say Mass for the workers, attempting to preach to them in their native tongue. "I would go down on Sunday mornings, and Saturday afternoons," he later recalled. "I did that for about a year then when the end of the war came and they were moved out then they asked for a church of their own."[92]

Renwald and Falcon managed to acquire the former St. Stephen's property, which had been sold in 1930 to a Japanese theater. When the owners defaulted on their mortgage due to Japanese internment, city officials offered it back to the Diocese of Sacramento. Renwald and Falcon jumped at the offer. With the monies that had been previously collected, a new chapel became a reality. A committee of Mexicans led by Falcon, Southern Pacific Machinist Susano Garcia, Jose Gonzales, and Juan Navarro cleaned, equipped, and renamed the building Our Lady of Guadalupe Chapel. In April 1945, Bishop Armstrong came to celebrate Mass. The Catholic newspaper reminded its readers:

In former days St. Stephen's was attended by great numbers of Sacramento residents … Already many old-time residents have expressed their pleasure at the knowledge that the venerable and hallowed building has been restored and will again be dedicated to the work of God.[93]

The chapel was the cause of community rejoicing. At the first Guadalupe celebrations in December 1945, lay members took charge of the public celebrations, raising money for a large oil painting of Our Lady of Guadalupe, which was hung over the main altar. On a rainy day in December, hundreds turned out at the cathedral for the solemn Mass followed by a procession from the cathedral to the new Mexican chapel. The paper reported:

> The great crowds of Mexican people ... who had arrived at the cathedral in spite of the rain and threatening weather, insisted on marching in procession to the new building at Third and O Streets. At the head of the procession was borne a large picture of the Virgin of Guadalupe surrounded by flowers carried by four girls dressed as angels, and surrounded in turn by a group of boys and girls dressed as Indians.

Among the marchers was Zacharias Esparza, who, "though 75 years of age and suffering from a broken leg," insisted on walking with his crutches from his home nearly a mile from the cathedral and then another mile to the Third and O church site in the procession." The paper noted also that "workers for the Southern Pacific Railroad ... some 300 strong ... [carried] a streamer with huge letters *Trabajadores Catholicos Mexicanos*."[94] Joining with them was a spectrum of Mexican cultural and social organizations that had taken root in Sacramento: *Hijas de Maria, Club Atletico Mexicanos, Sociedad del Santo Nombre de Jesus, Alianza Hispano-Americana, Club Fermenil Adelitas, Congregacion de N. Srs. De Los Dolores*, and *Damas de la Corte de Honor*. After the ceremonies of blessing and the enthronement of the painting, people visited the new church all day. In the evening, 300 devout Mexican Catholics returned to recite the rosary. Until a new Guadalupe Church was built in the 1950s, this was the spiritual center of the Mexican *colonia*. The inauguration of the new church included clergy support but was driven heavily by Falcon and other leaders. Unlike other ethnic groups, they had no opposition from the local clergy—although the church was under the administrative thumb of the cathedral church. The old buildings, though shabby, and always in danger of fire, nonetheless provided a location for their gathering and the perpetuation of their social and cultural links.

Falcon died in 1952 at the age of fifty-nine, but by that time, the ministry to Latinx Catholics was well established with full-time bilingual priests and access to a nearby Catholic school. By 1958, the community moved from the old buildings on Third and O to a newly built church at Seventh Street and T. Falcon and Keating's memories were preserved by a grateful community. Falcon's role and that of Martinez was pivotal.

Caffaro, Williams, Falcon, Martinez, and Diepenbrock were all men and women whose contributions of money, land, pastoral care, and determination earned them an important niche in Sacramento Catholic history.

The Fallen Away Catholic: C. K. McClatchy and Defending the Church

A common cliché about Catholicism runs like this: "once a Catholic always a Catholic." The point here is that while people may reject Catholic teachings and church attendance, Catholicism's rituals, organization, unique vocabulary, and culture leaves a strong imprint on people raised Catholic. This was especially true in the American West, where adherence to church teachings and attendance was often tenuous and older religious practices easily fell away. The history of California is famous for its fallen-aways, including James Duvall Phelan, mayor of San Francisco and later United States senator. Long serving Sacramento Judge Peter Shields and even former governor and Jesuit seminarian Jerry Brown were not noted for their adherence to traditional Catholicism. Perhaps the most visible drop-out was the long-time editor and publisher of the *Sacramento Bee*, Charles Kenny (C. K.) McClatchy (1858–1937).

Charles K. McClatchy was a son of Sacramento. Born in November 1859, he attended Sacramento public schools. His father James had dabbled in journalism, law enforcement, and finally bought a share in the city's evening paper, the *Bee*. After his death in 1883, his sons, Valentine and C. K., consolidated their hold on the paper and directed its destinies until their partnerships dissolved in the 1920s. C. K. held on to the paper until his death in 1937 and dominated the editorial policy of the *Bee* for more than a generation. His opinions were clear and expressed in the tone of ordinary reporting. McClatchy's agenda alone, usually progressive, but also bigoted at times, dictated the policy of the *Bee*—not an editorial board.

C. K. was born a Catholic, baptized, confirmed, and married at St. Rose Church. He was reared by a devoutly Catholic mother. His wife,

Ella Kelly, was also extremely devout. He had all three of his children baptized and two of them had Catholic priests as godfathers. McClatchy enjoyed warm relations with most of Sacramento's bishops and his family donated handsomely to church monuments in the city. Although he attended the Jesuit Santa Clara University, McClatchy dropped out of active practice of the faith long before his mature years—as did his brother Valentine. Whatever religious beliefs he held were more akin to the moralistic religious views espoused by writers like Charles Dickens. Religious doctrines and regulations meant nothing to him. He judged the authenticity of religious persons based on their conformity to the words and example of the "Gentle Nazorean." C. K. was friendly to some Catholic clergy. He traveled extensively visiting Catholic sites, enjoying audiences with two popes, and spending time in the Holy Land.

But he could be scornful of religious people and ideas and did not hold back criticizing clergy who irritated him. As editor of the *Bee*, he occasionally singled out the pope and the Catholic hierarchy as targets of his invective. He waged noisy battles with one of California's most prominent clergymen, Father Peter C. Yorke of San Francisco, who accused him of being an apostate. However, C. K. had no tolerance for religious bigotry, which he felt left a stain on the reputation of the city. When the need arose, he could vigorously defend the church. In fact, it was on the pages of his powerful newspaper that he was about the only public voice defending the church.

Anti-Catholicism was a part of Sacramento's history. When Catholics were attacked and their loyalty made suspect, how did Catholics respond? Unlike other areas of the country where Catholics mobilized and pushed back, Sacramento Catholic clergy and leadership were largely silent. It was McClatchy who took on the most virulent instances of anti-Catholicism in the city's history sponsored by the American Protective Association and the Ku Klux Klan.

Anti-Catholicism in Sacramento History

Being Catholic in Sacramento was sometimes a perilous proposition. In the nineteenth century, the church had faced organized opposition from the Know Nothing party movement, which targeted the loyalty of Catholic Americans. This agitation lasted only a few years.[1] For the most part, Sacramentans were highly tolerant or indifferent to various religions, especially in the tumultuous early days of the city. Religion was a layer of civilization that many men readily threw off on the mining frontier. Early missionaries and preachers who came to work among the Argonauts did not find a warm reception. Overt hostility to the Catholic Church emerged more strongly in the late nineteenth and the early twentieth centuries. The first generation of Sacramento life witnessed public fears that Catholic teachings could threaten the American way of life. These concerns were often found in the *Daily Union*, which lamented the slow growth of Protestant churches while Catholic numbers were advancing:

> We see the rapid strides which foreign customs and the notions of Catholic countries are making in this state. If California has ever been wholly reclaimed from the usages of that religion in which it was founded with so much constancy and heroism nearly a century ago, it has certainly passed out of the hands of the descendants of those who stood side-by-side in the days of the Reformation, and the dominant ecclesiastical power today is what it was ten and twenty years ago.[2]

Anti-Catholic speakers found ready audiences in the state capital. Catholic "interests" were conjured up to account for the relatively small-bore political corruption and occasional tawdriness of city government. The immigrant character of the church made it a target and its "strange" religious beliefs held it up to ridicule. A frequent trope was the image of the foreign born "Catholic boss" secretly manipulating the affairs of the city or of "hordes" of immigrant Catholics whose strange surnames were dominating city jobs. The dailies ran regular stories of murder, divorce, marital infidelity, larceny, arson, gambling, excessive drinking, violations of the Sunday Sabbath, and prostitution that emanated from the city's foreign-born neighborhoods. Since many of these newcomers were Roman Catholics, it was not a big leap for some to begin linking urban pathologies with the habits bred into immigrants by the church. The city consensus, expressed in the public press, favored Americanization and the rapid shedding of "foreign" habits.

Nowhere was this view on better display than during the city's annual Fourth of July celebration. This city-funded festival drew together a diversity of Sacramentans to the city plaza to hear patriotic speeches and to celebrate American identity. Public schools, such as Lincoln Elementary at Fourth and Q Streets, were right in the heart of the most ethnically diverse area of Sacramento. At Lincoln, classes were conducted in English and civics instruction reinforced lessons of public patriotism and praised American national identity. During the progressive era (1898–1918), local insistence on homogeneous Americanism was strongly endorsed by the McClatchy-run *Sacramento Bee*. Valentine McClatchy was one of the strongest voices in California pressing for the exclusion of the Japanese from the Golden State, while his brother C. K. launched querulous investigations over the nature of history texts that seemed to favor the British in the Revolutionary War used at Sacramento's only high school. During World War I and in its immediate aftermath, when nationalistic passions ran higher than ever, insistence on the assimilation of ethnic groups was pressed as a sign of patriotic loyalty.

The American Protective Association (APA)

Populist nativism during the 1890s coalesced into a political organization called the American Protective Association (APA). Founded by Henry F. Bowers in Clinton, Iowa in March 1887, the APA exploited fears generated by heavy immigration in the 1880s. They also targeted the visible growth of the Catholic Church, linking the largely immigrant church with urban corruption. Employing often crude anti-Catholic rhetoric, the APA warned of the corrosive effects of a growing Catholic population, especially in urban politics and public schools. The organization built strength throughout the East and Midwest, winning representation in municipal governments in Milwaukee, Detroit, and Kansas City. It also came to California.[3]

The first inklings of anti-Catholic agitation came from a group of Protestant pastors called the Ministerial Union in 1891. The union combined prayer and fellowship with plans for collective action on issues facing the city.[4] They expressed regular concern for city morality and sometimes bluntly blamed social problems on Catholic ethnic groups. Rev. R. M. Stevenson of Westminster Presbyterian preached a sermon on George Washington's birthday, February 22, 1891, titled "Our Country and Our Church" which derided the impact of immigration on the country. He pointed out that the number of Italians, Hungarians, Russians, and Poles was outpacing the older immigrant groups. "Not only is the tide of immigration swelling with rapidity, but it is bringing us the most filthy and degraded and undesirable classes." He warned of the dangers of taking in "a great mass of people whom we cannot assimilate." He singled out the saloon among the many evils of this mass of immigration. "Nothing so increased the number of criminals and the number of paupers as the saloon, and it is a great producer of lunatics and idiots."[5] Stevenson was echoed by other pastors and revivalists who amplified his jeremiads on social conditions in Sacramento, linking urban pathologies with the presence of the largely Catholic immigrant groups in their midst. When the city erupted into unexpected turmoil during a bitter railroad strike in 1894, fears of immigrant radicalism flared.

The APA came into California in early 1893. The Catholic San Francisco *Monitor* sounded the first warning of the movement's activities in the state.[6] A more blunt warning was issued on January 27, 1894.[7] In Sacramento, Bishop Manogue was one of the first to bring home to Northern California's large Irish Catholic population the danger of the group by comparing them Northern Ireland's "Orangemen."[8]

These attacks and political mobilization against the Catholic Church escalated, no doubt worrying the local Catholic clergy, but the only one to speak up and challenge it was Charles McClatchy. He relentlessly reported on the activities of the APA and printed the incendiary and bigoted words of local Protestant ministers who took verbal swings at the Church from the safety of their Sunday pulpits. When the APA entered local politics, he called out and exposed them and their ideas.

McClatchy Battles the APA

McClatchy had begun reporting on APA activities in 1894 when he noted the activities of an alleged former priest, Joseph Slattery, and his wife, Elizabeth, supposedly a former nun. This duo appeared in the capital city as speakers at a series of anti-Catholic lectures at the Pythian Hall on Ninth and I Streets. Slattery addressed the crowd of about 300 one afternoon, and his wife Elizabeth spoke in the evening.

Slattery, of Irish birth, claimed to have been a priest who converted to Protestantism in 1879. He showed up around Easter in 1894 and ridiculed Catholic beliefs and ceremonies, especially the Council of Trent's assertion of the *ex opere operato* efficacy of the sacraments. This doctrine teaches that the sacraments mediate the power of Christ even if the priest is unworthy. Slattery also attacked clerical celibacy and took aim at the Irish, claiming "Ireland might have Rome rule, but she should never have Home Rule, while there was an honest Orangeman left in the Emerald Isle."[9]

The evening talk by Mrs. Slattery was replete with stories of her former life as a Poor Clare nun in England and the pressure she felt to enter the convent which she did "in a moment of impulse and loneliness." She also recounted ribald stories of "Father Pat Smith who never drew a sober breath" and Sister Loyola "who was over fond of Guinness Stout." Elizabeth titillated crowds with suggestions of sexual misconduct when she alluded to "occurrences that could not be dwelt upon before a mixed audience" and "implored those who had daughters to beware of convents and nuns, and declared that every convent should be open to governmental inspection."[10] Neither speaker made much mention of the APA until the very end of their talks, and then only in a few words. McClatchy took a dim view of the Slatterys reporting their allegations with a sarcastic tone.

The Slatterys moved on to San Francisco, but their rhetoric opened up a space for local Protestant clergy to give vent to similar concerns about Catholics. Sometime in 1894, two chapters of the APA were organized in Sacramento. A third chapter, Council No. 16, was composed exclusively of African Americans and reached about sixty members. The organization trotted out boilerplate accusations about Catholic loyalty in late April, Reverend John B. Koehne of the Congregational Church, one of Sacramento's most accomplished intellectuals, spoke approvingly of the organization and discussed such anti-Catholic themes as "The Priest and the Flag," "The Jesuits Oath," and "Masonry and the Papacy." Other local preachers also injected a note of suspicion about Catholic loyalty to America. "The Priest and the Flag," in particular, reprinted verbatim in the *Record-Union* and summarized in the *Bee*, issued a stark warning about Catholic loyalty and questioned the compatibility of Catholic institutions with the American way of life. Speaking directly of Sacramento's foreign-born Catholic population, Koehne declared: "We should not shut the gates on account of birth, but against those who are under the dominion of a foreign potentate or pontiff. They are not Americans. Some men who are born here have foreign ideas—Italian ideas."[11]

Koehne argued that Catholics were becoming too numerous and too dominant in the state capital. Their presence was threatening the hegemony of native-born Americans and weakening the hold of Protestantism on Sacramento's social and cultural life. There was a hint of jealousy:

> If our Protestant business men are asked to contribute toward building a church or raising a mortgage on it, they say "Oh, you are always begging" … But if asked to contribute to build a Cathedral their contributions flow freely. No one ever, on the contrary, heard of a Catholic aiding to build a Protestant Church.

Catholic influence, he insisted, was pervasive at every level of Sacramento life, including (and especially) McClatchy's *Bee*. "The hand of the Catholic church was on their mouths. They would give columns to the ordination of a bishop and a few lines to the memory or work of the most eminent Protestant Divine."[12]

McClatchy noted this invective but took aim at the threat of APA infiltration of the state and local Republican Party. The former head of Westminster Presbyterian Church, Reverend Henry H. Rice, reiterated Koehne's concerns about Catholic power and warned darkly that the Jesuits were scheming to take over the country. He pointed to the increasing number of Catholic citizens in major American cities and specifically noted that "millions and millions of dollars have been taken from the treasury in New York City and applied to support Catholic denominational schools." Rice firmly asserted, "This political ascendancy has been brought about premeditatedly, for I have no doubt that Catholics combine to elect Catholics to office."[13]

Catholics in Sacramento's public schools were a prime APA target. Rev. Rice's successor at Westminster, Rev. R. M. Stevenson insisted that the APA was a necessity to curb Catholic influence:

> For instance, in this city the Catholic church manages to have at least one half of the public school teachers. I think that the priests use their influence to debar parents from sending their children to the public schools. Now there is an inconsistency in priests discouraging people from sending their children to public schools, and yet they want their people to teach our children in the public schools.[14]

Pastor Charles F. Oehler of St. John's Lutheran Church echoed Stevenson's complaint:

> While it is a fact that the Catholic Church is against the public schools it is also a fact that girls educated in Catholic convents and who are prejudiced against the public schools are allowed to teach in them ... Catholics are prejudiced against public schools ... it is a question whether Catholics, for that reason are competent to teach in the public schools.[15]

Others interviewed—including T. A. Atkinson of the Methodist Episcopal Church, W. S. Hoskinson of the English Lutheran Church, A. P. Banks of First Baptist, J. E. Denton of First Christian, and Walter Baugh of the Fourteenth Street Presbyterian—denied any APA/Protestant affiliation. However, some, like Hoskinson, suggested that there was some substance to fears of Catholic power and political influence.[16]

McClatchy stepped up his exposure and ridicule of APA principles and candidates during the off-year national election of 1894. The *Bee* obtained copies of the APA state ticket endorsements and the directory of members for Sacramento's APA lodges. McClatchy listed the names and occupations of the city's APA leadership, rank and file. Among them were twelve candidates for various state and local offices, including three Democrats, five Populists, three Republicans, and one Citizens' Party member. On the list as well were ministers A. P. Banks, R. M. Stevenson, and J. B. Koehne. Harry Knox, a strike leader in the previous summer's labor disturbances at the railroad yards, also appeared in the list of 157 members.[17]

One last bit of election-eve drama took place when three ministers—J. H. Reider of Calvary Church, A. P. Banks of First Baptist, and J. L. Trefren of Central Methodist Episcopal—attempted to round up political support for the APA at a joint service in the Methodist Church. Reider and his deacon invoked the aid of the Almighty for the APA through prayer: "O Lord God, Father Almighty, grant us victory in the great battle that is now before us and guard the ballot box at next Tuesday's election." Reider's sermon, entitled "Daily Bread" warned his hearers away from voting for men "who would tear down what we have built up ... no candidate should be elected who would tear down the glorious institutions of our country."[18] Later, Reider's support for APA principles apparently was not forceful enough for some of his congregation, and when the minister refused to become an outright member of the APA, he was pushed out of his pulpit by an APA cabal.

But in 1894, Protestant support was strong. At an evening service on election eve, Banks the Baptist warned Sacramentans about Catholic political power: "men who have taken possession of our land are foreign and strange to our institutions." He then urged his fellow citizens to "Gaze upon the spectacle of he who stands behind the incense in yonder Cathedral, and you will see whose hand is upon the politics of this country." The Methodist Trefren was even more dramatic in his indictment of Catholic political power:

> Every brick formed into a Catholic Cathedral is a political machine.... Suppose the Catholic Church ruled today, would I be here speaking tonight and you worshiping God according to the dictates of your conscience? No sir! A thousand times no! No you would have to walk up those stone steps [pointing in the direction of the Catholic Cathedral] or you couldn't worship at all.

As the congregation left Trefren's church, they were given APA literature along with the state and county list published in the *Bee*.[19] The election results were mixed but provided enough APA victories to give the movement heart. Of the nineteen candidates they endorsed (some of whom denied affiliation with the organization), only six actually won election (one of whom denied being an APA member) and one tied.[20]

Official Catholic voices in Sacramento were strangely muted in the midst of the rising invective. Perhaps clerical leaders were content to let the *Monitor* and the *Bee* carry on the verbal pyrotechnics, for they said little. In part, this was due to Manogue's illness, which by November had left him completely bedridden. However, Father Thomas Grace and other cathedral clergy, along with the Mercy Sisters and the Christian Brothers, did not speak openly on the matter. Not so much as a single Catholic sermon appears to have been recorded denouncing the APA. However, after the election other voices did speak in reaction to the election results. A Sacramento gathering of the Catholic Knights of America, highlighted by the appearances of both Father Ferdinand Serds of Oakland, spiritual director of the group, and A. J. McMahon of San Francisco, state secretary of the Knights, reaffirmed the patriotism and loyalty of American Catholics. C. K. McClatchy was present and delivered a toast to "The Press." In it, he affirmed his duty to uphold the Constitution and the "elemental principle" of that document, civil and religious liberty.[21]

A few days after the banquet, the city dedicated a new flagpole in the Civic Plaza. There, Robert T. Devlin—a prominent Catholic businessman, attorney, and later state senator—made an even more forceful statement of Catholic rights: "And what is the freedom symbolized by the Glorious Stars and Stripes?" he asked.

> It is the freedom to express honest thoughts, to recognize no dominion of man over man, to enjoy our natural rights, to respect the rights of our neighbors, to make the laws by which we shall be bound, to choose as sovereign our servants in public place, to commune with our Maker as we wish, to worship God according to the dictates of our conscience or to worship not at all.

Seeking to calm passions stoked by fears of runaway Catholic power in Sacramento, Devlin reassured the crowd that Catholics supported, "Free schools, free thought, free speech. These are the foundation stones on which our glorious country rests. Destroy one of these and the whole structure falls." But he warned:

> Whoever would stifle honest thought or deny his fellow-men the same freedom he claims for himself, or attempts to deprive them of enjoying the inalienable rights vouchsafed to all and preserve that for which this nation was baptized in blood is a traitor to that flag.[22]

Buoyed by their modest successes in the 1894 campaign, APA mobilization continued into 1895 as Sacramento prepared for mayoral elections. The kickoff event took place at the fortress-like Pythian Castle on Ninth and I Streets. Rev. Banks opened the meeting with a prayer and was followed by speech from Deputy County Sheriff, W. W. Coons. B. F. Huddelson of Oakland, president of the APA, addressed the subject of "Good Citizenship and the Right of Free Speech." Coons and Banks kept APA forces alive in the city and won a signal victory later when they dominated the planning for its Fourth of July celebrations.[23] By the end of July, another public event was held at Turner Hall, featuring Rev. J. M. Taulbee, a Methodist preacher who was also state president of the APA in Kentucky. In a rambling and occasionally ungrammatical discourse, Taulbee compared APA resistance to Catholicism to the heroic actions of the patriots of the American Revolution. Taulbee's martial battle cries pompously called for the exclusion of Catholics from political life by "the rattle of musketry and the roar of cannon."[24]

Taulbee's invective stung Catholics to defend their patriotism. On the tenth anniversary of the founding of the Sacramento branch of the Young Men's Institute (YMI), the local organizers welcomed Father William McKinnon of nearby Rio Vista, who had replied to other APA slurs on American Catholic patriotism.[25] Taking as his theme the YMI motto, *Pro Deo et patria* (for God and Country), he vigorously defended the organization from accusations of disloyalty to American values:

> I know that there exist fanatics at the present day. In our own state they are numerous and noisy and they say that American institutions are endangered by our organization: that we are a body of Catholic young men and therefore are not loyal. It is our glory and our pride to be Catholics but we are none the less loyal for that. Every hope of our hearts, every prayer of our souls is a prayer for the prosperity and perpetuity of the American Republic.... I voice the sentiments of the Young Men's Institute, that I as a Catholic priest, yield to no man my love and devotion to my Church, nor do I yield to any man in my loyalty to my country. Yes, I love this grand old Republic; I love her institutions; I love her liberty; I love my country's flag and long may it wave over my country in exalted glory and forever remain the banner of down-trodden men, giving hope and cheer.[26]

APA organization for the upcoming municipal elections continued at a rapid pace. In late August 1895, APA President Huddleson appeared once again in Sacramento to meet with the councils of the APA at the Odd Fellows Temple to "give the Order pointers for the coming election." One report estimated attendance at the meeting and its subsequent banquet at the Pythian Hall to be 900.[27]

As Sacramento headed into the nominating and campaigning phases of its municipal elections, it was clear that Huddleson's "pointers" served a good reason. On the eve of the city Republican primaries, the *Bee* noted:

> It is quite evident that the APA intends to take an active part in the contest tomorrow. All or nearly all of the known leaders of the organization have

been working with might and main today, interviewing the members and the belief is quite strong that an effort is to be made to capture the Republican primaries and then have full control of the Convention to be held next Monday night.[28]

The organization waged a ward-by-ward battle for the Sacramento city government and pressed Cyrus Hubbard, a hardware merchant and Civil War veteran, for the mayoral post.[29] The effort failed as the convention nominated J. W. Wilson as its standard bearer.

The APA then endorsed a ticket of favorites who had been nominated by other parties. Hubbard secured the nomination of a hastily contrived Citizens' Party in late September. McClatchy opened a full-throttled attack on the mayoral candidate:

> The fitness—or rather unfitness—of C. H. Hubbard to be Mayor of any progressive community, is not necessary here to discuss. Every man who knows this nominee—every business man who has ever had dealings with him knows that he is entirely unsuitable in every way to be Mayor of any city that desires to progress.[30]

To flush out Hubbard's true allegiances, McClatchy released a list of APA picks in the October 14 edition of the *Bee*.[31] The editor then sent a reporter to ask Hubbard if he was "in sympathy with the acknowledged objects of this order which are primarily to keep members of a certain religion out of any political office." Hubbard replied evasively, "*The Bee* has the wrong idea of the APAs. They are just as much opposed to Methodism and Presbyterianism in politics as they are to Catholicism." But he added: "The Pope of Rome has a representative at every court of Europe and would like to have one in Washington. The Catholic Church must keep its hands out of politics."[32] McClatchy's reporters also tracked down city clerk candidate Oscar Flint and City Attorney John Quincy Brown to ask the same question, receiving an ambiguous answer from Flint and an outright denial from Brown. The one openly APA candidate, J. A. Roblin, running for the school board, positively affirmed his membership and pledged if elected to vote "to discharge every Catholic in the employ of the schools of this city."

As the campaign went into high gear, party politics splintered into several different directions, and the campaign evolved into a three-way contest when, with three weeks before the election, former mayor Benjamin U. Steinman entered the race challenging Hubbard and J. W. Wilson (running as a regular Republican). Nativist feelings bubbled to the surface as the campaign intensified. J. E. Denton of the First Christian Church, who had denied APA membership the previous year, unloaded on the Irish and the Catholic Church in a sermon on the Sunday evening before the election:

> Let us as Protestants stand together against every Catholic in the land.
> Let us be true to the APAs. The APA is against the Irish. It is time for
> Americans to take office and for the Irish to take to the woods.... Let
> us for once have an American government, an American state, and an
> American city where we can hang our banner on the outer wall, "No
> Irish need apply.[33]

Matters grew even worse when another APA speaker, former state Deputy Attorney General Oregon Sanders, delivered another anti-foreign/anti-Catholic diatribe before a crowd of 500 at the Old Pavilion. Sanders indulged in the crudest rhetoric heard to that point, mimicking the accents of ethnic Californians, sneering at "Dagoes," and deriding Irish immigrants as having "a Gothic brow and hair on his [their] teeth." Sanders demanded the direct election of the president, "because he was afraid a time might come when there might be a sufficient number of Catholics chosen as electors." He also warned that churches were becoming obscenely wealthy because of tax exemptions for their properties, which he accounted, tallied up to $2 million:

> They bury a Dago there and call it a cemetery. When in the course of
> time that property becomes worth millions of dollars that festive Dago
> experiences a premature resurrection and he is carted off to the sand
> dunes, while the cemetery is cut up into town lots and sold.[34]

The gross nativism of these speakers may have undercut whatever appeal the movement might have had in the city. Cyrus Hubbard would probably have been defeated by Republican candidate J. W. Wilson had former mayor Benjamin Steinman not jumped into the fray and divided anti-Hubbard votes, allowing Hubbard to squeak through to claim mayoral victory.[35] However, despite his election, the 1895 contest marked the crest of APA activity and anti-Catholic rhetoric in Sacramento. The only openly announced APA member, J. A. Roblin, who ran for trustee of the Eighth Ward, lost handily. Some APA-endorsed members won, including C. C. Perkins, who ran for the Fifth Ward slot on the board of school directors, Daniel Webster Carmichael as treasurer, J. Frank Brown as city attorney, D. McKay as trustee of the Fourth Ward, and school director William H. Sherburn of the First Ward. However, all denied being members of the APA.

Following the election, Mayor Hubbard tried to repay his debt to the APA. One story circulated by the *Bee* involved a hapless Catholic in the railroad shops who for some unknown reason had campaigned for Hubbard. However, when he attempted to seek a patronage appointment, however, he was turned down because of his religion. Hubbard denied the story, but admitted to the *Bee,* "Of course you know that the APA was the backbone of my election and that I am inclined to favor them in any way."[36] The new mayor made some languid efforts to reform the police department and looked especially into efforts to prevent drinking on the job. McClatchy decried these efforts as "a rigid system of espionage" and a feint to remove Catholic officers whose jobs were protected by tenure provisions of the city charter. "In fact," McClatchy wrote, "it is freely asserted around the streets that seven obnoxious members of the police force will go if Mayor Hubbard can get a sufficient number of the Board of Trustees to stand in with him."[37] Hubbard met with failure in his attempt to appoint G. W. Rallton, a railroad ticket agent, prominent Episcopalian and APA member, to the police force.[38] Nonetheless, McClatchy continued to keep an eagle eye on the mayor, scrutinizing his every appointment, and bashing him in print whenever he stepped out of line.[39] Hubbard was replaced after a single term by William Land, a local hotelier.

The brief term of Mayor Hubbard signaled the end of formal APA activity in Sacramento. Thanks to C. K. McClatchy the city turned away from nativists and anti-Catholic rhetoric and embrace a new season of urban reform.

Prohibition and the Rise of the Klan

Anti-Catholicism and nativism ebbed until World War I awakened a new concern for public morality and anxieties about the loyalty of some Sacramento citizens. Indeed, well before the passage of the Eighteenth Amendment to the Constitution, Sacramento had carried on a vigorous debate over the presence of drinking establishments in their midst. Women's groups like the local branch of the Women's Christian Temperance Union (supported by Margaret Crocker) and the Church Federation, a successor to the Ministerial Union, periodically spearheaded crusades to restrict the growth of taverns, especially in residential neighborhoods, and continually urged city officials to crack down on saloons that operated without licenses. McClatchy himself, though addicted to drink his entire life, was also critical of taverns that admitted women and were open to children. However, these efforts generally were in vain as periodic votes always registered strong opposition to any curtailing of the right to purchase and consume alcoholic beverages. Indeed, saloons and taverns abounded in Sacramento, many of them in the West End—the home of the immigrant population. Efforts to enforce restrictions on taverns got a new wind during World War I when military officials put pressure on the local government to "clean up" the "immoral" conditions in Sacramento's West End. A major investigation of the problem, spearheaded by Simon Lubin (son of the department store head) revealed many problems with enforcement of laws against prostitution, gambling, and public intoxication.[40] The Eighteenth amendment to the Constitution was ratified during the war as a food conservation measure. It was to be enforced by the Volstead Act, which took effect in January 1920, after a raft of "blow-out" parties.[41]

But illegal liquor continued to be bought and sold in Sacramento, causing one state officer to characterize the city as the "wettest" in the state. This flaunting of the law angered other Sacramento citizens who saw it as an affront to public morality. The leaders of certain of the Protestant churches and the Church Federation continued their opposition to liquor, blaming it as the prime source of the vice and immorality of the city. More vocal prohibition leaders urged the spotlight be turned on those of the city who violated the law and city officials who allowed them to get away with it. For many of them, this meant the Catholic Church and those sympathetic to the church in local government.

Not surprisingly, Catholics were not of one mind on the subject of Prohibition (some favored it). But, mirroring the wider Sacramento populace, by and large Catholics tended to oppose prohibition. Every now and then, a Catholic priest would publicly denounce the Eighteenth Amendment, and his words would be repeated verbatim in the *Bee* by C. K. McClatchy who himself was a bitter opponent of the law.[42] But, once again, religious communities like the Catholic Church, which had large immigrant constituencies, were held in suspicion as those most likely to inhabit speakeasies and other places of ill-repute.

One rumor circulated throughout the city that the Knights of Columbus, a popular Catholic men's fraternal club, had "gone on record" against the enforcement of the prohibition laws. Local Methodist minister W. D. Redburn summed up the distaste for Catholic "immorality" when he declared: "Nearly all of the bawdy houses, bootleg joints and other dives are owned or controlled by Romanists. A member of the Catholic church may go to Mass in the morning and lie drunk in the gutter all day, Sunday or any other day."[43] When a Methodist lay preacher delivered a diatribe against the Catholic Church to a large audience in Sacramento in late April 1921, editor Thomas Connelly of the *Catholic Herald* lamented the appeal of these hateful messages:

It is hard how any thinking American can give accommodations to those whose sole purpose is to vilify a large and respectable body of their fellow citizens. Yet ... that is what has happened here in the beautiful city of Sacramento![44]

An especially distasteful source of anti-Catholic animus among the city's Protestant churches continued to be Westminster Presbyterian Church, especially under the pastorate of William E. Harrison. Harrison became Westminster's senior pastor in 1914, succeeding the scholarly and dignified John T. Wills. Coming to Sacramento from Abilene, Texas, Harrison was, according to the church historian, "energetic, emotional, and uninhibited" and anxious to build up church membership. Among his more successful techniques was importing the charismatic evangelist Aimee Semple McPherson to lead a revival in his church (a move which met with disdain from other Protestant ministers), showing movies in the church sanctuary, and Catholic bashing.[45] Postwar Sacramento, jittery from threats of radicalism and suspicious of the foreign-born, was primed for Harrison's kind of preaching. Catholics were once again targeted as the cause of urban woes as they had been during the Know-Nothing and APA "explosions." However, this time, the popular appeal and the tenacity of organized anti-Catholicism suggested something deeper than a periodic burst of bigotry. The violation of Prohibition gave new impetus to anti-Catholic sentiments that still lurked among some Sacramento citizens. It was not only illegal, but according to some, immoral.

The Popularity of the Ku Klux Klan

The emergence and popularity of the Ku Klux Klan in Sacramento was an ominous sign for the city's Catholics.[46] Revived in Atlanta and then nationally just before World War I, this organization made great inroads in many communities and states throughout the 1920s. Its members exercised considerable influence over state and local elections in a number of states outside the rural south. Klansmen were found in Massachusetts, Michigan, Indiana, and Wisconsin. Although seen by many as hooded bigots, slightly ridiculous in their sheets and declamations as 100 percent American, Klan membership still had a great appeal to men and women. Many enjoyed the fraternal contact of its local units (Klaverns) the organization and saw the group as a guardian of public morality. Klan organizations made their first appearance in Southern California in early 1921 and were soon recruiting members and making dramatic public appearances in white-sheeted Klan regalia at funerals and in various churches.

Klan organizers appeared in the state capital that same year. They worked hard to avoid the taint of their original racist bigotry. They even painted an African American church on the West End as a gesture of good will and portrayed themselves as good citizens who demanded proper enforcement of Prohibition laws as a condition for social order. The Catholic Church was an embodiment of all that opposed biblical Christianity and the source dysfunction in the community. Klansmen engaged in vigilante raids on suspected distillers and labor radicals. The appeal of Klan efforts to recruit Sacramentans astounded their opponents in the press and local government. When the first Klan rally was held in Sacramento County on May 5, 1921, on Lower Stockton Road, nearly 4,000 people attended.[47] Editor McClatchy spoke out immediately, exposing them and tracking down their activities, often splashing their exploits on the front page of the *Bee*.[48]

Through a half-year of 1922, the *Sacramento Bee* waged war on the local Klan by keeping the media spotlight on the organization. It highlighted Klan activities in the area and condemned them in harsh terms. For example, in April 1922, McClatchy's reporters wrote: "It is known that a number of citizens, most of them high in the business life of the community, not only have been approached but importuned by agents of the Klan to apply for membership in the organization."[49] But mysteriously, no public Catholic voice was raised in protest—only McClatchy and his allies in city government kept up the public pressure. As he had with the APA, McClatchy was determined to expose them and run them out of business.

On Palm Sunday April 9, 1922, the *Bee* reported in detail the highly theatrical debut of the Klan in Sacramento. Pastor William E. Harrison of Westminster Presbyterian Church was preaching to a crowded evening service of 300 when six hooded men dramatically entered the church in silence. They marched to the altar and handed him a sealed envelope containing a new $50 bill. With it was a note commending his work as a minister. After Harrison read the letter aloud, the congregation burst into applause. Harrison himself later claimed he had no advance knowledge of the incident and knew little about the Klan, but he aroused suspicion when in response to a question about the Klan, he sounded moderately supportive of the organization.[50]

McClatchy's reporters tracked the advancing organization of the Sacramento "Klavern" to one Edgar Fuller, a secretive but genial man, who was the local "Kleagle," or Klan organizer. Fuller had come to Sacramento early that March 1922 and had begun organizing Klansmen from a rented room at the Traveler's Hotel. Within a few days of his arrival, he presented himself to County Sheriff Ellis Jones, seeking permission to carry a concealed weapon. Jones, who routinely granted such requests, formally deputized Fuller. The latter may have planned and participated in the showy Palm Sunday debut of the Klansmen at Westminster Church. Tracked down by a *Bee* reporter and queried about the purposes and beliefs of the organization, Fuller's reply reflected the moral righteousness of the Klan program: "We are not anti-Catholic, anti-Jew, or anti-Union labor, as has been charged, but are simply anti-wrong." But he left no doubt that his tolerance was conditional. "We believe in the tenets of the Christian religion, that lets out the Jews. We believe in the separation of church and state, and that lets out the Catholics."[51] His activities were closely monitored by McClatchy who suspected him of criminal activity.

McClatchy's alarm was picked up by city officials such as City Manager Clyde Seavey and Police Chief Bernard McShane, who viewed the Klan as lawless vigilantes and also as an embarrassment to a city burnishing an image as a friendly and progressive community. Despite intense opposition from the press and local government, Fuller enjoyed great success in recruiting for the "Invisible Empire" in Sacramento. Klan activity quickened in 1922 and won the active endorsement of some Protestant ministers. A revival held at the Nazarene Church at Twenty-eighth and S Streets, highlighting "Cowboy" evangelist "Bud" Robinson, praised the Klan as an organization that enforced laws.[52] While Robinson preached, Fuller held a major initiation of new Klan members at Muddox Hall in suburban Oak Park. Nearly 300 men knelt before the fiery cross and swore allegiance to the Invisible Empire. Although reporters were kept out, they watched the people going in and out carefully and noted that the number included two Sacramento police officers, a former chief of police, and the city harbormaster, Albert Greilich.[53] The initiation rite, witnessed at a distance by Police Chief McShane, spurred City Manager Clyde Seavey to order all municipal department heads to investigate reports of Klan membership among their ranks.

McClatchy's efforts to expose Klan members in Sacramento received a tremendous boost when a police raid on Klan headquarters in Los Angeles turned up statewide dues records. These revealed that nine Sacramento public officials, including several police officers and firemen, were listed as paying Klan initiation fees.[54] This discovery propelled a stalled anti-Klan ordinance in the city council forbidding the wearing of disguises or masks (with exceptions for entertainment purposes) to final passage on May 4, 1922. The next day, District Attorney Hugh Bradford made public the names of local members of the Klan—a list containing some 144 names, which included businessmen, police, and other public officials.[55] Seavey, McShane, and Fire Chief Michael J. Dunphy suspended the Klan members among their ranks and moved to have them, along with harbormaster Greilich, dismissed.[56] On the evening of May 5, Seavey went before the council to press for the dismissal of seven police officers and three firemen.[57] The *Bee*, a rival paper, and the *Sacramento Star* kept up a flood of unfavorable publicity against the group. Yet, the Klan was undaunted. Despite the barrage of criticism and invective on the front page of the *Bee* and even threat of city action, the Klan staged another group initiation on Natomas Company property near Folsom on May 16. McClatchy, never one to back down in a public fight, sent two courageous *Bee* reporters to infiltrate the event and they copied the license plate numbers of the vehicles parked along the road and published the names of the owners in the May 18 edition.[58]

A similar technique by the *Sacramento Star* covered a joint meeting of the Sacramento and Stockton Klaverns at the John Elliott Ranch near Franklin.[59]

To the dismay of many, Seavey's efforts to have Klansmen purged from city service failed. Strong defenses of the Klan were heard from some Protestant churches that viewed the organization as a protector of public morals. At Wesley Methodist Church in the city's Colonial Heights neighborhood, for example the Reverend W. B. Redburn urged his congregants to defend the Klan and praised their help in cleaning up the worst aspects of city life. "In Sacramento the bawdy houses are running wide open, gambling is rife and bootlegging is openly carried on. The City Manager knows this, the Council knows it, the police know it." He concluded, "To remedy this condition one must remove the causes." The Klan was ready, willing, and able to act.[60] On the city council, five of the nine members of the body voted to reject Seavey's request. The four who did vote to eject Klan members included Catholics Harold Kiernan, Daniel Sullivan, Jewish mayor Albert Elkus, and C. W. Anderson.[61] Later, Superior Court judges C. O. Busick and Catholic Peter J. Shields held that membership in the Klan was not forbidden by the city charter.[62]

The furor over the attempted city employee firings encouraged further anti-Catholic invective of ministers like Redburn and Harrison. On June 11, 1922, both ministers bitterly attacked Seavey, Elkus, and the "Jesuit controlled" *Sacramento Bee*. Harrison reserved especially strong words for Seavey, accusing him of being a member of the Knights of Columbus in Pennsylvania, and arguing that if "someone is to be dismissed for belonging to an un-American organization, Seavey ought to be fired and the policemen promoted."[63] Seavey, in fact, was not a Catholic and avowed that he had never visited Pennsylvania much less been a Knight of Columbus. Harrison later attacked the mayor for supporting the city manager's efforts to remove the Klansmen from the city payroll:

There is a growing conviction that in all controversies between Protestants and Catholics the Jews side with the Catholics. The Jewish controlled film industry is seeking to belittle Protestant ministers, but does not attack Catholic priests ... The unswerving loyalty of Mayor Albert Elkus to Rome suggests that he should go to Mass rather than to the synagogue.[64]

Reverend Redburn was even more vitriolic about the Catholic Church in his defense of the Invisible Empire. "Romanism is absolutely unchristian." He urged Protestants to overcome their differences and unite to oppose a unified Catholic Church and to put their efforts into the moral improvement of cities, all of which he preached were compromised by the presence of Catholics.[65]

The fight soon spilled over to the city's schools when city school superintendent Charles C. Hughes fired Edwin Anders, a substitute teacher at Sacramento High School. Anders's dismissal came in the wake of controversial comments he made to a history class that impugned the morality of Catholic priests: "Protestant ministers often marry and have families while Catholic priests do not marry but sometimes have families as they did in the Philippines."[66] Anders spilled his tale of woe to Harrison, whose church he attended, and the pastor leapt to his defense. Since Anders's case had to be heard before the school board, Harrison marched to the office of school board member J. B. Giffen to demand justice. It so happened that Superintendent Hughes was in Giffen's office when Harrison appeared, and immediately the minister began to importune both officials for Anders reinstatement. When Hughes refused, Harrison denounced the superintendent as a "Romanist and papist" and threatened, according to Hughes, "to get" him.[67] Harrison later denied threatening Hughes but did defend Anders. "Edwin Anders' words may have been indiscrete," he said, but he defended the "truth" of his assertions, insisting: "I can appreciate some people's desire to blue pencil human history before it is taught and I know something of the strength and chicanery of the traditional elements of our free schools."[68]

Yet despite the strong opposition of the *Bee,* Klan activity continued into the election season, with Klan-backed candidates retaining some incumbent seats.[69] Large induction ceremonies continued to be held, including one in May 1923 on the heels of a state convention of the Knights of Columbus.[70] Klan activities spread to nearby Roseville and even though Kleagle Fuller departed the scene in 1924, due to a falling out with local Klan members, Klan activity percolated beneath the surface of Sacramento life. Perhaps most noticeable were the successful efforts of local Klan supporters in city and county government to raise assessments on non-exempt Catholic properties. County Assessor B. C. Erwin, a Klansman, had bragged at a local Klavern meeting that he had "assessed St. Joseph Catholic cemetery in this city for $10,000 and was going to force the Catholics to pay taxes on it." Indeed, there was a spike in the assessments on various Catholic properties in the city.[71]

Catholics fought back lamely. Connelly's poorly circulated *Catholic Herald* fired a few salvos at the Reverend Harrison and the Klan, denouncing "this small but officious contingent of bigots and busybodies" of the "malodorous and disreputable order." Connelly also defended city manager Seavey from efforts to remove him from office.[72] However, the Klan was not run out of town nor were Klan activities stigmatized to the extent that Seavey and McClatchy hoped. The simple fact that may have dawned on Catholic Sacramentans was that their fellow citizens passively tolerated this anti-Catholic organization and many actively supported it as an instrument of urban reform. Sacramentans of the 1920s, it seems, had taken seriously Klan rhetoric linking Catholicism with public vice and social dysfunction. Some Catholic Sacramentans probably shook off the Klan episode as so much nonsense, but other signs from the community were also suggesting that the Catholic niche was not as secure as it had once been.

In the end, the Klan would be toppled by internal scandals and financial misconduct. By the end of the 1920s, it would fade away nationally and locally, but for the time it flourished and threatened Catholics in Sacramento, it was only McClatchy and a few allies in city and county government who defended them.

Public Leaders

Many lay men and women stepped forward to provide leadership on issues of common concern and respond to important needs. A significant number of these were women.

In recent years, the voices and presence of American Catholic women have been explored by historians and others. Much of this has been focused on the critical work done by American religious sisters. Religious orders of women were numerous and influential in US Catholicism. American sisters were critical to the growth of the church in the United States especially in education and health care.[1] Such was the case in the city of Sacramento where two groups stood out, the Sisters of Mercy and the Franciscan Sisters, who opened schools, day care centers, and a hospital.

But lay women also left their mark. Two Sacramento Catholic women Minnie Fogarty and her friend Mary V. Leonard are prime examples. Fogarty was the niece and housekeeper of her uncle, Bishop Patrick Manogue.[2] She was a sharp-minded and witty woman who had a keen eye for local Catholic realities and put her sometimes acerbic opinions in the public sphere.

In late January and early February 1889, a holiday fair was held to raise money to furnish the cathedral. The returns were modest, about $800, but the occasion gave an opportunity for the two women to issue a sassy daily paper called *The Cathedral Chimes*. Selling for a dime, the little magazine contained a number of articles the women themselves characterized as "Bright, Spicy, Entertaining." They especially took potshots at a number of Sacramento organizations and prominent citizens, such as the Sacramento City and County Improvement Association, the Museum Board, and the local militia. They also zeroed in on prominent public figures such as Judge John Wesley Armstrong (a local jurist who had been active in bringing the state capital to Sacramento), *Bee* co-publisher Valentine McClatchy, and local shipping merchant Thomas Dwyer. Their main line of attack was to single out these and other worthies for their stinginess in furnishing the new church. "[Anthony] Coolot gave $1,500 to help along the new cathedral," one quip read. "He probably thinks this will entitle him to a $2,000 seat in heaven."[3] No doubt they shared Manogue's disappointment with the penury of Sacramento Catholics.

But Fogarty and Leonard did not confine themselves to complaining or teasing about church affairs. They also went after those who seemed to hold Sacramento back by their bad policy decisions. One such entity was the Funded Debt Commission, established by the state legislature in 1872, this board was tasked with helping the city pay off the enormous, bonded indebtedness run up by raising the city streets to protect it from floods (*i.e.*, levee construction and strengthening and raising the grade of many streets and buildings). This process was lengthy and expensive and resulted in a high tax burden on property that made it difficult to sell or develop. Who could afford to purchase such indebted property in Sacramento? How would the city ever advance under this staggering burden? Consequently, large tracts of foreclosed land reverted to the Funded Debt Commission, which kept the land off the market until delinquent taxes could be paid (rather than selling it at auction and trying to recoup some tax revenue). The result was that the tax burden got worse and Sacramento property became even more prohibitive, thereby further stalling the pace of urban growth. Fogarty and Leonard spoke out against this self-defeating policy and their sarcasm spilled out on the pages of *The Cathedral Chimes*:

> Stranger: "Who owns that beautiful block of land?"
> Old Citizen: "That, Mr. Indiana belongs to the Funded Debt Commission."
> Stranger: "And the water system, that keeps the lawn in such splendid condition?"
> Old Citizen: "Also to the Funded Debt Commission."
> Stranger: "Is there anything in your city that those gentlemen don't control?"
> Old Citizen: "Not that I ever heard them admit."[4]

But the women's choicest invective was saved for the ineffectual Sacramento City and County Improvement Association (a predecessor of the Chamber of Commerce), which produced nothing but "splendid" reports about itself while the city stagnated. "And so it stands," the women wrote, "a Samson in resolution, a deserter in the ranks in action. It needs a galvanic battery to infuse some life in it; for, as it is, it is lingering along on the bloat-giving properties of its own jawbone."[5] In the final issue of the *Chimes*, the women observed:

> As to the politicians, office-holders and those who continually dab [*sic.*] in politics—either for its alleged betterment or their own advancement— if it has hurt their feelings in any way; if it has, by the slightest caused them a tinge of pain; if it has touched them in a tender spot; if it has rubbed salt into their own overpowering super sensitiveness; if it has given one moment's annoyance to any of this class—it most heartily apologizes to its readers for not having done more of it.[6]

The paper was highly successful, raising a total of $775.00 for the new cathedral.[7]

This waggish and not so subtle indictment of the Sacramento City and County Improvement Association reflected the frustration felt by others. The little *Cathedral Chimes* went out of existence, but like a bee, it stung and annoyed. Sacramentans were tight with their money.

Mary Rooney O'Neill

Among the social forces reworking Sacramento in the early years of the twentieth century was the emergence of women in the workforce and as agents for social and political reform. In 1910, census figures identified 476 men and nine women in this "professional" category. By 1920, 1,673 men and forty-four women were counted. The number of women in the workplace increased steadily, many in secretarial or clerical jobs (e.g. telephone operators) but especially in education. Already in 1874, the state legislature mandated stricter school attendance, curricular reform, and new school buildings. Improved pedagogical methods provided by a growing array of state and private normal schools. One of Sacramento's most prominent Catholic women was the first female superintendent of schools, Mary "Minnie" Rooney O'Neil.

Mary Rooney was born of Irish immigrant parents John Rooney and Mary Clark in 1862.[8] Her parents were Sacramento hop farmers who sent young Minnie to school at the Mercy Sisters St. Joseph's Academy. In 1878, she was among the first three women of the academy to receive a teaching certificate.[9] She taught general subjects in public schools in both Perkins and Brighton (Sacramento County) until her marriage to Thomas O'Neil in 1887. O'Neil was a prominent local artist who undertook the creation of the original frescoes in the Cathedral of the Blessed Sacrament and then served one term as Sacramento County sheriff and tax collector. The O'Neils were closely associated with the cathedral and intimate friends with Bishop Thomas Grace, who had succeeded Bishop Manogue in 1896. In 1905, O'Neil suddenly dropped dead of a heart attack, leaving Minnie with seven children under the age of seventeen.[10] Pressed by the financial plight of her large family, Minnie threw her hat into the ring for the elective post of county superintendent of schools. She won handily and was re-elected in 1910, serving until 1914. She was appointed assistant superintendent of city schools in 1916, a position she held until her death in 1932.

O'Neil stayed connected to her Catholic network of friends and acquaintances and assisted in the development of a broader role for women in Sacramento's Catholic community. In 1920, the Diocese of Sacramento sent her to Washington, D.C., where she participated in the formation of the influential National Council of Catholic Women (NCCW)—a federation of Catholic women's organizations from around the nation that advanced Catholic issues in the public sphere. Among these were the care of "working girls" in industrial cities, religious education for public school youth, and charitable giving to Catholic immigrants.[11] When O'Neil returned to Sacramento, she helped organize the Sacramento branch of the NCCW (the Diocesan Council of Catholic Women), in which she was active until her health declined.[12] Minnie O'Neil's professional career and public actions reflected the emergence of a strong Sacramento middle class that flourished on the tide of improving wages. As historians Dian Self and Elaine Connolly suggest, Minnie O'Neil's professional rise was also associated with the dominance of Catholic women in the ranks of public-school teachers as well as the increasingly vocal role they played in city life and politics especially through demands for suffrage.

Catholic Women and Care for the Poor

Women have always been leaders in benevolence: care for the poor and disadvantaged. Care of the poor in Sacramento County followed the asylum model pioneered in New York in the early nineteenth century. In 1853, Sacramento County opened its first public hospital on I and Seventh Streets. In 1860, it purchased 60 acres on upper Stockton Road, southeast of the central city, and built a larger county hospital and "poor home" (a residential shelter for the homeless) and sponsored a farm whose produce fed the "inmates," as the residents were called. County care for the indigent was augmented by various private city-based agencies as well as by a proliferation of private social welfare institutions. These included the Marguerite Home (for aged women) founded by Margaret Crocker, and the Peniel Rescue Mission for "wayward girls" in her donated mansion. Religiously based organizations such as the Episcopalian Home of the Merciful Savior for invalid children and the Protestant Orphan Asylum, sponsored by the Congregationalists dealt with needy or abandoned children. One of the earliest charitable organizations was the non-denominational Howard Benevolent Association, founded in 1857 to dispense charity in times of need. Assisting people with food, clothing, shelter, and related needs, the organization collected money through fund-raisers and voluntary contributions—including donations from the state legislature.

Catholic efforts on behalf of the poor can be seen in the Sisters of Mercy who, though mainly educators, provided some of the first Catholic social welfare assistance in Sacramento. The practice of the "Visitation"—the outreach to the poor by pairs of sisters, who visited their homes, jails, and even executions—was an important source of visibility for the sisters in the city. In Sacramento, two very prominent Catholic women became leaders in the city in caring for the poor and for young people: Mary Judge and Nettie Hopley.

Mary Judge

Mary Judge was the city official in charge of relief for the city for many years. The daughter of a local Irish immigrant farmer, her family eventually moved to the capital and lived on the city's east side (1221 D Street).[13] Her father worked on the construction of the state capitol and later the railroad. She was educated in the Mary Watson public grade school and regularly attended Mass at the Cathedral of the Blessed Sacrament. A forceful and decisive woman, she began work as a laundress and worked long hours for little pay.

In 1911, she was appointed head of the Sacramento County Relief Office—originally the county board of charities. She was the only employee for many years. Later, she managed a staff of fifty and she held her post for much of her life and apparently never took a day off in twenty-five years. She was specially remembered for her heroic work during the influenza epidemic—going door to door to meet with those stricken. Judge had a reputation as a curmudgeon because she was a rigorous dispenser of public largesse. She eyed applicants warily and was especially critical of the transients who came to Sacramento on railroads or through river traffic. Her relief decisions were highly personal. She might help you once, but if she suspected that you were "milking the system," she might throw you out of her office bodily. But then she might track you down and help you out of her own purse.

Bee editors who viewed her with respect noted in a tender tribute: "She had a heart as big as all outdoors and innumerable were her acts of kindness," But, as the encomium continued: "Miss Judge had no patience with those who sought to chisel assistance ... the phony "needy" avoided her office."[14] At times, their demands grew vocal and threatened violence, but the doughty Judge faced them down with her rhetoric and her own clenched fists. Eventually, things got out of control and the unemployed formed an Unemployed Organization and stormed her office, led by local activist Nora Conklin. Conklin provoked a mini riot in July 1933 when she marched to the relief office. Judge confronted her and police and sheriff deputies dispersed the crowd. Conklin led many demonstrations against Judge and was hauled before the law under the Criminal Syndicalism Act. Judge also courageously disarmed a would-be assassin of the county executive by offering him $5 for his gun.

Judge eventually realized that her methods of dealing with the poor were ineffective. She retired and died in 1945. When she died, she left her home and a bank account of $140 to a niece.[15] Judge was highly motivated by her Catholic faith, and her legendary generosity drew from the sources of her belief.

Nettie Hopley: Catholic Women and Benevolence

Mary Judge could be very harsh with those she presumed to be lazy and unambitious. Just the opposite approach was taken by other Catholic women who practiced benevolence to the poor. As late as the Great Depression of the 1930s, Sacramento still relied heavily on private voluntary organizations to assist in the care of the indigent, mentally ill, and orphaned. The view of poor people was generally negative, at least as expressed in the newspapers. Poverty was still considered a form of moral failure.

One particular leader who challenged this view stands out: Nettie Hopley, a teacher and principal at the diverse Lincoln School on the West End. Born in Sacramento, the daughter of a furniture dealer, she was a faithful parishioner of the cathedral. She began teaching at the age of nineteen and did not retire until 1938. Hopley knew well the realities of discrimination and poverty that thrived on the west end. In the area around Lincoln School (4th and Q), the demographic shifts had produced a stunning diversity of Sacramentans: Chinese, Japanese, Koreans, Filipinos,

94 *Indomitable Sacramentans*

Serbians, Greeks Italians, Portuguese, African Americans, French, Mexicans, Armenians, and Hindus. She treated them all with kindness and when children misbehaved her first impulse was not corporal punishment but curiosity about what caused this behavior. In one account, the case of an Italian lad who skipped band practice, she discovered the boy was ashamed of his shabby clothes. She of course helped him, and he went on to a career as a gifted local musician. In a tribute in the newspaper, it was written:

> She took a strong personal interest in the problems of hundreds of boys and girls who completed their grade education under her direction and many an errant foot was put on the path of rectitude and integrity through her understanding of adolescent problems and adolescent temptations.[16]

Hopley, perhaps more than other Catholic women devoted to benevolence had a good grasp of the effects of poverty on children.[17] In 1938, when she retired as principal of Lincoln School, over 500 people attended a testimonial dinner in her honor at the Elks Temple. Gently teased but lovingly praised, her admirers included former students going back nearly to the turn of the century.[18] One who memorialized her was Ernesto Galarza, a former student. He wrote of meeting her as a recently arrived first grader. As she rose from her chair to speak with him and his mother, he recalled:

> Rising from her chair she soared. And what she carried up with her was a buxom superstructure, firm shoulders, a straight sharp nose, full cheeks slightly molded by a curved line along the nostrils, thin lips that moved like steel springs, and a high forehead topped by hair gathered in a bun. Miss Hopley was not a giant in body but when she mobilized it to a standing position, she seemed a match for giants. I decided I liked her.[19]

Hopley brought her characteristic empathy and kindness to the poor through an effective but understudied Catholic organization called Catholic Ladies Relief Society (CLRS). In the beginning, about one hundred Sacramento Catholic women signed on for active membership in this organization. "Although Catholic in name, we adopted as our principle, work of an entirely non-sectarian character, neither creed, class nor color interfering with our sympathetic interest in the applicant," noted the founding branch.[20] In a rare display of "ecumenical" amity, the common needs of Sacramento's poor brought the Catholic charity into immediate contact with not only the well-established Howard Benevolent

Association but also such familiar private aid associations as Traveler's Aid, the Salvation Army, the Tuberculosis Association, and the Red Cross. It also shared information and made referrals to the Ann Land Fund, a large endowment left for the indigent of Sacramento in the name of wealthy hotelier William Land's deceased wife.

In its first year, CLRS No. 1 assisted sixteen impoverished families and cared for one orphan. As the city grew larger, the demands for financial help also grew more numerous. Ultimately, CLRS provided a social service worker and a staff of officers to review and coordinate the dispensation of relief. Other activities launched by the CLRS included a popular used-clothing drive that began in 1906, netting hundreds of discarded items every year for distribution to the poor; daycare services for cannery workers; and the distribution of Christmas baskets. Work at county institutions such as the hospital and the poor house, and the local and diocesan orphanages, as well as countless hours of mending, sewing, and repairing clothing fell to the members. From the time of its founding to the Great Depression, the CLRS operated as one of the major dispensers of private charity for the indigent of Sacramento.

Rebecca Coolot

A third woman, well-known to Catholics at the time and well-connected because of her family ties and wealth was Rebecca Coolot. Born in in Livermore, Rebecca Eliot was brought to Sacramento by her parents. Her father worked for the Southern Pacific. In 1902, she married the son of Anthony Coolot (Augustine or Gus) in a magnificent ceremony in the cathedral. Marrying into this prominent and well-connected Sacramento family gave her a number of advantages that she used for the good of the city. She had one child who died in infancy, but she soon threw herself into various kinds of social work and joined every Catholic women's group in the city, and even non-Catholic ones including the Tuesday Club and the Federation of Women's Clubs. In 1914, she joined the Ann Land Commission. During both world wars, she served on the local war-price and rationing board.

Her enduring work was with the coordinated collection for charitable activities first known as the Community Chest (today the United Way). Charles Virden, president of the Chamber of Commerce, who had spearheaded World War I war-bond campaigns in Sacramento, had helped form the Community Chest in 1923. At Rebecca's urging in 1924, Bishop Patrick Keane brought the main Catholic social welfare agencies—Grace Day Home and the Catholic Ladies Relief Society—into the pool of agencies slated to receive chest funds.[21] "Becky," as she was known, was part of the first board of directors and came to be called as the "Godmother of the Community Chest." The chest worked admirably throughout the prosperous 1920s.

In 1951, she and others urged a further consolidation of charitable, health, and character-building organizations in a common fund drive. The United Crusade was formed in 1952, and Coolot sat on the board until her health faltered. She continued to press for a Catholic share of the funds. When her husband "Gus" died in 1931, she was free for more public service, including the boards of various charitable agencies like the Children's Receiving Home. She helped set up the Catholic Charities Bureau in Sacramento, the same body that would hire Frederico Falcon as a social worker. Through her efforts, St. Patrick's Home, an orphanage run by the Sisters of Mercy of Omaha in Grass Valley was relocated to a new facility in Sacramento. Coolot donated generously to the diocese.

She held great sway with Bishop Robert Armstrong, whom she lectured quite freely. Once, when she observed the bishop nodding off during meetings, she insisted that he get a medical evaluation. "My Gus did the same thing." Her intervention revealed not only the diabetic condition of the prelate and other ailments that led to the decline of his health and death in 1957. When Father James Casey, the editor of the *Catholic Herald*, wrote a sarcastic column about her, she complained to Bishop Armstrong, who dismissed him. Armstrong so appreciated her efforts on behalf of the church and made her the recipient of papal honors (*Pro Ecclesia et Pontifice*) awarded to her in a colorful ceremony in the cathedral. Coolot, who died in 1964, was one of the most visible and prominent Catholic women in the city. Her strong advocacy assured a steady stream of revenue to Catholic Charities and poor relief.[22]

Judge, Hopley, and Coolot saw service to the poor as integral to their lives. Each of them approached this challenge in their own way—public administration, education and benevolence, and consolidated fundraising.

Catholic Fraternalism in Sacramento

Sacramento had a welter of fraternal organizations that provided fellowship and social opportunities for men. The Masons, the Red Men, the Odd Fellows were all influential lodges. The most significant Catholic fraternal order to come to Sacramento was the popular Knights of Columbus, which inspired a new generation of upwardly mobile Catholic men to service of church and community. Founded in New Haven, Connecticut, in 1882 by Father Michael McGivney, the knights were

Above: Early Sacramento. (*Public Domain*)

Right: Peter Hardeman Burnett. (*Public Domain*)

Dr. Gregory Phelan. (*California Room, California State Library, Sacramento*)

Fr. Peter Anderson. (*Cathedral of the Blessed Sacrament*)

Above: J Street from the Levy, Old Sacramento. (*Center for Sacramento History*)

Right: St. Rose Church, 7th, and K Streets. (*Center for Sacramento History, 1984-024-4280*)

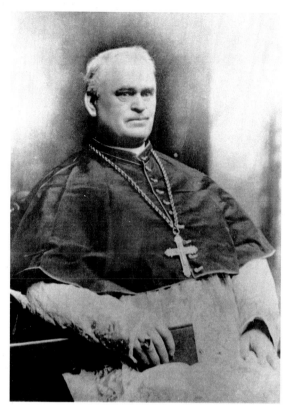

Bishop Patrick Manogue.
(*Nevada Historical Society*)

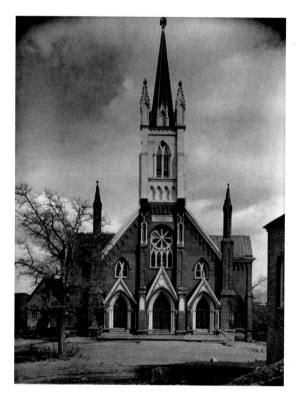

St. Mary of the Mountains
Virginia City. (*Library of
Congress*)

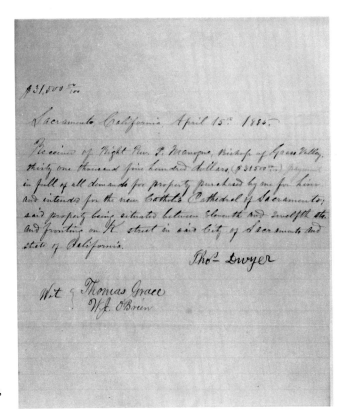

Dwyer Letter. (*Center for Sacramento History, 2007-037-001*)

Theresa Fair. (*Nevada Historical Society*)

Left: James Fair. (*Nevada Historical Society*)

Below: A portion of the Cathedral house donated by Theresa Fair is visible behind the Cathedral. (*Sacramento Public Library*)

Above left: Birdie (Virginia) Fair. (*Nevada Historical Society*)

Above right: Tessie Fair Oelrichs. (*Find a Grave*)

Marie Louise Hungerford
Bryant Mackay. (*Nevada
Historical Society*)

John Mackay. (*Nevada
Historical Society*)

CATHOLIC CATHEDRAL, SACRAMENTO.

Cathedral of the Blessed Sacrament. (*Public domain*)

Anthony Coolot. (*Sacramento Bee, December 4, 1900, p.6*)

Above: Golden Eagle Hotel.
(*Center for Sacramento History,*
1970-001-0146)

Left: Leland and Jane Stanford.
(*Center for Sacramento History,*
1981-086-029)

Above: Harris Weinstock and David Lubin (*left*). (*Center for Sacramento History, 1983-146-0945*)

Right: News clip regarding Westminster Chimes, donated by Mary Bithell. (*Sacramento Bee, December 23, 1901, p.4*)

WESTMINSTER CHIMES WILL TELL THE HOUR

GREAT CLOCK TO BE PLACED IN CATHEDRAL TOWER.

The great four-dial clock, the gift of Mrs. Mary Bithell, which is to ornament the tower of the Cathedral of the Blessed Sacrament in this city, has arrived, and will be placed in position next month.

This great clock is of complicated mechanism and it will require several days to place it in position.

The clock will strike the quarter-hour in the mellow Westminster chimes and will have a mechanical contrivance which will permit of the chiming of the bells being stilled at will.

Why the Germans Celebrated.

EDITORS BEE: Taking some interest in the position of the Germans in this city as American citizens, allow me to give you an extract from the German paper, the Sacramento Journal, in regard to the reasons why the Germans of this city arranged a celebration last week, in regard to which the Reporter takes the opportunity to question their worth as citizens of this Republic. The Journal explains them in the following manner:

News clip: "Why the Germans Celebrated." (*Sacramento Bee, February 7, 1871, p. 2*)

Melchior Diepenbrock. (*Find A Grave*)

Above: St. Francis Church. (*Center for Sacramento History,* 2007-037-003)

Right: News clip regarding St. Stephen's dedication. (*Sacramento Bee, December 3, 1900, p. 5*)

MISS BOWDEN LEFT ESTATE OF $200,000

Many Bequests Are Made To Catholic Institutions And Various Friends

An estate valued at more than $200,000, left by the late Miss Ellen Bowden, is divided among five charitable institutions and eighteen relatives and friends. So her will, offered for probate, reveals. Miss Bowden, died October 28. The will was offered for probate by Attorneys Thomas A. Farrell and Gerald M. Desmond, counsel for the estate.

St. Joseph's Convent is bequeathed $1,400 in cash and a number of religious pictures; the Stanfor Home is given $100; the Grass Valley Orphanage is given $400, and the Catholic Aid Society $100.

The Rev. Phillip E. Brady, pastor

News clip regarding Miss Bowden's estate. (*Sacramento Bee, November 6, 1926, p. 9*)

Bishop Thomas Grace. (*Personal collection of the author*)

Rev. Father
E. Mela, D.D.

Right: Fr. Eugenio Mela. (*Sacramento Bee, October 10, 1910, p.8*)

Below: St. Mary's Church 7th and T Streets. (*Center for Sacramento History, 2007-037-006*)

Left: St. Mary's Third Church 58th Street. (*Center for Sacramento History, 2007-037-007*)

Below: Manuel and Josie Waxon Williams. (*Portuguese Historical & Cultural Society*)

Above: St. Elizabeth Church interior. (*Center for Sacramento History, 2007-037-013*)

Right: Frederico and Cleofa Falcon. (*Courtesy of Socorro Zuniga*)

Charles K. McClatchy. (*Center for Sacramento History, 1982-005-4606*)

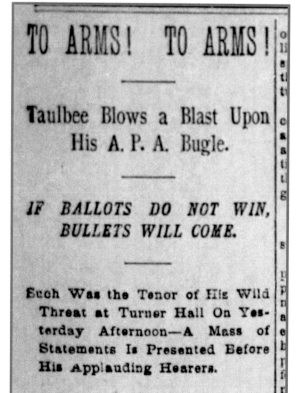

TO ARMS!   TO ARMS!

Taulbee Blows a Blast Upon His A. P. A. Bugle.

IF BALLOTS DO NOT WIN, BULLETS WILL COME.

Such Was the Tenor of His Wild Threat at Turner Hall On Yesterday Afternoon—A Mass of Statements Is Presented Before His Applauding Hearers.

News clip regarding American Protective Association activity. (*Sacramento Bee, July 31, 1895, p. 6*)

GOLDEN ✧ NOTES

Volume 27, No. 2   Summer 1981

THE
KU KLUX KLAN
IN SACRAMENTO,
1922

Right: The Ku Klux Klan in Sacramento. (*Sacramento Historical Society Golden Notes Vol 27 No 2*)

Below: News clip regarding KKK visit to local church. (*Sacramento Bee, April 10, 1922, p. 1*)

Six Ku Klux Klansmen Visit Local Church And Present Pastor With $50

Hooded and Robed Figures Enter Suddenly During Service and March Silently and With Precision to Pulpit; Note Commends Work of Minister.

'KLEAGLE' FULLER IS MAN OF MYSTERY AND MANY OVERCOATS

Phantom Visitors Flit by His Door; He Tiptoes About; He's an Officer of the Law

Unheralded and unknown, except perchance to a small group of the faithful, a knight errant of the Ku Klux Klan, arrived in Sacramento on the eighth day of last March and established headquarters at the Travelers Hotel.

To this shrine of Ku Kluxism came a steady stream of visitors to whom his presence soon became known. He was besieged with telephone calls and almost every mail brought him numerous letters.

The "Man of Mystery."

He was seen little by day and less by night. His name was Edgar I. Fuller, self-admitted "Kleagle," and organizer for the Ku Klux Klan. He

SEAVEY TO ASK COUNCIL TO OUST TEN KLANSME

City Manager Will Prese Cases of Three Firemen ar Seven Policemen at Meetir This Evening

Unanimous consent of the Cl Council for summary dismissal three firemen and seven police off cers whose names appeared on t list of Kleagle Edgar Fuller as ha ing applied for membership in t Ku Klux Klan and paid the $10 in tiation fee will be asked of the Cou cil to-night by City Manager Cly L. Seavey.

Above left: News clip regarding Kleagle Fuller. (*Sacramento Bee, April 12, 1922, p. 1*)

Above right: News clip regarding Seavey and the Klan. (*Sacramento Bee, May 18, 1922, p. 1*)

Ku Klux Klan And Its Poisonous Hatreds

The Ku Klux Klan, with its cheap theatricals, began its campaign of separating the foolish from $10 each last evening in Sacramento by the dramatic appearance of six sheeted figures during the regular services at the Westminster Presbyterian Church.

The pastor was presented with $50, which will probably be charged to advertising purposes, for sudden public appearances with an air of mystery are part of the Klan's methods of securing recruits and funds.

the Negro, the foreign-born, the Catholic and the Union Labor Man all at once, care to make such a mental condition known.

Based upon cheap theatricals, the Ku Klux Klan makes a great mystery of its ritual and its mummery, with terrible oaths of secrecy to its joiners, and with constant exhortation from Imperial Wizard Simmons to keep the secrets inviolate.

Yet two copies of the ritual and oaths and secrets are on file for public inspection at Washington, where

News clip: "Klan and Poisonous Hatreds." (*Sacramento Bee, April 10, 1922, p. 18*)

Minnie Fogarty Gormley. (*Find a Grave*)

Mary Judge

A Sacramento Legend . .

Mary Judge. (*Sacramento Bee, October 10, 1941, p. 24*)

Nettie M. Hopley

Left: Nettie M. Hopley. (*Sacramento Bee, June 30, 1942, p. 4*)

Below: Lincoln School 5th and Q Streets. (*Center for Sacramento History, 1999-082-049*)

Above: Rebecca Coolot (with hat). (*Center for Sacramento History, 2007-037-014*)

Right: William F. Gormley obituary. (*Sacramento Bee, July 30, 1935, p. 1*)

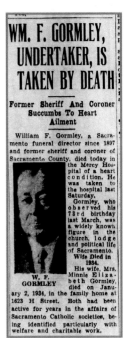

WM. F. GORMLEY, UNDERTAKER, IS TAKEN BY DEATH

Former Sheriff And Coroner Succumbs To Heart Ailment

William F. Gormley, a Sacramento funeral director since 1897 and former sheriff and coroner of Sacramento County, died today in the Mercy Hospital of a heart condition. He was taken to the hospital last Saturday.

Gormley, who observed his 73rd birthday last March, was a widely known figure in the church, lodge and political life of Sacramento.

Wife Died in 1934.

His wife, Mrs. Minnie Elizabeth Gormley, died on January 2, 1934, in the family home at 1623 H Street. Both had been active for years in the affairs of Sacramento Catholic societies, being identified particularly with welfare and charitable work.

W. F. GORMLEY

Thomas Connelly and family. (*Center for Sacramento History, 1983-121-001*)

Christ the King Retreat House. (*Center for Sacramento History, 1983-001-01885*)

Marie Dachauer
Bee Photo

Right: Marie Dachauer. (*Sacramento Bee, April 4, 1959, p. 11*)

Below: Cenacle Retreat House. (*Center for Sacramento History, 2007-037-008*)

Left: Marie Harris.
(*Archives of the North American Province of the Cenacle*, PH218_036)

Below: First retreat at Cenacle Retreat House. (*Archives of the North American Province of the Cenacle*, PH218_026A)

Right: Anton Dorndorf. (*Bishop Armstrong High School Yearbook 1959*)

Below: News clip regarding tribute to King Humbert. (*Sacramento Bee, August 9, 1900, p. 5*)

talian Residents Pay
Tribute to Humbert.

Portuguese Festa. (*Center for Sacramento History, 1977-047-006*)

Above left: Cesar Chavez and Father Keith Kenny at Our Lady of Guadalupe Church, April 1966. (*Archives Diocese of Sacramento*)

Above right: Young Men's Institute shirt. (*Center for Sacramento History, 2016-039-003*)

icy
a
po
Bo
con
set
tio
wa
ro
m
ar
at
fre

MORE THAN 1,500 JOIN HOLY NAME PARADE IN CITY

Superior California Catholic Men Attend Annual Services

More than 1,500 Catholic men and boys of Sacramento and Superior California marched in a parade and attended special services in the Cathedral of the Blessed Sacrament yesterday.

The event was the third annual demonstration in honor of the Holy Name of Jesus. The program from the cathedral was broadcast over The Bee Radio Station.

Bay Priest Speaks.

Rev. Thomas F. Burke, C. S. P., of Old St. Mary's Church in San Francisco, was the principal speaker at the cathedral services. He declared the Holy Name Society was not formed solely for the suppression of swearing and cursing, but for the furtherance of the Catholic faith generally. He stressed the ideals of the society, which call for reverence of God, patriotism to country, and protection to home and family life.

Bishop Robert J. Armstrong of the Sacramento Diocese thanked the men for their attendance.

Rolph Heads Parade.

The parade, which formed at St. Francis Church, Twenty-sixth and K streets, and proceeded to the cathedral, was headed by Governor James Rolph, Jr. Acting Mayor Arthur Ferguson represented the city.

The parade was reviewed by

to
Ol
ad
co
se
di
so
do
th
ti
lo
th
pe
nu
it
co

ch
bo
th
ha
Th
ap

tri
m

Se
ar

ch
th

ch

K
M

CATHOLIC men of Sacramento and Superior California staged a parade and rally here yesterday under the auspices of the Diocesan Union of Holy Name Societies. The picture above shows the first division of the parade which formed at St. Francis Church, Twenty-sixth and K streets, and proceeded to the Cathedral of the Blessed Sacrament, Eleventh and K streets, where special services were held. In the lower picture are Governor James Rolph, Jr., Bishop Robert J. Armstrong and Acting Mayor Arthur Ferguson, who marched and then reviewed the parade.

Bee Photos

ROOSEVELT NOTE ON MOONEY CASE TAKES NO SIDES

Governor Rolph Receives Long-Awaited Letter; Has No

CANNON'S DOUBT OVER CANA WINE STIRS CRITICISM

Grape Growers' League Assails Statement Of Bishop

News clip regarding Holy Name Parade 1933. (*Sacramento Bee, January 9, 1933, p. 1*)

Catholic Patriotic Rally. (*Center for Sacramento History, 2007-037-016*)

Opposite above: Fr. Patrick Peyton rosary crusade. (*Center for Sacramento History, 2007-037-012*)

Opposite below: Catholic rally at Edmonds Field. (*Center for Sacramento History, 2007-037-017*)

Eleanor McClatchy and Dunbar Beck. (*Center for Sacramento History*)

conceived as a mutual aid and benefit society, as well as a social club for men and their wives. The organization's branches, called councils, spread rapidly from their New England base and became popular nationwide. Adopting an organizational framework that provided for regional and local governance, the Columbians became an attractive outlet for many Catholic men, providing a good alternative to the Masons, the Odd Fellows, and other anti-clerical social organizations that the church pronounced off-limits to Catholics. The knights first came to the West Coast in 1902 and established councils in San Francisco and Los Angeles within a week of each other in January of that year.

At the urging of cathedral rector Father John Quinn, the Sacramento Knights of Columbus council 953 was founded in 1905 by a San Francisco deputy of the organization, Neal Power. Included in its earliest leadership were Southern Pacific ticket agent James O'Gara; insurance agent Joseph A. Blair; lighting contractor Joseph Hobrecht; and realtor Frank E. Michel. These early leaders typified the category of men who gravitated to the knights.[23]

Michel was born in Sacramento in 1879, attended Christian Brothers School, and then went on to St. Mary's College in Oakland, where he graduated in 1900. Soon after his graduation, he returned to Sacramento and entered the real estate business as an employee of the W. P. Coleman Company. In 1904, he became an insurance agent and a partner of Isador Nathan in the firm of Nathan and Michel. He often advised diocesan officials on matters of real estate transactions. Michel was an active force in Sacramento business and cultural life, serving for a time as secretary of the E. B. Crocker Art Gallery board of trustees, member and president of the Sacramento County Civil Service Commission, and as a member of the Sacramento Real Estate Board and the Southside Improvement Club. He served not only as the local "Grand Knight" of the Sacramento council, but also participated in its statewide leadership. He helped to plant the organization in Stockton as well. Michel's links with the Knights connected him to other city professional organizations, such as the Sacramento Parlor of the Native Sons of the Golden West. He was also secretary of the city's Serra Club, an organization dedicated to encouraging young men to enter the priesthood, and the Holy Name Society, a devotional and educational organization for men.[24] Other leaders of the knights in Sacramento included architect Harry Devine, Public Utilities Board head Peter Mitchell, and physicians F. E. Shaw, and James W. O'Brien.

Catholics as City Professionals

An array of prominent local Catholics became well-known as important figures in the city's rising professional classes. Robert T. Devlin was born in Sacramento in 1859, the son of a prosperous grocer. After graduating from Sacramento High School, he read law in the firm of longtime Sacramento attorney George Cadwallader and in 1881 opened his own firm, Devlin & Devlin, with his brother William. Devlin cemented his social prominence by his marriage to Mary Ellen Dwyer, the daughter of transportation magnate Thomas Dwyer.[25] Devlin's interests and activities led him in a number of directions. A skilled attorney, he also was an active supporter of the Southern Pacific, which in turn made possible his career in local politics and land dealing. He served on the commission to revise the city charter in 1891 and invested heavily in the development of the city's Oak Park neighborhood. From 1884 to 1912, he was a member of the state board of prison directors.

From 1900 to 1904, he represented Sacramento County in the state senate, retiring from the legislature to accept an appointment from President Theodore Roosevelt as United States attorney for the Northern District. Devlin held this position until a change in administrations in 1912 and then returned to private practice, eventually expanding his firm to include other partners. Touted frequently as a candidate for higher judicial office in both the federal and state systems, Devlin developed a national reputation as an expert on property law. His *Treatise on the Law of Real Property Under the Constitution of the United States* became a required text in many law schools. Likewise, his *Devlin On Real Estate* was a popular text. Devlin was a member of every prestigious club in the city and a highly respected and prominent member of St. Francis Parish. Active in law, politics, banking, and church life, Devlin represented the symbiosis between Catholic identity and civic life on the very highest levels.

Perhaps the most representative Catholic figure of this generation, however, was Irish-born William F. "Billy" Gormley.[26] He was born March 5, 1862, in Irvinestown, County Fermanagh. Gormley's father, Thomas, a millwright and pattern maker, came to El Dorado County California in 1871. The Gormley family reunited in 1872, and two years later, they moved to Sacramento, where Thomas found steady work with the Southern Pacific Railroad. Apprenticed at age fifteen to a bookbinder, young William soon found a substantial job as assistant foreman of the State Printing Office, one of the more sought-after government agencies. Gormley grew up with Sacramento in the 1870s and 1880s and represented a second generation of the Irish presence at St. Rose Parish. He became closely associated with Sacramento's bishops by marriage, a factor that helped him greatly in later business dealings. When Bishop Manogue moved to Sacramento in 1886, he brought with him his young niece, the earlier mentioned Minnie Fogarty, whom he had raised since she was twelve. Minnie was the daughter of Manogue's deceased sister, and she became the priest's housekeeper while he lived in Virginia City. Gormley apparently tried to woo the young maiden away from her prelatical uncle, but Minnie refused to budge until Uncle Patrick died in February 1895. Less than one year later, Father Thomas Grace officiated at their wedding. The couple eventually had three children: Manogue, Thomas Grace, and Mary Gormley.

Not surprisingly, Bishop Grace played an important role in Gormley's life. In 1897, for example, the bishop convinced the young man to become a funeral director, a decision that brought the family great economic security. As the sole Catholic undertaker in Sacramento for many years, Gormley made a great many friends among the clergy and the Catholic community at large. After a series of moves, in 1925, Gormley built a new permanent $45,000 funeral home on Twentieth and M (Capitol Avenue), across the street from the episcopal mansion. Gormley was probably the most visible and prominent Catholic layman in Sacramento from 1897 until his death in 1935. He was an inveterate joiner, attaching himself to the San Francisco Bookbinder's Union in 1885 and the Sacramento Council of Federated Trades.[27] He was a devout parishioner of the cathedral, where he served as an usher. He participated in the founding of nearly every major Catholic men's organization in the city. He belonged to the Ancient Order of Hibernians, the Elks, and was also an important force at the Chamber of Commerce and in the counsels of the local Democratic Party. Whenever there was money to be raised or an issue to promote, Gormley was always on the dais to offer his support.

Gormley may have settled for the funeral home business as a way to make a living, but he also cherished political ambitions. He made the most of his connections with the Sacramento clergy and his position as the city's chief Catholic funeral director before facing competition from other ethnic morticians, and he busied himself in local politics. He had entered local politics at the urging of the Democratic County Central Committee as a candidate for county coroner in 1898. Although he was defeated, he made a strong showing against a Republican candidate.[28] In 1902, he threw his hat into the ring once again for the coroner's post and won handily. He held this post for twelve years. In 1908, he won reelection with a warm endorsement from the *Leader*, Peter C. Yorke's pro-labor San Francisco paper:

Wm. F. Gormley, who aspires to succeed himself in the office of coroner, is one of the most popular men in [Sacramento] county. Billy Gormley,

as he is familiarly known, is a friend of everybody and everybody is his
friend. He is one of those kind-hearted, genial, whole-souled individuals
whom it is a pleasure to know.[29]

In February 1910, he was appointed county sheriff after incumbent David
Reese died unexpectedly. The appointment was temporary, but Gormley
found he liked the job even though another man Edward Reese, the son of
the former sheriff, was appointed.[30] In 1914, he stepped in again after an
incumbent died. He ran for the post himself in in the 1914 and defeated
the permanent replacement, James Donnelly.[31]

Gormley served one full term as county sheriff. It was his fate to preside
over local law enforcement during the period of mobilization for World
War I and its aftermath. He was at the heart of one of the most distressing
episodes of wartime dissent when an explosion at the governor's mansion
in 1917 led to accusations of sabotage against the local chapter of the
Industrial Workers of the World. Gormley assisted city Police Chief Ira
Conran in incarcerating sixty members of the organization on relatively
flimsy evidence and later spoke publicly on behalf of congressional
legislation to have the group outlawed. C. K. McClatchy endorsed
Gormley's reelection in the primary of 1918:

> That it would be a very bad thing for Sacramento and her reputation to
> have Gormley defeated at this time. They assert that if he is defeated it
> will be used by the I. W. W., their aiders and abettors and sympathizers
> and those corkscrew intellects that believe that whatever is wrong; that
> every convict should be out of jail because general society is guilty—that
> this element will use the defeat of Gormley as a proof of the truth of its
> accusations that these I. W. W. were shamefully treated in Sacramento
> and will say to the world that the citizenry of Sacramento County has
> proven the truth of these assertions.[32]

However, his opponent, Republican Ellis Jones, rode a wave of discontent
with the Democratic Party and argued that Gormley was too affluent to
effectively serve the people. Jones coasted to victory in the August 27, 1918,
primary by a majority of over 2,500 votes.[33] After his defeat, Gormley
retired to the funeral home business, but the day-to-day operations were
handled by his sons Manogue and Thomas. He had indeed grown wealthy
through investments and other sources and spent the remainder of his life
in any number of civic and political interests.

Catholics as Urban Boosters

Sacramento's civic life quickened as it entered the twentieth century. A revivified Chamber of Commerce in 1902, made the promotion of Sacramento a key priority. Public officials, businessmen, educators, and religious leaders—all were expected to advance the cause of the city in their respective spheres of influence. Recognizing that a more prosperous Sacramento benefited everyone, few balked at the task of "booming" the city and urging its beautification.

Catholic boosterism in Sacramento reached a high point with the work of Thomas A. Connelly. Connelly made an early imprint by launching Sacramento's first Catholic weekly, the *Catholic Herald*. Born in Philadelphia in 1858, Connelly was educated in parochial schools and at the University of Notre Dame.[34] In the 1880s, he found work in Baltimore at *The Catholic Mirror*, a lay-owned Catholic weekly.[35] There he met and married Mary Eucebia Fink at nuptials attended by none other than Cardinal James Gibbons of Baltimore. Connelly's friend, author and diplomat Maurice Egan of Notre Dame, helped him find a position as editor of a troubled *Catholic Universe*, a weekly of the Diocese of Cleveland. His work revived the paper and increased its circulation.

In 1898, Archbishop Patrick Riordan of San Francisco invited Connelly to assume direction of the largest Catholic newspaper in the West, the *Monitor*. With some misgivings but assured by promises of support from Riordan, and the promise that he could hire a capable business manager, Connelly uprooted his by then large family and moved to the Pacific Coast. Arriving in June 1899, he kept a low editorial profile but made changes in the image and style of the *Monitor* that broadened its appeal. However, the paper's finances were never healthy, and Riordan did not make good on his promise to hire a capable business manager. Moreover, it was Connelly's fate to edit the paper during the disastrous earthquake and fire of 1906. In spite of the calamity, the paper missed only a few issues because Connelly quickly set up a new shop across the bay in Oakland. He managed to resume publication by May.[36]

Connelly moved easily among laity and clergy—especially Irish clergy—with whom he shared an ethnic background and Irish patriotism. Connelly was a fervent Irish nationalist. But more than anything else, he was a booster. Much of his career as a Catholic journalist was devoted to promoting the glories of life in the American West, especially in California. He regarded the church as an agency of civilization and a force for social and cultural influence. Few in California's Catholic establishment saw the link between the spiritual and practical aspects of Catholicism and society as clearly as Connelly.

Sadly, for him, his hopes of making the *Monitor* a strong business proposition failed. Even his personal finances were in disarray, and in 1901, he borrowed $1,000 from the archdiocese at 4 percent interest to cover his bills.[37] In 1907, when his publishing contract came up for renegotiation, Archbishop Riordan finally agreed to hire a separate business manager, but for reasons of personal pride, Connelly now refused the support and asked for additional time to bring the *Monitor* back to fiscal health, even to foreswearing his own salary.[38] But Riordan would not hear of it, and so in June 1907, Connelly was replaced by Wisconsin journalist Charles A. Philips, with Sarsfield F. MacCarthy as the business manager.

Separated from the *Monitor*, Connelly moved to Sacramento where he became an associate editor of *The Wednesday Press*, a non-sectarian booster publication founded in 1902 by the Sacramento Valley Development Association (SVDA) and edited by Everett Irving Woodman. This organization, founded in 1900, was a cooperative venture of six counties in the Sacramento Valley—Colusa, Yuba, Sacramento, Sutter, Glenn, and Yolo—to promote the region's economic and social development. In 1903, *The Wednesday Press* moved to Sacramento, and in June 1907, when Connelly joined the staff, W. A. Beard, a local developer and publicist, succeeded Woodman as editor and publisher. Beard introduced a new format and by autumn, the name was changed to the more grandiloquent *The Great West*. From June 1907 to February 1908, Connelly provided copy for Beard, writing glowing articles that promoted regional growth and development. Connelly made sure that the importance of religious institutions was calculated into the mix of advantages advertised as incentives for people to move to California.[39]

Work on *The Great West* could not have provided enough sustenance to feed the large Connelly family and so he purchased a small press on 305 J Street, renamed it the Capital Press, and began to bid for printing jobs from state and local government. Living in Sacramento allowed him to build closer relationships with persons he had known during his years heading the *Monitor*. He was a daily communicant at the cathedral which was near his printing office. Connelly forged an even closer relationship with Bishop Grace and Father John Ellis, pastor of the parish. Connelly also developed strong ties with the same network of Catholic fraternal organizations that boosted the careers of other Catholic professionals in the city. When the journalist approached Bishop Grace in early 1908 with plans to start the *Catholic Herald*, Grace replied:

> Your determination to begin at once the publication of a Catholic weekly in Sacramento is indeed timely. The city is growing rapidly and proportionate to that growth is the increase in the Catholic population

... With at least ten thousand Catholic people in Sacramento alone, not to speak of the countless others outside who look to the Bishop of Sacramento in all their spiritual needs, I anticipate for *The Herald* a bright and useful future.[40]

As soon as the weekly was launched in early 1908, Connelly devoted much of his time to it, but he also kept the printer's job to maintain a steady cash flow.[41] The *Catholic Herald* rolled off the presses in Connelly's shop for two decades until his death of cancer on December 17, 1929. Its circulation never appeared to rise much above 4,000 copies, but it traveled far beyond the city and environs of Sacramento and was strategically circulated in the East. While the paper covered national and local church news, as well as Irish events, it was never a diocesan-sponsored organization. Cathedral rector Monsignor Thomas Horgan observed that Connelly was never able to sell the paper to the local clergy. Therefore, Connelly devoted a lot of ink to boosting Sacramento and encouraging local Catholics to participate in city development. Connelly joined ranks with other city promoters who launched a campaign to combat Los Angeles's efforts to attract new citizens to the southland. "For a long time the only part of California that the outside world knew much about was that portion lying south of the Tehachapi," he complained in 1913. "All the vast territory of the San Joaquin and Sacramento valleys and the coast counties from Santa Barbara to Del Norte has been a terra incognita to the average citizen in the East—and yet from our point of view this end of the State is far more desirable than the south."[42] As he wrote in one of his earliest editions, "No city in America today faces a future pregnant with larger promise than Sacramento."[43]

Connelly diligently promoted the city and encouraged Sacramentans to get on the development bandwagon. One motif of his editorial style was to gently criticize those who did not share as positive a view of the city as he did. In one of his first editorials, "For a Greater Sacramento," he chided "the deplorable lack of local patriotism and proper civic pride" in the community for not enthusiastically backing new Western Pacific railroad yards.[44] He supported public water and power and the development of new streets and civic buildings. He frequently tried to mobilize the Catholic community to support large development projects, such as a water filtration plant, and create their own projects that would benefit the city or the Sacramento Valley at large. Connelly exulted as loudly as any member of the Chamber of Commerce when in 1913 the city passed a bond issue for a major capitol extension project. "It shows that the old Silurian spirit is dead and that a new, live, up-to-date city has taken its place." He urged a positive vote for the passage of additional municipal bonds for more sewers, better improvements in the recently annexed Oak Park, and favored a municipal ice plant and more electric power. "Sacramento needs only some local improvements to make it not only a first-class city, but an ideal city."[45]

Beginning in 1909, he launched a thick annual edition of the *Herald* that highlighted the best of the new developments, both sacred and secular. These annuals also included pieces on residential growth and agricultural developments in the valley. Connelly was especially supportive of Catholic building projects whose style and architecture enhanced the Catholic presence on developing Sacramento. For several years, he touted elegant drawings of a proposed Catholic clubhouse for the downtown (that never materialized). He championed efforts to build a new St. Francis Church in a mission style that would enhance the touristic appeal of Sacramento as it was paired with a recently restored Sutter's Fort.

It would be too much to say that Connelly was a dynamic force in Sacramento. His paper had limited circulation, even among local Catholics. Priests tended to disregard him, disliking his writing on "secular" subjects. He had a son who became a priest and a prominent military chaplain in World War II, but he spent most of his life away from the diocese. Connelly died on December 17, 1929, and in early 1930, Bishop Robert Armstrong contracted with the popular Denver-based *Catholic Register* chain to produce a weekly diocesan paper that was more restricted in its reporting. Its editors had a much narrower view of the function of Catholic journalism and stayed away from commenting on local issues and doing little or none of the regional and urban boosterism that had been Connelly's trademark.

Harry Devine: Catholic Architect

Harry Devine literally put the Catholic Church in Sacramento on the map in the twentieth century. Born March 22, 1894, Harry Devine was the son of James Devine, a *Sacramento Bee* printer for forty-four years. The devoutly Catholic Devines were parishioners of the cathedral and sent their son to Christian Brothers School. He later entered the University of California for advanced study, interrupting his work only to serve in the navy during World War I. He returned to his studies and completed his degree in architecture in 1919. Devine was hired by the architectural firm of Dean & Dean in Sacramento.[46]

Young Harry Devine worked for the firm until the death of his father in 1926. His inheritance allowed him to open his own firm and enjoy a virtual monopoly on Catholic Church design for many years, often presenting architectural plans free of charge.[47] He also earned a share of the increasing volume of city work, designing schools, public buildings, banks, and later department stores and parking structures. Devine left his imprint all over Sacramento.[48] His most elegant work was the new Sacred Heart Church on 39th and J in Sacramento.

The Sacred Heart pastor, Father Michael Lyons, gave Devine the nod to design the new church while Lyons threw himself into fundraising, enlisting transportation magnate William Dwyer, whose son would soon enter the seminary, to direct the appeal. Dwyer was successful in securing a number of pledges, but as the Depression's grip began to tighten on Sacramento, many could not pay.[49] Later, the $10,000 from Ellen Bowden's will would provide seed money for the new church.[50] Nonetheless, however grateful he was for Bowden's money, Lyons took steps to scrap her beloved name "St. Stephen's" by maneuvering the Altar Society to petition that the church be called "Sacred Heart," a name popular with the Sacramento Irish and recently abandoned by a failed Croatian church. The William Keating Company secured the construction contract in December 1930, and by March the building was advanced enough for the laying of the cornerstone.[51] Devine built an Italian-style Romanesque church with a handsome campanile and delicately carved moldings over the entrances. The cruciform church could hold 750 people. Located at the southwest corner of Thirty-ninth and J Streets, the Church of the Sacred Heart occupied a 100-foot frontage on J Street and 340 feet on Thirty-ninth.

The success of the Sacred Heart construction resulted in Devine being awarded additional church contracts in other cities including Sacred Heart in Gridley, St. Anthony's in Ryde, St. Thomas in Oroville, and St. Joseph's in Lincoln. School contracts included Mount St. Mary's in Grass Valley and St. Patrick's Home in Sacramento. Devine also enjoyed a fruitful relationship with the burgeoning school system of Sacramento when he erected the new California Junior High School in 1933. Devine's office buildings, parking structures, and public institutions contributed substantially to the up building of Sacramento, particularly as the state government grew and the local population increase after World War II.

Seeking Peace in the Suburban Sprawl

Parishes and prayer centers were not the only lay-led expression of local Catholicism. Catholics, especially after World War II sought places of refuge and rest and opportunities for prayer and spiritual development. The "retreat" movement had its origins in the Catholic Action movements of the 1920s and 1930s and by religious orders, who often found their houses inundated with visitors wishing to experience the quiet and savor the somewhat "exotic" liturgical solemnity of their chapels.[52] Such groups got involved in building retreat houses and delivering lectures and sermons in a structured context for the earnest seeker.[53]

The retreat movement in Sacramento got off to a slow start with the first efforts spearheaded by the local Franciscans in a small retreat center for men located outside the city. Interest in a local retreat house for Catholic men next came from a prosperous retail paint dealer, Raymond, and his wife Irene Wilkins. Ray Wilkins, a native of Plymouth County, Iowa had come to California in the 1930s and established himself as a successful paint dealer in Sacramento since 1941.[54] His business prospered and at one point, he had two stores: one in downtown Sacramento and another in Del Paso Heights. In 1950, he took on a partner, Maurice Dubey, and then eventually sold the business to him and devoted his life to charitable causes. A sister of the Cenacle related Wilkins' role in the origins of Christ the King retreat house:

> Mr. and Mrs. Wilkins came in to see us and have been most kind … I am sure you will be interested in the story of the first retreat in Sacramento … Mr. Wilkins was the instigator and he asked to use a Catholic Camp up on the mountains … early in June 1948 ninety men in cars carrying blankets, sheets, and towels and all sorts of things made their way up to the camp…they stayed there for three full days and loved it so much they prevailed upon the Bishop to ask the Passionists to come and open a regular house.[55]

Wilkins knew the Passionist fathers at Sierra Madre, California, near Pasadena, and had begun making retreats at their newly opened retreat center in 1935. In 1945, Wilkins took the initiative in bringing a retreat house for men to Sacramento. On his own, he actively pursued this idea with the head of the Congregation of the Passion (the Passionists), a religious order dedicated to hosting retreats and offering spiritual direction. His timing was perfect. The Passionists, on the verge of a major expansion program, were looking for places to develop.

Passionist Father Angelo Hamilton came to Sacramento and found a 41.5-acre plot about 13 miles north of Sacramento.[56] Owned for many years by the Cross family, the acreage lay right in the heart of the emerging suburb of Citrus Heights. Cross, who lived in San Francisco, was anxious to dispose of the property but did not want to see it subdivided into housing lots or the destruction of its handsome scrub oaks. He gladly sold the property to the Passionists in early 1948, which included a frontage on the main thoroughfare in the area, Auburn Boulevard.[57] The first community arrived sometime in the summer of 1948 and later moved into a small caretaker's cottage on the last Sunday in October, the Feast of Christ the King in the Catholic liturgical calendar.

The Catholic newspaper included an appealing sketch of the proposed retreat house and monastery done by William S. Lenoir, a local commercial artist. However, like the Franciscans earlier in the century, the Passionists had their own in-house architect, Father Neil Parsons, C.P., of Chicago.[58] On Palm Sunday, April 10, 1949, ground was broken for the retreat house and monastery, and Parsons shuttled back and forth between Sacramento and Sierra Madre as both structures went up at the same time.

The $350,000 modified Spanish-style structure was completed in late April 1950, and on Sunday, May 7, Bishop Armstrong dedicated the beautiful new complex in the presence of 700 people. On May 26, the first scheduled weekend retreat for men got underway. Scores of retreatants, middle-class government workers, local retailers, and others descended upon the facility, crowding its quarters every weekend. Parish priests exhorted their parishioners to take a "quiet weekend with the Lord."[59] By 1951, 848 men had attended thirty-eight retreats at Christ the King. Another important contributor to the retreat house was Jerry Olrich, the head of landscaping at the state capitol and a good friend of Wilkins. He and a volunteer crew began to shape the grounds into a comfortable and quiet space for prayer and meditation. Olrich also procured four granite pillars which were former entryways to the state capitol. Olrich's crew and ingenuity provided a peaceful haven for retreatants which continues to this day as a quiet oasis in the middle of a busy neighborhood. In 1955, an additional forty-room wing was added to the facility, indicative of its popularity.[60] In 1957, additional structures were transported onto the property for even more rooms.[61]

The Cenacle: Marie Dachauer and Marie Harris

The success of Christ the King hastened parallel efforts to secure a retreat facility for Catholic women. The initiative for this came from two women, Marie Dachauer and Marie Harris.[62]

Dachauer, the child of German immigrant parents in Milwaukee, worked for many years at Sacramento's Enos department store. Her priest brother, Jesuit Andrew Dachauer, who had entered the Jesuits in California, encouraged her to get involved with a local charity. Through him she met a Filipino Jesuit, Luis Toralla, a chaplain in the U.S. Army who related the sad plight of those who had Hansen's disease (leprosy) in his native land. Dachauer became interested and traveled to a leprosarium in Carville, Louisiana where she learned more about the dreaded illness. Later, she traveled to Japan and the Philippines to investigate conditions there as explained by Father Toralla. She came back convinced that she had found her calling. She formed an organization called the Friends of the Lepers and eventually quit her job in the department store after the group officially incorporated in 1947. She remained "moving spirit" behind this work for the rest of her life. She attracted volunteers and used the cathedral basement as a headquarters where she organized relief and shipments of medical supplies.[63]

A deeply spiritual woman, she had been interested in retreats for many years. She heard of the Cenacle in the fall of 1947 and made a retreat on Long Island, New York, at the American motherhouse of the nuns of Our Lady of the Retreat in the Cenacle. This religious community dedicated to retreats and spiritual direction of women.[64] Unlike most congregations of religious women, many of the members of this society were called "mother" rather than the more common "sister." Their distinctive religious attire included a pie plate-shaped coif that framed the face. Dachauer was so impressed by the experience that she mentioned the idea of a Cenacle coming to Sacramento to Mother Ida Barlow, Provincial of the Midwest Province in the fall of 1947. In 1949, a friend, Marie Harris, a fellow member of the Young Ladies Institute, a club for Catholic women, and accompanied her to another Cenacle retreat in Vancouver. Both women again mentioned the possibility of beginning a retreat house for women in Sacramento. Barlow was unable to commit, but Harris and Dachauer worked hard over the next few years to make retreat opportunities available to Catholic women. In summer 1951, Dachauer and Harris formed a Sacramento Laywomen's Retreat League.[65]

Harris was born in Asheville, North Carolina in 1920.[66] Her father was a surveyor for the U.S. Geological Survey and eventually moved the family to Sacramento. Marie, a graduate of Sacramento High and of Dominican College in San Rafael as well as a business school, began a career as an accountant and was hired at McClellan Field just as World War II broke out. She was the first female accountant at the field and worked there for three decades. When she retired, she was the chief of accounting for the Sacramento Air Logistics Center and won numerous awards for her performance. A devout Catholic, she participated in many parish groups and events. She was especially attracted to the range of adult education programs held in the Aquinas Center, an adult learning center and library in the cathedral basement. Harris took the leadership role in the women's retreat effort in early 1952 and phoned Mother Ida Barlow again, asking for a Cenacle in Sacramento.

After meeting with Dachauer and Harris in 1952, Barlow made the trip to Sacramento to inspect the possibilities and meet with local church officials.[67] The following year, Barlow and her treasurer, Mother Mary Angela Roduit, arrived in Sacramento. They discovered an 8-acre property at 5430 Fair Oaks Boulevard, owned by Mrs. Dudley V. Saeltzer, Jr., the widow of a wealthy Sacramento physician.[68] The property was run down, but the sisters loved the two-story home and the quiet acreage. However, the initial asking price was in excess of what they could afford to pay. After some dickering and a novena to St. Anthony of Padua, they secured the Saeltzer property, and Mother Barlow laid plans for a $350,000 program of extensive remodeling and expansion that added eleven new rooms, which could accommodate forty-six retreatants with community quarters for the resident sisters. In late October 1953, Jerry Olrich provided landscaping. "Yesterday Mr. Oldrich [sic.] who has charge of Capitol Park came up to see us," wrote Mother Ida to her superiors. "He is going to give us all the trees and shrubs we need to landscape the entrance to our grounds, which has never been done and is certainly not a thing of beauty."

Harris and Dachauer were on hand to help the first sisters move in. The sisters related, "yesterday was 'the day'! In the morning we had Marie Harris and Marie Dachauer here helping us put some order in the confusion of boxes and all the kitchen equipment sitting in the corridor."[69] By late February 1954, the sisters began running days and evenings of recollection. Over 650 women attended the initial programs and public interest in the retreat house built steadily. After the July 31 dedication, the first weekend retreat at the new facility was held in mid-August of 1954 conducted by Father Richard Dwyer.[70] A year later, nearly 1,500 women had walked through the doors of the Cenacle Retreat House.[71]

The image of the somewhat remote retreat houses, located in spacious acreage and somewhat cut off from the hustle and bustle of suburban life, were perfect tributes to the work of these women and their followers. Christ the King Retreat House would be surrounded by housing developments, apartments, and commercial structures that took away even the little privacy it had. The Cenacle (and the episcopal residence near it) literally fell to the demands of Sacramentans for housing on the valuable property along Fair Oaks Boulevard.

Dachauer returned to her main work with the Friends of the Lepers. Harris continued a life of activism becoming one of the "Grandmothers for Peace" who picketed Sacramento's military installations.

Music: The Legacy of Anton Dorndorf

Catholic churches in Sacramento enhanced local culture with their numerous and varied musical performances. Grand celebrations at Christmas and Easter at the Cathedral of the Blessed Sacrament, heavily attended, always highlighted polyphonic music accompanied by the cathedral organist, Lizzie Griffin, and occasional symphonic ensembles. From high in the second loft of the cathedral church, various choirmasters attempted to provide a touch of elegance to the comparatively unadorned liturgical life of the huge church. A far more exuberant tradition of religious music was to be found at St. Francis Parish. Modeling the traditional German love for elaborate musical presentation, ordinary Sunday worship and the high holy days alike were moments of great splendor for the church. St. Francis's Parish organ had been provided with funds donated by retired steel master Andrew Carnegie, who included the provision of these instruments along with his other well-known benefactions.

In the tradition of many German parishes, St. Francis had a paid choirmaster who raised the level of performance to high standards. For many years, this was Anton Dorndorf (1906–1970).[72] The German-born Dorndorf had music in his veins. As a small boy he had been a member of the Boys Choir of St. Elizabeth Church in Krefeld, Prussia under mentor Arthur Luis who was choirmaster and organist there for many years. This would forge a lifelong friendship between the two men and both of them would come to California, Luis to the Franciscan church of St. Boniface in San Francisco, and Dorndorf to Sacramento.

Dorndorf had received a liberal arts education in the best European tradition at the classical gymnasium in Krefeld, where the course of study included mathematics, natural sciences, modern languages, fine arts, and Latin. He graduated from this institution with the distinguished *Abitur* degree, which was considered the necessary passport to a successful career in any branch of higher learning. Dorndorf, an outstanding boy soprano, was chosen competitively from the schools of Krefeld to participate in a municipal youth chorus that presented major musical works such as Handel's *Elijah*. Dorndorf took solo parts in some of these productions and continued to sing in the choir and study piano and organ until he came to America in 1926. He entered the Music Conservatory College of the Pacific, where he took his AB degree in 1934. He became the musical director of the Turners in Sacramento, married, and had a son. Dorndorf's talents came to the attention of the friars at St. Francis Church where he accepted the role of organist and choir master for the church. His skills built the St. Francis choir's reputation over the years, and he produced elaborate choral Masses at Christmas and Easter. Often broadcast live over radio, the crowds that pressed into the church on those already heavily attended holy days were larger than ever.

During the summer months, Dorndorf moonlighted with radio and movie greats such as Fred Waring and Walter Schumann. He also composed some of his own music. Admiring the style of the eighteenth-century composers like Haydn and Mozart, he composed a *Kyrie* and *Gloria* for a "Mass in the Dorian Mode" and a *Laudate Dominum* after the style of Haydn. His talents as a choir director extended to local Catholic elementary and high schools employed him to direct their choirs. In the mid-twentieth century, wherever there was a large public rally of Catholics, Dorndorf's baton was in evidence. Traveling from school to school and parish to parish to introduce and teach musical numbers to both young and old, Dorndorf led the massed choirs of adults and children in providing music for several preeminent occasions, including Bishop Robert Armstrong's Silver Jubilee, the 1950 Eucharistic Congress celebrating Sacramento's centennial of Catholicism, and the annual Holy Name and Marian Rallies.[73] Dorndorf also organized and directed the Bishop's Boys Choir, composed of lads from around the city who rendered sacred music for high holidays and special episcopal functions. Dorndorf was, in many respects, the quintessential expression of the vibrant Sacramento Catholic culture of his era.

Celebrate! Celebrate! The Catholicism of the Streets

Catholics in Sacramento occasionally let their faith spill out on to the city streets and other public venues. These events involved clergy but were often organized and coordinated by lay persons, especially those involving school children. This took many forms: an expression of ethnic identity, a demonstration of a militant faith, or a proof of good citizenship.

Ethnic Celebration: Faith and Sacramento Life

Early Irish Catholics of Sacramento combined traditional faith with support for nationalism. Initially, the religious motivation for Irish public religion was deeply affected by the religious revival in Ireland in the mid-nineteenth century known as the "Devotional Revolution." This nineteenth-century religious revival among Irish Catholics reflected a quickening of local faith and the importation of many pious practices from Rome as well as the resuscitation of older home devotions.[1] This had been encouraged by the powerful Cardinal Paul Cullen of Armagh and priests who followed his lead. One historian argues:

> The devotional revolution ... provided the Irish with a substitute symbolic language and offered them a new cultural heritage with which they could identify and be identified and through which they could identify with one another. This is why, for example, Irish and Catholic have become almost interchangeable terms in Ireland despite the attempts of Nationalists to make Irish rather than Catholic the inclusive term.[2]

This would be true in Sacramento. Public celebrations of Irish identity in Sacramento provide, as historian John Delury notes, "valuable insights into the Irish immigrants sense of themselves and their community."[3]

Beginning in 1857, Sacramento's modest celebrations of Ireland's patron St. Patrick were closely linked with the demand for Irish freedom from England. In March 1865, 350 persons marched in a parade led by the Emmet Guard. The event expressed loyalty to the saint and a nostalgia for the "Auld Sod." At the same time, the parade offered public support to the growing Fenian organization, a brotherhood of men who favored Irish nationalism. The cause of Irish nationalism burned bright, and it was often led (and occasionally obstructed) by church officials. Ireland's long quest for independence from Great Britain found strong support from Sacramento's church leaders in the seventy-year period from 1850 to the 1920.[4] The St. Patrick's Day celebrations in Sacramento became more militant even as they were devotional. They usually began at St. Rose Church with a Mass and a rousing sermon from one of the Irish priests. The ranks of marchers were augmented by Catholic school children, taught by Irish Sisters of Mercy and Christian Brothers who added liberal doses of their own fierce nationalism to the children's school lessons. One of the most vocal proponents of Irish nationalism in Sacramento was Brother Justin McMahon, a fiery orator who regularly denounced the British and who helped head up relief collections for the victims of English tyranny in Ireland.

In 1854, the famous Irish nationalist Thomas Francis Meagher visited the city and inspired the formation of several nationalist organizations that were highly popular with Sacramento's Irish.[5] By the 1860s, Sacramento had two predominantly Irish militia companies, the Emmet Guard and the Sarsfield Grenadier Guards, and a smaller Fenian Circle.[6] These met at St. Rose Church and contributed their services and presence to public religious events. The parade of 1875 saw and even more militant display with four hundred Sacramentans marching and including not only militia units, but also newly formed popular associational groups such as the Ancient Order of Hibernians, the Hibernian Benevolent Association (a short-lived Irish insurance group), and the Father Matthew Total Abstinence Association. The highlight of the parade was a float with thirty-two young women dressed in white (representing the thirty-two counties of Ireland) and three additional female representations of the Goddess of Liberty, the Maid of Erin, and the Maid of Honor. Patriotic quotes adorned the float taken from Irish national heroes Daniel O'Connell and Robert Emmet, and American patriot, Patrick Henry. The celebration marched to the Agricultural Hall at Sixth and M while marchers sang patriotic songs and speeches were delivered.

Italian Celebrations

Italian community visibility was marked by local organizations that celebrated Italian national identity. By 1887, there were already enough Italians to form the third chapter of *"Societa M. S. Bersagliere Italiana,"* or Bersagliere Guards, an Italian mutual benefit and fraternal society that provided widow's benefits and whose members dressed in elaborate military uniforms for participation in public events.[7] As a mutual aid society, they helped with funeral expenses and some benefits. Because feelings between Italian nationalists and the Catholic Church were strained for decades over the seizure of papal domains in Italy during the period of Italian unification (1860s), open association with church events was not quite as visible for Italians as for the Irish. However, there were occasions when Catholic faith and Italian community consciousness met.

One such was when Italian citizens publicly mourned the assassination of King Humbert of Italy in August 1900. Luigi Caffaro presided at a meeting of 200 Italian citizens at Smith's Hall to plan for a public commemoration. Two hundred Sacramento Italians accompanied by the Second Infantry Band, marched in procession from Tenth and M Streets to the cathedral. Six black horses drew a funeral carriage with a catafalque covered by a canopy that held the royal crown of Italy, around which were draped wreaths of ivy. Decorating the pedestal upon which the casket rested were the shields of Italy and America. Bishop Grace agreed to hold a solemn high Mass of Requiem at the cathedral on the day of the monarch's internment.[8] Mourners marched into the church to the tolling of bells and listened attentively as Father John Quinn delivered a stirring eulogy to the late king and stern condemnation of the anarchism that had slain him.[9]

Portuguese Celebrations

While the Irish or the Italians, who used public displays to advocate nationalistic aspirations, the Portuguese replicated popular devotions from the Azores or the mainland, accompanied by distinctive dancing and foods. The Portuguese had a number of popular devotional societies which including the *Irmandade do Divino Espirito Santo* (IDES) founded in 1893 in Freeport, Sacramento County, and the Order of the Divine Spirit (ODES) begun in 1904 in Sacramento. They prepared annual religious celebrations, such as the popular Holy Spirit festival held around the Feast of Pentecost (roughly fifty days after Easter). The celebrations were elaborate and well attended. One such celebration took place in 1901 at

John Brown's (Azevedo) 100-acre ranch at Arcade between the Freeport Bridge and Clarksville. It included a Mass by Father Thomas Dermody of the cathedral, followed by a procession led by one of the Brown daughters who had been chosen queen that year. Afterwards, "the tables were spread and it was estimated that between 5,000 and 6,000 people enjoyed the feast." As the Arcade band played popular tunes, people danced, held raffles, and celebrated.[10]

In 1904, the Portuguese of Sacramento held their first religious festival in honor of the Holy Spirit. Organized by the newly founded ODES, the celebration was held on a vacant lot at Fourth and U Streets owned by builder Manuel Jacinto. Three years later, a small one-story Portuguese hall, later enlarged by additions, was constructed on a lot on W between Fourth and Fifth streets. In 1908, the celebration was held at St. Mary's Church and included a large parade, a Mass and dancing in the new hall.

Mexican Celebrations

The high point of the year's activities occurred on the feast of Our Lady of Guadalupe each December. A Mexican cultural and national feast, the festivities centered on the apparitions of Mary on the hill of Tepeyac outside Mexico City in 1531. Hosted at the Cathedral of the Blessed Sacrament, this event was preceded by a week-long mission (a series of revival-style sermons), a solemn Mass and procession in honor of the patroness of Mexico, which brought the Mexican community together in the capacious church.[11] For the celebration of 1930, a men's choir and orchestra, a dramatic club, and a boy's string orchestra provided entertainment for about 1,300 people who attended. "In the evening a musical program was given in the cathedral hall featuring the orchestra of the Mexican Holy Name Society."[12]

For the feast of the Holy Name of Jesus in January, 250 Mexican "Holy Name" men "marching in perfect alignment" turned out for a mammoth parade down K Street. Leading them were the members of the band and an enormous float depicting the hill of Tepeyac near Mexico, on which the apparition of Our Lady of Guadalupe took place in the sixteenth century.[13] The band rendered music for parades, festivals, and religious services for the *colonia*.[14]

Mexican Catholics also spilled into Sacramento streets reflecting the same nexus of religion and culture expressed by other ethnic groups. Under Frederico Falcon, Mexican youth were taught to play instruments and formed a thirty-five-piece Holy Name (Santo Nombre) Marching Band. Resplendent in their "natty uniforms of blue and white," the young men made a debut of sorts in the annual Holy Name Parade held in January 1935.

When the Mexican community finally took possession of its own church in 1945, the celebrations became even more intense. Typical was the celebration in December 1946. The day began with a 6:30 a.m. "*las mananitas*" serenade before the church. A High Mass celebrated by a Carmelite priest from Texas who had also conducted the mission for the Spanish-speaking people followed. Another High Mass was celebrated at 10 a.m. In the evening at 7:30, a symbolic crowning of a statue of the Blessed Virgin was held. Thousands attended these annual celebrations, and the entertainment afterwards was often presented by Jose (Pepe) Delgado, a favorite Sacramento-based Mexican entertainer, and Ramon Magdaleno and Alejandro Vasquez, leaders of a local orchestra. Frederico Falcon himself performed musical numbers, as did church organist Mary Ortiz.[15]

Later celebrations incorporated floats from all the various Mexican groups and societies in the city. In 1953, the celebration began with the traditional Mass offered at the Third and O site with an imported preacher. Delgado was once again on hand to lead the singing, and news accounts reported "hundreds of Mexicans from Sacramento and outlying areas" were in attendance. The next day, a procession formed in front of the church and marched down Fourth Street to J Street and then to the Cathedral of the Blessed Sacrament. In the parade, colorful floats were built by a network of Spanish-speaking groups such as the predictable *Sociedad Guadalupana* and *Sociedad del Santo Nombre*, but also a Mexican Mr. and Mrs. Club, the *Club de Senoritas*, the *Club Libertad*, and the Spanish-speaking association of war veterans, *En Memorial* American Legion Post No. 610.[16] These celebrations continued for many years, providing a focus for many of the energies of the community and a gathering point for its rich associational life.

Although not always acknowledged by the local press and the mostly Anglo Sacramento population, the varied and meaningful ethnic observances contributed to some degree to the city's culture. Indeed, the idioms of minority populations (e.g. jazz performances in African American clubs, food, and festivities of Portuguese and Mexican celebrations, and otherwise "exotic" qualities of ethnic public ritual) would eventually come to be celebrated as part of the city's "diversity."

Celebrating the City's Mythic Past

Not all Catholic displays were strictly religious. Catholics actively celebrated Sacramento's celebration of its historic past. The reconstruction of Sutter's Fort in the late 1890s provided the city with a remembrance of its "ancient" past. The fort was an important symbol of the many links between Sacramento and the Mexican ranchos. Catholics eagerly supported the city's initiative to recreate the fort and cooperatively reworked the architecture of the nearby St. Francis Church in accordance with the romantic myth.

Shortly thereafter, one of the first demonstrations of Catholic participation in recognizing Sacramento's history came in 1908 with the city's hosting of the Grand Council convention of the Young Men's Institute (YMI), a popular Catholic organization. An astounding 10,000 conventioneers descended on the state capital for the conclave, whose goal was to celebrate the union of their Catholic identity and American patriotism. The high point of the conference took place in the newly rebuilt Sutter's Fort. The hosts enacted "A Night in Forty-Nine," a dramatic presentation that called for the interior of the stockade to be illuminated with hundreds of dazzling electrical lights strung in festoons from an enormous staff radiating in gold, red, and green, the official colors of the institute. Scores of young YMIers dressed as Forty-niners, Native Americans, and in other period costumes, while the female branch of the organization, the Young Ladies Institute, served as hostesses dressed as Native American women to serve the conventioneers. The day after the Sutter's Fort performances, 7,000 white-garbed women marched in a loop down Twelfth Street to J Street, down J Street to Second Street, and then around the block to K Street. Invited marching bands pumped out patriotic and religious tunes, flags and banners were waved, and conventioneers jammed into the cathedral to witness a Pontifical Mass celebrated by Bishop Grace and preached by Monsignor Thomas Capel, a popular local orator. Three thousand Catholics then attended a luncheon hosted by the YLI women in the capacious Agricultural Pavilion of the state fairgrounds.[17]

Marching for the Holy Name of Jesus and Christ the King

The Catholic culture of the mid-twentieth century shifted slightly from ethnic issues and refocused around certain devotional practices and pledges of moral action for the common good. Such was the character of the Holy Name Society, a voluntary organization of Catholic men on a parish sponsored by the Dominican Order. Sacramento's first Holy Name Society was founded at Immaculate Conception Parish in 1910. The group encouraged frequent communion and Holy Name men came together for monthly communion breakfasts. There they took the Holy Name Pledge, which bound them to avoid coarse and vulgar language and especially not taking the name of Jesus in vain. A liturgical feast of the Holy Name took place in January commemorating the bestowal of the name "Jesus" on the son of Joseph and Mary. This organization grew in popularity and Holy Name Men, many of the businessmen and professionals strategized ways to bring their message of good language and efforts at public morality to a wider public. The Holy Name was a popular organization for Catholic men, and Junior Holy Names was created for teens.

In 1930, Bishop Robert Armstrong created a Diocesan Union of Holy Name Societies. Latinx Catholics formed their own version of the groups. The first meeting of the group, held at Immaculate Conception Church on Holy Name Sunday in January 1930, was led by George Meiers. This group planned big for the next year.[18] In 1931, the Diocesan Union organized a parade that called on men to march from St. Francis Church to the Cathedral. In 1932, the route was repeated and increasing number of Holy Name men came to participate from all of Sacramento and the surrounding region. Organized by laymen Henry Lynn and Henry Meyer this march included not only local clergy, but also Bishop Armstrong and Governor James "Sunny Jim" Rolph. The entire event was broadcast live from a local radio station. An address by noted Catholic layman, Joseph Scott capped the day.[19] In 1933, more than 1,500 joined the Holy Name Parade, and three years later, 2,000 joined in in 1936.[20] In 1937, the parade marched from St. Francis to the Cathedral, with 1,500 marchers, and included an escort from the city police and the California Highway Patrol.[21]

Long Live Christ the King

In 1925, Pope Pius XI instituted the liturgical feast of Christ the King in the church's calendar. Echoing a priority of Pope Pius X (1903–1914) and continued by his successors, this feast was expanded as a universal call to "Catholic Action." Catholic Action exhorted the laity to "reconstruct the social order" by active engagement in public issues, politics, and education. Sacramento Catholics, especially the Holy Name, picked up this challenge. The Holy Name switched their big public demonstration in January to the month of October. In October 1940, the Holy Name welcomed 5,000 Catholics to the Memorial Auditorium for a patriotic rally. In 1942, the Holy Name Men held a memorial service for those who had already perished in World War II.[22] Numbers increased as did the presence of military speakers and martial music at these events. No longer taking to the streets, Catholics began to rent big meeting spaces. In 1946, the rally was held at Edmonds Field, home of the Sacramento Solons. Organized by Al Westlake, a prominent layman in the diocese, the event was scheduled to welcome thousands to the baseball field.[23] By 1952, 10,000 participants were expected.[24] These demonstrations, although monitored closely by clergy who arranged for permits, rentals, and esteemed guests, were mostly handled by Holy Name Offices such as Maurice Bamberry, Ward D. Driscoll (who recommended the Memorial Auditorium venue), and Al Westlake. The Christ the King Rallies downtown faded as people moved away from the city to the growing suburbs, but new public venues for faith and patriotism emerged.

Catholic Anti-Communism: Prayers and Pageantry

Among the most unsettling post-World War II fallout shaping the Sacramento Catholic experience was the fears generated by the Cold War. Huge government investment in the California economy during the Depression and the Second World War perhaps might have ended when the threat of economic and totalitarian disaster no longer loomed large. However, the deterioration of the wartime alliance between the United States and the Soviet Union and the aggressive push of pro-Communist governments in Eastern Europe moved America into a state of permanent tension with the other superpower. Antagonisms took an even more ominous turn in 1949 when it was discovered that the Soviets possessed the technology to build and deliver a nuclear bomb.

For Californians, these developments were accentuated when Pacific basin tensions, born of the reshifting of geopolitics. Specifically, the 1949 "fall" of China to the communists and the outbreak of war in Korea in 1950 mobilized American defense industries and military installations. California's southland became home to a welter of defense industries requiring scores of workers. The military bases in the state were the nerve centers and debarkation points for thousands of servicemen and women *en route* to Korea, Japan, Vietnam, and other hot spots in Asia. More than most, Sacramentans were reminded constantly of the realities of the Cold War by the roaring of jet engines over the skies of McClellan and Mather fields, and the rush of activity and preparedness drills, such as air raid alerts, demanded by the various international crises. In fact, Sacramento's dependence on government work and military activity and its concomitant demands for security clearances and positive affirmations of loyalty to the United States may also have emphasized the anti-Communist threat more than in other locales.

Sacramento Catholics certainly joined the anti-Communist consensus of their neighbors, but their religious affiliation provided still another prism to focus and intensify the loathing many felt for Communism. To be sure, certain Catholic ethnic groups, such as the city's Croatian populace, had relations and friends who experienced the heavy grip of Communist domination. Incidents of anti-Catholic persecution behind the Iron Curtain also excited the antipathy of Catholic Sacramentans. In 1957, they donated over $3,500 for relief of the embattled Hungarians (whom Bishop Joseph McGucken characterized as "this brave and honest nation") and their imprisoned prelate, Hungarian Cardinal Josef Mindszenty.[25]

International incidents that aggravated the tensions of the Cold War were felt throughout Catholic Sacramento. On the editorial pages of the Catholic newspaper, frequent denunciations of communist thinkers, policies and leftist politicians in America were often illustrated by regular cartoons depicting Stalin or the Chinese communist leaders as foes of God. Pulpit orators, like Fair Oaks pastor Patrick Cronin, regularly condemned communism in his Sunday sermons. In 1954, the charismatic Italian Franciscan Antonio Lisandrini, (nicknamed the "Microphone of God") visited Sacramento at the behest of the Italian Catholic Federation. At a "standing room only" crowd in St. Mary's Church, he denounced communism and related with vivid detail his own narrow escape from communist agitators who heckled him and threw bombs at him during public addresses in Italy. Lisandrini told his audience, "Faith is necessary to fight communism." He believed fervently that "America was called on by Divine Providence to combat communism."[26] The audience applauded vigorously, demonstrating how clearly orators like Cronin and Lisandrini struck a chord in postwar Sacramento. Anti-Communist invective registered strongly with Sacramento Catholics. A letter to Armstrong, for example, from a disgruntled Broderick Catholic woman who protested the closure of her church by the local pastor noted, "How can we even hope to combat social injustice and the scourge of communism when our priests do things like this?"[27]

But the fears generated by the threat of communist subversion at home or even the prospect of nuclear war led Catholics everywhere to a new level of devotion to the Blessed Virgin Mary. Indeed, an explicitly anti-Communist version of Marian piety became one of the chief ways Sacramento Catholics demonstrated their hatred for this atheistic totalitarian system and means of combating it and bringing about its demise.

Devotion to Mary, the Mother of Jesus, had for centuries been a characteristic of the Catholic faith.[28] Scriptural evidence and theological development had given it a solid niche in the pantheon of Catholic life and culture. Its resilience, despite objections that it encroached on the unique privileges of Christ, is in part due to its resonance with religious impulses toward the feminine in worship and prayer but also because devotion to Mary displayed a remarkable adaptability to historical, regional, and cultural needs. Virtually every Catholic nation had its particular version of the "Madonna." Her intercessory powers and closeness to the person of faith have been almost instinctively appreciated over the centuries.

Along with the official "cultus" of the Blessed Virgin Mary, approved by Church authorities, a separate popular cult, manifested in apparitions, special messages, and utterances, flourished at this time. So also did the praying of the fifty-bead prayer called the rosary. As with Catholics the world over, the rosary was an important part of the spiritual world of Sacramento Catholics. Taught in schools and urged regularly from the pulpit, the recitation of the rosary in groups gathered to pray for peace was especially popular during the war years and continued long afterward. Indeed, so popular was the recitation of the Rosary that in 1951, FM radio station KCRA began a daily program during which a studio group recited the Rosary sponsored by the Diocesan Union of Holy Name Societies and the National Radio Rosary Organization.

The intensification of the cult of the Virgin Mary as an antidote to communism was urged in the 1950s by no less than Pope Pius XII himself. A vision of Mary had allegedly appeared in Cova da Iria, Portugal, to three peasant children during World War I. Explanations of the widely followed event spoke of the whirling of the sun and even some healings, but the main message that seized so many, especially after World War II, were the Virgin's instructions for Catholics to pray the rosary for world peace and the conversion of Russia. In the aftermath of World War II, devotion to Mary under the title of "Our Lady of Fatima" spread among American Catholics, and was reflected in books, organizations, a popular Hollywood movie, and countless exhortations from clergy and religious to heed the instructions of Mary. Sacramento Catholics needed little prodding to honor the Virgin Mary. All churches contained statues of Mary, and school children and adults were urged to pray to her for their needs. Public shrines, like the Lourdes grottoes on the grounds of St. Joseph's Academy and at St. Lawrence Church in suburban North Highlands, reminded Catholics of her powerful intercession.

Dr. William Ballou, a Sacramento physician who played an important role in both the building and naming of the parish school for St. Joseph's church in North Sacramento, "Our Lady of Fatima," was the chairman of a local branch of the nationwide Fatima Crusade Central Committee, which kept the cult alive and even helped spread it to the cathedral, St. Francis, St. Philomene's, St. Mary's, Sacred Heart, St. Joseph's, All Hallows, and Our Lady of Assumption parishes by 1953.[29] Fatima's popularity spread even beyond the Catholic ghetto when Gladys Gollahon's song "Our Lady of Fatima" rocketed to a place on the popular music charts. Gollahon came to Sacramento to accompany a theater group that performed a play about the apparitions and signed autographs for the Catholic youth who flocked around her.[30] Pope Pius XII declared 1954 a "Marian Year" to honor the centenary of the definition of the doctrine of the Immaculate Conception. Cold War themes of anti-Sovietism and Catholic patriotism were still going strong when in 1959 a Marian Rally recruited hundreds of school children from Sacramento's over-crowded Catholic schools and highlighted a youthful Father Keith Kenny as the chief preacher of the day.[31]

An important element of this distinctive type of Marian devotion was its unabashed American nationalism. The Second Provincial Council of Baltimore had proclaimed Mary the patroness of the United States back in 1846. But Mary's role as a special guardian of America had never been more dynamically accentuated than during the Cold War era. In Sacramento, public demonstrations signaling devotion to "faith and flag" took place, further symbolizing some of the character of the Catholic culture of the era. Replacing the Holy Name and Christ the King rallies in 1948 or 1949 were huge Marian rallies held at the newly opened Edmonds Field made available by Catholic architect Harry Devine who was a part-owner. Its wide grounds and welcoming grandstands were one of the places where Catholic Sacramento "went public." The time of year shifted again to take advantage of good weather for an outdoor event.

Service station owner Al Westlake of the Holy Name Society staged huge extravaganzas which always included a cast of hundreds, led by the local bishops. Typical of the blend of Catholicism, patriotism and anti-Communist fervor was the rally of 1951, right during the Korean War and the revelations of the Hiss and Rosenberg cases. Governor and Mrs. Earl Warren were among 7,500 gathered at Sacramento's Edmonds Field to hear future Sacramento bishop Joseph T. McGucken speak on the topic "This Nation Under God." Joining McGucken on the dais was Major General Junius W. Jones, commanding officer of McClellan Field Air Force Base, who led the pledge of allegiance.[32] Other invited guests included Senator and Mrs. Earl Desmond, Sacramento Mayor Bert Geisreiter, and Assemblymen John E. Moss (a future congressman), Gordon Feury, and Laughlin E. Waters. In the crowd as well were City Manager and Mrs. Bartley Cavanagh, James Galick, chairman of the Sacramento County Board of Supervisors, and county manager Charles Deterding.

A moment of high solemnity and pageantry arrived when Father Anthony Maio of the cathedral appeared in a special car with a police escort, carrying the Blessed Sacrament to the high altar in the middle of the field (erected by city workers at Bartley Cavanagh's direction). Preceding him was an "honor guard" of 200 vested altar boys carrying lighted tapers and 100 grammar-school girls wearing pastel formals. These third and fourth grade students were led by Patricia Barbeau, student body president from St. Joseph's Academy. In a moment of supreme union between flag and cross, after the Blessed Sacrament was enthroned on the altar, General Jones led the assembled rally participants in the pledge to the flag. McGucken, who had flown directly to Sacramento from a tour of Guatemala, rose to the occasion insisting that America turn to God in its hour of national peril and even alluded to the recent Hiss perjury trial when he stated "today we are dismayed by the revelations of treachery all over our country and the mounting numbers of those in high places accused and convicted of treason."[33] Chancery hands Father Thomas Kirby and Father Cornelius Higgins assumed the visible leadership, but the coordination of the event was in the capable hands of Westlake and his associates.

Public Art: Another McClatchy Legacy

The public Catholic sphere also manifested itself in religious art and architecture. Churches are notably among the most elegant buildings of a city. In Sacramento, worship sites such as Westminster Presbyterian on Capitol Avenue, St. John's Lutheran on Seventeenth and L, and the elegant First Baptist on Twenty-eighth and L were architectural gems of the first order. Catholic contributions to public culture also took the form of substantial additions to the urban space. The design and elegance of the cathedral, St. Francis Church, Immaculate Conception, and Sacred Heart Church were signs of Sacramento's increasing architectural maturation. Other Catholic sites became cultural landmarks of the city. The chapel of St. Patrick's Orphanage, later known as St. Rose Church, is a prime example. The interior design of the chapel was funded by the grieving family of Carlos McClatchy, the only son of *Sacramento Bee* editor and publisher C. K. McClatchy, who died unexpectedly at the age of forty-four in 1933. McClatchy's grief-stricken mother, Ella, and his sisters Eleanor and Charlotte, spent lavishly to decorate the heretofore unadorned interior chapel to honor his memory as well as other members of the McClatchy family. Ella McClatchy purchased the main altar, which was constructed of imported Siena and Numidian marbles. Above the altar were five statues—Christ and the four evangelists, Matthew, Mark, Luke, and John.[34]

Ella McClatchy's gift of the St. Rose altar was complimented by new Stations of the Cross donated by her daughters Charlotte McClatchy Maloney and Eleanor McClatchy. The stations were the work of New York artist Dunbar Dyson Beck. A graduate of Yale University's School of Fine Arts and a fellow of the American Academy in Rome, the accomplished Beck had attached himself to the McClatchy family, serving as an artistic consultant to the newspaper and the companion of Eleanor McClatchy. Beck's fourteen paintings, done on aluminum panels and set in frames of Spanish cedar, departed from traditional images that depicted a number of characters who participated in the *Via Crucis*. By contrast, Beck's modernistic Stations of the Cross highlighted only the face of Christ (with the exception of an appearance by Mary in the fourth station). Initially displayed in San Francisco's Gump Art Galleries before their memorial installation in St. Rose Church, they attracted some comment for their departure from the traditional format of religious art. However, the *Superior California Catholic Register* reassured its readers, "we can readily see that although the Stations are modern in design, their modernism does not in any way detract from a deeply reverent and spiritual interpretation."[35] At Eleanor's McClatchy's request, Beck also contributed artwork to the Stanford Home, settlement house under the direction of the Sisters of Social Service.

The McClatchy family later commissioned stained-glass artist Charles J. Connick to execute a series of windows that memorialized several other members of the McClatchy family. Connick, whose work also graced the Cathedral of St. John the Divine in New York and Grace Cathedral in San Francisco, created and executed the chancel group of three windows highlighting St. Rose and stories from her life. The seven windows of the nave illustrated an appropriate orphanage theme incorporating scenes from the childhood of Christ, while the two windows above the organ loft depict the orphanage's patron, St. Patrick, and the friend of the poor, St. Vincent de Paul.[36]

The "religion of the streets" is an important facet of public religion and a window into the role of religious beliefs in the lives of "ordinary people." Clergy and religious women were certainly organizers and motivators— but the numbers that turned out reflect just how deeply faith ran in the lives of Catholic laity. The traditional boundaries between religious and secular space were erased. The rich texture of Sacramento's cultural life was laid bare in ways that still amaze even years after these celebrations no longer exist.

Conclusion

What has been written here about Sacramento's Catholics can be said of every other religious body in the California capital. "Ordinary" people who are only marginally noted in press accounts of the origins and development of city institutions and movements were often critical to the success or failure of a city enterprise. Their accomplishments have been noted by some, but mostly passed over in favor of more easily sourced people of prominence or the skewering of press accounts.

This book attempts to awaken interest of the social and cultural impact of religion in the city. While church institutions spend a lot of time and money tending to their own internal affairs, Catholics (and other religious communities) also invested heavily in the city itself—in healthcare, education, concern for the disadvantaged, and especially the current phenomenon of homelessness that burdens the community and pokes at its collective conscience.

In an era when historical reckoning is taking place in the nation's understanding of race, ethnicity, and poverty, it is also a matter of simple justice to acknowledge the role of those whom official history has either ignored or thought uninteresting. Every church endeavor or building carries the names of now-forgotten benefactors and quiet souls who made possible what the current generation enjoys, uses, and builds on. Every generation of Sacramento's history brings for people who rise to the challenges of the moment. They are indeed "Indomitable Sacramentans," sharing in the distinct charism of this beautiful state capital.

Endnotes

Introduction

1 The main published works on Sacramento history include Severson, T., *Sacramento: An Illustrated History: 1839 to 1874* (California Historical Society, 1973); McGowan, J. A. and Willis, T. R., *Sacramento: Heart of the Golden State* (Woodland Hills: Windsor Publications Inc., 1983); Burns, J. F. (ed.), *Sacramento: Gold Rush Legacy, Metropolitan Destiny* (Carlsbad: Heritage Media Corporation, 1999). Interesting vignettes can be found in Davis, W. J., *An Illustrated History of Sacramento County, California* (Chicago: Lewis Publishing Co., 1890) and Willis, W. E., *History of Sacramento County* (Chicago: Historical Publishing Co., 1925). There are also short overviews of the city's history and a number of master's and doctoral dissertations dealing with various aspects of the city's past.

2 Dated but still very helpful is Joseph McGowan's *History of the Sacramento Valley,* 3 Vols. (New York: Lewis Historical Publishing Company, 1961).

Chapter 1

1 "Solemn Diocesan Eucharistic Congress, Centenary of the First Mass in Sacramento, 1850-1950, copy in the Archives of the Diocese of Sacramento.

2 There is no scholarly history of Sacramento to date. The most recent popular overview is my own work, *Sacramento: Indomitable City* (Charleston: Arcadia Press, 2003). See also Mark Eifler, *Gold Rush Capitalists: Greed and Gold in Sacramento* (University of New Mexico Press, 2002).

3 McGloin, J. B., S. J., "'Philos' (Gregory J. Phelan, M.D., 1822–1902) Commentator on Catholicism in California's Gold Rush Decade," *Records of the American Catholic Historical Society of Philadelphia* 67 (June 1966): pp. 109–116. "Pioneer Doctor Passes Away," *Sacramento Bee*, 7 November 1902,

p. 5. See also Weber, F. J., "Reflections of 'Manhattan'" (1) and (2), *Catholic California: Some Historical Reflections*, Archdiocese of Los Angeles, 1922, pp. 221–224.

4   Fragment of a Diary of Doctor J.G. Phelan of Sacramento City, 1850 Biography File, California State Library, Sacramento.

5   McGloin, J. B., S.J., "Anthony Langlois, Pioneer Priest in Gold Rush San Francisco," *Southern California Quarterly* XLIX (December 1967), pp. 407–424.

6   A copy of this letter is in the Archives of the Archdiocese of San Francisco (hereafter AASF), n.d.

7   "Philos," *Freeman's Journal*, August 29, 1850.

8   The baptismal register of St. Rose of Lima Parish records the baptism of "Pius Sierra Nevada O'Brien." Baptismal Registers, Cathedral of the Blessed Sacrament, Sacramento, California.

9   "Philos," *Freeman's Journal*, August 29, 1850.

10 *Ibid.*

11 "Meeting Held to Plan Erection of a Catholic Church," *Sacramento Transcript*, August 13, 1850; "California Correspondence, December 13, 1850," *Freeman's Journal*, February 22, 1850.

12 "California Correspondence, October 20, 1850," *Freeman's Journal*, December 14, 1850.

13 Anderson's hastily sketched diary is in the Archives of the Dominican Friars at St. Albert's Priory, Oakland, California. He mentions the Tenth and I site.

14 "California Correspondence, January 31, 1851," *Freeman's Journal*, March 15, 1851.

15 Two other churches would bear this name. A Catholic church in Roseville (Placer County) would open under this title. In the 1940s, Bishop Robert Armstrong would designate the chapel of St. Patrick's orphanage on Franklin Boulevard as a parish church with this name as well.

16 "California Correspondence, December 13, 1850," *Freeman's Journal*, February 22, 1851.

17 A hagiographical legend has grown around the "Martyr of Charity," an image burnished over the years by his Dominican confreres. The legend was highlighted in the 1950 celebrations of the centenary of Catholicism in Sacramento. Despite the legend, Anderson's importance is largely symbolic. "The First Priest to Work in Sacramento," *Superior California Catholic Register*, October 22, 1939, p. 4; "Father Augustine Anderson—City's First Martyr," *Superior California Catholic Herald*, April 26, 1950, p.3A. See also history of Dominicans in California. See also Fabian Stan Parmisano, OP, *Mission West: The Western Dominican Province, 1850-1966* (Oakland: Western Dominican Province, 1995), pp. 19–27. Parmisano suggests that even though he was traveling all over Northern California "he spent most of his time in Sacramento." However, the details of his itinerary are not documented.

18 "Sacramento Church Erected," *Alta*, September 29, 1852, p. 1.

19 "Tremendous Conflagration," *Sacramento Daily Union*, July 14, 1854, p. 2. The fire also destroyed the Congregational church of Joseph Augustine Benton.

20 "Our California Correspondence, July 14, 1854," *Freeman's Journal*, August 19, 1854.

21 "California Correspondence, October 15, 1853," *Freeman's Journal*, November 19, 1853.

22 "Another New Church," *Sacramento Daily Union*, September 13, 1854, p. 2.

23 "Attended Church," *Daily Bee*, August 8, 1859, p. 3.

24 Other brick churches followed. By 1857, the Southern Methodists joined the ranks of those with elegant new buildings, prompting the *Evening Bee* to write warmly, "Nothing adds more to a city than fine churches, and we trust our citizens one and all will lend their aid in building the one proposed." See "New Church of New Methodist Episcopal Church," *Daily Bee*, March 8, 185, p. 4. Finally in 1859, the Seventh Street Methodist church moved to new quarters at Sixth between K and L. The Gothic church, known as the Sixth Street Church, was 52 feet across and 100 feet deep. Topped by a distinctive spire that rose 165 feet over the flat city, it was an early Sacramento landmark.

25 "City Intelligence," *Sacramento Daily Union*, March 8, 1862, p. 3.

26 "A Catholic Fair," *Daily Bee*, March 26, 1857, p. 3; "Church Improvements," Daily Bee, September 30, 1857, p. 3; "Catholic Church," *Daily Union*, March 10, 1857, p. 2.

27 "Catholicity in California—Dedication of a Church in Sacramento— Hospitality of the City to Mgr. Alemany," *Freeman's Journal*, April 12, 1851.

Chapter 2

1 Doyle, E., "Building the Cathedral," *Catholic Herald*, September 30, 1976, p. 4.

2 Olson, J. S., "Pioneer Catholicism in Eastern and Southern Nevada, 1864–1931," *Nevada Historical Society Quarterly* 26 (1983), pp. 159–171, presents a good summary of the mining booms and the pace of Catholic development in this region.

3 Gaffey, J., "A critical look at Bishop Manogue," *Catholic Herald*, September 23, 1976, p. 4.

4 Kline, C. R."Patrick Manogue: Priest, Pastor, Bishop, 1831–1895" (unpublished MA thesis, University of California, Berkeley, 1960), p. 54. See also Bucchanieri, V. A., "Nevada's Bonanza Church, Saint Mary's in the Mountains" pamphlet (Gold Hill: Gold Hill Publishing Co., 1997).

5 Patrick Manogue to Augustine Schulte, April 30, 1885, AASF.

6 Doyle, E., "The bishop builds his cathedral," *Catholic Herald*, September 16, 1976, p. 4.

7 "Death of Mrs. Theresa Fair," *San Francisco Examiner*, September 14, 1891, p. 3.

8 "Mrs. Fair's Will," *San Francisco* Chronicle, September 18, 1891, p. 10.

9 "Bishop Manogue Returns," *Monitor*, January 21, 1891, p. 5.

10 "Bishop Manogue Dead," *Evening Bee*, February 27, 1895, p. 1.

11 Obituary, *San Francisco Call*, September 14, 1891, p. 8; "Death of Mrs. Fair," *San Francisco Chronicle*, September 14, 1891, p. 10. "Many Fainted in the Crowd," *San Francisco Examiner*, September 17, 1891, p. 3.

12 For the relationship between Marie Hungerford and Manogue, see Crouch, G., *The Bonanza King John Mackay and the Battle Over the Greatest Riches in the American West*, (New York: Scribner, 2018), pp. 166–167.

13 Another account of Marie Hungerford Bryant's life is found in Lewis, O., *Silver*

Kings: The Lives and Times of Mackay, Fair, Flood, and O'Brien Lords of the Nevada Comstock (Reno: University of Nevada Press, 1986), pp. 71–80.

14 Crouch, *Bonanza King*, pp. 220–221.

15 "Mrs. J.W, Mackay's Handsome Donation," *Nevada State Journal*, February 6, 1906, p. 3.

16 "Millionaire A. Coolot Passes Quietly Away," *Saturday Bee*, December 1, 1900, p. 1; "The Late A. Coolot," *Sacramento Record-Union*, December 2, 1900; "Augustine E. Coolot," Sacramento County Biographies, Rootsweb.Ancestry. Com.

17 "Anthony Coolot Left No Will," *Evening* Bee, December 4, 1900, p. 8.

18 "Millionaire A. Coolot Passes Quietly Away," *Saturday Bee*, December 1, 1900, p. 1.

19 "Col. M'Nassar Dead," *Evening Bee*, May 22, 1896, p. 5; "Death of a Good Citizen," *Sacramento Daily Record-Union*, May 23, 1896, p. 3; "Colonel McNasser Dead," *San Francisco Call*, May 23, 1896, p. 5.

20 "Mrs. Ellen Dwyer Answers the Call," *Evening Bee*, April 30, 1906, p. 5.

21 "The New Cathedral in Sacramento," *Monitor*, January 9, 1889, p. 4; "Dedicated! Sacramento's Grand Cathedral," *Monitor*, July 3, 1889, p. 5.

22 "Sacramento Cathedral," *Monitor*, December 5, 1888, p. 5.

23 "Obsequies of Bishop Manogue," *Sacramento Daily Record-Union*, March 6, 1895, p. 3; "Death of an Eminent Prelate;" *Sacramento Record-Union*, February 28, 1895, p. 3.

24 "The New Cathedral in Sacramento," *Monitor,* January 9, 1889, p. 4.

25 Manogue apparently was a heavy drinker in his earlier years but later became a temperance advocate (although not a very loud one). One anecdote relates that his conversion to temperance came when he poured a few drops of liquor from his personal flask down the throat of a desert horned toad whereupon the animal promptly died. "From that moment on, I put the ban upon all intoxicating liquors. If a few drops had such a deadly effect on that reptile what must be its ultimate effect upon the human being." "A Temperance Sermon," *Evening Bee*, March 6, 1895, p. 2.

26 "Death of James Bithell," *Sacramento Daily Union,* July 3, 1896, p. 5.

27 "Westminster Chimes Will Tell the Hours, *Evening Bee*, December 23, 1901, p. 5.

28 "Mary E. Bithell, Pioneer is Dead," *Sacramento Bee*, July 9, 1912, p. 1.

29 "Mary Bithell," *Sacramento Star*, July 30, 1912, p. 2; see also the Bithell Probate, Wills and Probate, Center for Sacramento History (hereafter CSH).

Chapter 3

1 This point is made in Hardwick, S. W., "Ethnic Residential and Commercial Patterns in Sacramento with Special Reference to the Russian-American Experience" (unpublished Ph.D. diss., University of California, Davis, 1986), pp. 49–55.

2 For general information on Germans in California, see Gudde, E. G., *German Pioneers in Early California*, Historical Bulletin No. 6 (Hoboken: Concord Society, 1927).

3 See McCoy, F. N., "A History of the First Five Years of the Sacramento, California Turnverein, 1854–1859". The actual figures are as follows: 1852:

730; 1860: 1,374; 1870: 1,634; 1880: 1,838; 1890: 2,182; 1900: 1,957. These statistics are to be found in Pierini, B., "Germans: A German History of the Sacramento Area," Sacramento Area Ethnic History Survey, 1984, Center for Sacramento History (CSH). See also Carol Cosgrove Terry, "*Die Deutschen Enwanderer* in Sacramento: German Immigrants in Sacramento, 1850–1859" (unpublished MA Thesis, University of Nevada, Las Vegas, 2000). Terry's work covers only the decade of the 1850s and makes little mention of German Catholics. Her work does give a detailed description of German demographics, employment, and social expression in Sacramento for those years. Her main focus is on the Turnverein which may or may not have been an acceptable social outlet for Catholics.

4   Bruce Pierini, "Italian History and Demographics of the Greater Sacramento Area," Sacramento County Ethnic History Survey, 1984, CSH.

5   *Ibid.*

6   "California Correspondence, August 31, 1854," *Freeman's Journal*, October 7, 1854.

7   "A New Catholic Church," *Daily Bee,* March 16, 1871, p. 3.

8   "German Catholic Mission," *Daily Bee,* May 23, 1871, p. 3.

9   "The German Celebration," *Sacramento Union*, February 2, 1871, p. 3. For a fuller description, see Sister Marie Vandenbergh, R.C. "Attitudes and Events Leading up to the Establishment of Christian Brother's School in Sacramento, 1871–1876" (unpublished MA thesis, Sacramento State College, 1968).

10 Gaffey, J. P., *Citizen of No Mean City: Archbishop Patrick Riordan of San Francisco, 1891–1914* (Consortium Books, 1976), p. 191.

11 Clementine Deymann to Michael Richardt, October 19, 1894, St. Francis File, Archives of the Friars Minor, Santa Barbara Province, California (hereafter AOFMSB).

12 "M. Diepenbrock Taken By Death," *Sacramento Bee*, January 20, 1928, p. 1.

13 "Melchior Diepenbrock," in Willis, pp. 462–466.

14 The details of these administrative foundations are found in Marion Habig, *Heralds of the King: The Franciscans of the St. Louis-Chicago Province* (Franciscan Herald Press, 1958), pp. 221–236. The details of the interactions among the friars and with Bishop Manogue are to be found in the Archives of the Franciscan Order, Santa Barbara. See also Schutz, O. M., "German Catholics in California: The Origins of St. Elizabeth's Parish, Oakland and the Early Move to a Multicultural Parish," *U.S. Catholic Historian* 12 (Summer, 1994) (3), pp. 63–72.

15 Manogue to Richardt, August 18, 1893, "St. Francis, Sacramento File," AOFMSB.

16 Father Leo to Father Prior, May 6, 1894, "St. Francis, Sacramento File," AOFMSB. For information about the German cohort in Marysville, see Terry, C. C., "*Die Deutschen Von* Marysville: The Germans of Marysville, 1850–1860," *Psi Sigma Siren* 1 (January 2003), pp. 1–31.

17 Father Leo to Michael Richardt, May 6, 1894, AOFMSB.

18 *Ibid.*

19 Patrick Manogue to Clementine Deymann, September 13, 1894, AOFMSB.

20 Born Patrick McClory on November 15, 1847, he had entered the largely German Franciscan band at Teutopolis, Illinois on September 24, 1869. He professed his solemn vows as a Franciscan in 1873, and on June 29, 1875, he

was ordained to the priesthood in St. Louis. Until he arrived in Sacramento in 1894, he had served at parishes in St. Louis, Cleveland, and Chicago. "Father Augustine McClory, OFM, 1847–1907," Chronology of Sacred Heart Province and History of St. Francis and St. Boniface Churches, AOFMSB.

21 Clementine Deymann to Michael Richardt, October 19, 1894, "St. Francis-Sacramento File, AOFMSB.

22 Clementine Deymann to Michael Richardt, November 3, 1894, "St. Francis-Sacramento File," AOFMSB.

23 Augustine McClory to Michael Richardt, November 8, 1894, "St. Francis-Sacramento File," AOFMSB.

24 Clementine Deymann to Michael Richardt, September 28, 1894, "St. Francis-Sacramento File," AOFMSB.

25 Godfrey Hoelters to Fr. Commissarius, November 15, 1900, "St. Francis-Sacramento File," AOFMSB.

26 Godfrey Hoelters to Fr. Commissarius, March 4, 1901, "St. Francis-Sacramento File," AOFMSB.

27 *Ibid.*

28 Godfrey Hoelters, OFM to Bishop Thomas Grace, February 10, 1909, AOFMSB.

29 "The German Catholics," *Monitor*, September 21, 1907, p. 1; "Catholics Meet Today," *Sacramento Union*, September 8, 1907, p. 16; "German Catholics in Convention," *Sacramento Union*, September 9, 1907, p. 2.

30 Brother Eugenius to Fr. Provincial, July 12, 1896, "St. Francis-Sacramento File," AOFMSB.

31 Circular of Father Humilis Weise OFM to the parish, December 7, 1919. AOFM SB. St. Francis File.

32 Galarza, E., *Barrio Boy* (Notre Dame: University of Notre Dame Press, 1971), pp. 198–199.

33 "Ellen Bowden Active in Catholic Church, Dies," *Sacramento Bee*, October 30, 1926, p. 12.

34 The inheritance, thanks to good investments, was still $70,000 strong when she died in 1926. Bowden's generosity to Brady would continue throughout the priest's life. In 1907, when he was building a new Sacred Heart Church in Red Bluff, Bowden gave $1600 to equip the new edifice with pews. She also paid for a stained-glass window of St. Patrick in honor of her parents. The next year, after the church was completed, Bowden underwrote Brady's expenses for a lengthy trip to Continental Europe and a home visit to Ireland. He later returned and related details of the trip for a fund-raiser for the convent of St. Stephen's. In 1926, Brady was chosen as the founding pastor of a new parish in East Sacramento, which would be named "St. Stephens." Bowden left a considerable sum in her will for the new parish and named Brady as the executor of her estate. See "Illustrated Lecture," p. 8. *Leader*, July 4, 1908, p. 5; a copy of Bowden's will, which is on file at the Center for Sacramento History. The monies gathered for St. Stephen's, later renamed Sacred Heart, are referred to in the Catholic press. Brady seemed to be especially adept at winning huge financial considerations for the cathedral. In the early twentieth century, he managed to snare a huge amount of the estate of Johanna Carroll, the daughter of a large Sacramento business owner.

35   "City and Coast," *Monitor*, April 28, 1900, p. 68.

36   Raymond Renwald, "St. Stephen's: Church with eight lives," *Catholic Herald*, November 4, 1976, p. 4; "St. Stephen's Story: Hard to Top," *Catholic Herald*, November 11, 1976, p. 4. Renwald knew the community well, but in neither of these articles does he acknowledge the role of Ellen Bowden.

37   "Miss Bowden Left Estate of $200,000," *Sacramento Bee*, November 6, 1926, p. 9.

38   Ellen Margaret Bowden, Wills and Probate, CSH.

39   "Reverend Brady, Noted Priest to be Laid to Rest," *Sacramento Bee*, October 7, 1929, p. 6.

40   *U. S. Census of Population, Sacramento, 1910, 1920, 1930, 1940.* Additional demographic analysis is found in Pierini, pp.67ff. See also Susan Hardwick, "Ethnic Residential and Commercial Patterns in Sacramento with Special Reference to Russian-American Experience" (unpublished Ph.D. diss., University of California, Davis, 1986).

41   Hardwick, "Ethnic Residential" lays out the changing residential "clustering" of the Italians of Sacramento, pp. 97–98; 130–133.

42   "On European Trip," *Sacramento Star*, July 2, 1907, p. 1.

43   Mention of the school's precarious condition is made in "Italians Plan Grand Benefit," *Sacramento Union*, March 12, 1909: "The school in Sacramento has been established over a year and is not on what is considered a firm basis." For efforts to induce the teaching of Italian in the public schools, see "Italians Want Language Taught in High School," *Sacramento Bee*, June 8, 1916, p. 4.

44   John Dwyer, "Michael Gualco, pioneer priest of Chico," *Catholic Herald*, October 14, 1976, p. 4.

45   Gualco soon became one of the leading citizens in this agricultural community, not only by building and beautifying his church, but also by working with city leaders to attract a branch of the State Normal School to the community. Since the relationships between these teacher training institutions and Catholics were often stormy, Gualco was especially vigilant over the intellectual life of his flock—often attending classes and challenging professors. Moreover, he held sessions in his own parlor to explain Catholic teaching and practices. "Father Gualco and the Church He built," *Catholic Herald*, January 29, 1921, p. 5.

46   "Impressive Ceremonies at Cathedral Attend Visit of the Apostolic Delegate,' *Evening Bee*, May 18, 1903, p. 1. Later, this beautiful lamp was discarded in the renovations done in the 1970s. It hung for a time in a local home and was purchased back and reinstalled when the cathedral was renovated in 2005.

47   Thomas Grace to Patrick Riordan, April 17, 1905, Riordan Papers, AASF.

48   Michael Gualco to Diomede Falconio, September 24, 1905, Apostolic Delegation Files, IX, Diocesi Sacramento Apostolic Vatican Archives, Rome (hereafter AVA).

49   Massimo made his way to London to study English and then his plans called for him to come to Sacramento for ordination. However, after four months, Grace determined that he did not need him and released him, urging him to join the Salesians in London. Massimo struggled in London and eventually secured passage to New York where he was adopted by the Diocese of Dallas, Texas, and ordained in September 1907.

50   Mela, who used his second name Eugene, was born in 1873, and became a priest of the Archdiocese of Milan and a seminary professor of Latin at

a college in Torino, Italy. Taverna was born in Castellazzo, northern Italy, in 1876. He studied with the Salesians in Turin and afterwards entered the seminary at Alexandria in Piedmont. In 1900, he was ordained and served in the diocese until Gualco contacted him and asked him to come to Sacramento. "Father Taverna Silver Jubilee," *Catholic Herald*, January 2, 1926, p. 1.

51 Eugene Mela to Diomede Falconio, May 6, 1906, Apostolic Delegation Files, IX Diocesi Sacramento, AVA.

52 At one point, opposition to the church and to Mela resulted in an unpleasant incident in April 1907. As Mela was walking along Third Street, three drunken Italian men began verbally insulting him, calling him *ladrone* (robber). Mela approached the trio and asked why they spoke in this way and one of them, Vincent Riola, physically assaulted the priest. Riola, who claimed to be an anarchist, was arrested and hauled to court, but the charges were dropped. "Priest Fears Anarchists," *Evening Bee*, April 22, 1907, p. 4.

53 "Church Edifice Finished," *Evening Bee*, May 26, 1907, p. 4.

54 "Dedication of New St. Mary's Church," *Sacramento Union*, June 8, 1907, p. 12.

55 Eugene Mela to Patrick Riordan, July 23, 1907, Riordan Papers, AASF.

56 Gualco was at this time in the midst of a huge battle with Bishop Grace over the title to the hospital he had erected with the assistance of some Daughters of Charity who had come into the diocese without Grace's permission. It seems that these sisters had taken the property in their own name, and Grace had demanded that it be retitled in the name of the Diocese of Sacramento. The story of the hospital and the sisters' involvement is related in a letter of Thomas Grace to James Cantwell, March 27, 1920, Edward Hanna Papers, AASF.

57 Michael Gualco to Diomede Falconio, August 1, 1907, Apostolic Delegation Files, IX Diocesi, Sacramento, AVA.

58 For Gualco's complaint that the Italians in Reno and McCloud and the Germans in Woodland were being ignored, see Gualco to Falconio, June 7, 1910. Grace's reply to Falconio is dated July 26, 1910, Apostolic Delegation Files, IX Diocesi Sacramento, AVA.

59 Quoted in "Father Mela Called," *Catholic Herald,* November 2, 1918, p. 8. The same edition carried the notice of the death of Editor Thomas Connelly's son at a military camp in Washington of pneumonia.

60 "Church Festival Will be in Tent Pavilion," *Sacramento Bee*, October 19, 191-, p. 12. "Festival of Santa Maria Church Draws Large First Night Crowd," *Sacramento Bee*, October 20, 1910, p. 10. The Italians received much help from local Irish dignitaries, including Thomas Gormley who spoke at the affairs. Gormley by this time had a deep investment in the Bank of Italy, later renamed the Bank of America.

61 Pierini, *op. cit.*, p. 158.

62 Holmes, L. and D'Alessandro, J., *Portuguese Pioneers in the Sacramento Area* (Sacramento: Portuguese Historical and Cultural Society, 1990) pp. 11–20.

63 *Ibid.*, pp. 26–27.

64 *Ibid.*, p. 69.

65 Hardwick, pp. 134-137.

66 Holmes and D'Alessandro, *op. cit.*, pp. 239–40.

67 *Ibid.*, p. 158.

68 "Feeling High with the Portuguese," *Sacramento Bee*, 20 April 1909, p. 5.

69 Holmes and D'Alessandro, *op. cit.*, p. 91.

70 "Henrique Jose Reed DaSilva" in Weber, F. J., *Encyclopedia of California's Catholic Heritage* (Mission Hills and Spokane: St. Francis Mission Society and the Arthur H. Clark Company, 2000), p. 317.

71 DaSilva was apparently part of the royal family of Portugal. See "A Royal Bishop's Work," *Monitor*, July 27, 1907, p. 1.

72 "Greatest of All Grand Councils," *Catholic Herald*, August 22, 1908, p. 1.

73 "Bishop DaSilva," *Cathedral Monthly Tidings*, August 1908, p. 5.

74 *Ibid.*

75 DaSilva even opened one of the sessions of the Senate with a prayer at the invitation of Senate Chaplain Henry Wyman, C.S.P. "Bishop DaSilva Goes Back to San Francisco," *Sacramento Bee*, March 10, 1909, p. 2.

76 Numbers vary. Mela said ten, the Portuguese said twenty-five. "Feeling High with the Portuguese," *Sacramento Bee*, April 20, 1909; "Portuguese Members Strike Against Priest," *Sacramento Union*, April 20, 1909, p. 5.

77 "Portuguese Make a Reply," *Sacramento Bee,* April 22, 1909, p. 6.

78 *Ibid.*

79 Eugene Mela to Diomede Falconio, May 6, 1909, Apostolic Delegation Files, IX Diocesi Sacramento, AVA.

80 "Many Hundreds of Portuguese Join Festival of Holy Ghost," *Sacramento Bee,* May 24, 1909, p. 13.

81 Azevedo, who had been recruited for service in California while still a seminarian at the Portuguese seminary in Angra do Heroismo, Terceira, had arrived in 1902. He was sent first to St. Patrick's Seminary in Menlo Park in order to acculturate and learn English. In 1904, Grace ordained him and then dispatched him to the northern most reaches of the diocese—Yreka and Fort Jones. He later went to assist at Sutter Creek. Azevedo was the natural choice for service to the new community and would become a fixture in Sacramento's city life until his death in 1957. Living with his sister and assisted by members of his own family whom he brought to Sacramento, he provided substantial leadership to the growing Portuguese community.

82 "Portuguese Church Will be Dedicated," *Sacramento Bee*, February 1, 1913, p. 1.

83 Kouba, J., S.D.S. "The Hispanic Presence in the Diocese of Sacramento," *Catholic Herald*, November 17 and 24, 1986.

84 "Our Lady of Guadalupe Festival Next Sunday in Catholic Church," undated clipping, *c.* 1920, from *Yolo Independent*. This account records the visit of Bishop Grace to the church in Washington (the first name for Broderick). The prelate sat on a "specially constructed throne built by the Spanish people." Present also were Agustin Ruiz, vice consul of Mexico, and a small ensemble with organ, violins and clarinet. "Bishop Keane Will Officiate in Local Catholic Church," undated clipping from *Yolo Independent* relates the celebration of 1923. ADS.

85 Kouba, "The Hispanic Presence," carries an account of his oral history with the Falcon children.

86 "Report of Mexican Activities in Sacramento," *Superior California Catholic Register*, December 28, 1930, pp. 5 and 8.

87 Catholic Ladies Relief Society, No. 1, Report of the Works in General, October 1, 1926 to October 1, 1927, History Book, 1927–1931, ADS.

88 Minutes of the Thirty-ninth Session of the Grand Council of the Catholic Ladies Relief Society of the Sacramento Diocese, History Book, 1927–1931, ADS.

89 *Ibid.*

90 Gonzales, M., *Mexicanos* (Indiana University Press, 2019, 3rd ed.), pp. 147–149; see also Balderrama, F. E. and Rodriguez, R., *Decade of Betrayal: Mexican Repatriation in the 1930s* (Albuquerque: University of New Mexico Press, 1995).

91 "$25,000 Campaign Underway for New Church," *Superior California Catholic Register*, June 22, 1930, p. 8.

92 Transcript of interview with Monsignor Raymond Renwald, by Olivia Wheatley, May 15, 1981, St. Thomas More Parish, Paradise, copy in St. Thomas More File, ADS.

93 "New Church of Our Lady of Guadalupe Will be Dedicated," *Superior California Register*, April 8, 1945, p. 3.

94 "Faith of Mexico is Seen at Impressive Dedication Rites," *Superior California Register*, April 15, 1945, p. 5.

Chapter 4

1 Hurt, P., "The Rise and Fall of 'Know Nothings' in California, *California Historical Quarterly* Vol. 9 (March 1930), pp. 16–49.

2 "California Protestant Churches," *Daily Union*, August 21, 1858, p. 1.

3 The best source for the origins, ideology and national scope of the APA is Kinzer, D. K., *Episode in Anti-Catholicism: The American Protective Association* (University of Washington Press, 1964).

4 "Pastors' Union," *Daily Record-Union*, October 28, 1890, p. 3.

5 "Our Country and Our Church," *Daily Record-Union*, February 24, 1891, p. 5.

6 "Spirit of the Time," *Monitor*, April 15, 1893, p. 3 "A Brave Repudiation of the APA Conspiracy," October 14, 1893, p. 4; "Bigotry Now and Forty Years Ago," November 4, 1893, p. 4; "The Late Elections," November 18, 1893, p. 4.

7 "Topics of the Times," *Monitor*, January 27, 1894, p. 1

8 "British Volunteers, Orangemen and the APA," *Monitor*, November 25, 1893, p. 4.

9 "Working Up the APA," *Evening Bee,* March 26, 1894, p. 4. By contrast, the report of the talk in the *Record-Union* was much less inflammatory: "Although he arraigned the church, he was much more moderate in his attack on it than his audience supposed he would be." See "Ex-priest Slattery," *Sacramento Daily Record-Union,* March 26, 1894, p. 4

10 "Against the Nuns," *Evening Bee,* March 26, 1894, p. 4. The *Daily Record-Union* carried no account of Mrs. Slattery's talk.

11 "The Priest and the Flag," *Evening Bee*, May 14, 1894, p. 4.

12 "Rev. Koehne's Sermon: He Preaches the Fifth of His Series Last Night," *Sacramento Daily Record-Union*, May 14, 1894, p. 3

13 "Churches and the APA," *Evening Bee,* October 6, 1894, p. 8

14 *Ibid.*

15 "The A.P.A. Not Official," *Evening Bee,* October 8, 1894, p. 2.

16 *Ibid.*

17 "Names of Members of Sacramento Lodges," *Monitor,* November 3, 1894, p.1 5 (supplement). McClatchy had earlier taken special aim at the African-American Council. Dismissing claims that the council had sixty members, McClatchy denied that it existed at all. To those few blacks who belonged to such a prejudiced group, McClatchy scolded: "As well almost might the Israelites renounce their Creator as for these Negroes to deny civil and religious liberty to men who shed their blood that these ingrates might be free, to women who nursed them tenderly in many a hospital and many a fearful battlefield." He concluded harshly, "Let them [the black APAers] remember that if this council has sixty members it presents to this community sixty ample and sufficient reasons why the Negro should never have been given a freedom which he has proved he did not deserve, nor granted the blessings of citizenship which he cannot appreciate." "Sixty Good Reasons," *Evening Bee,* September 29, 1894, p. 4.

18 See "The APA Intriguing Against a House of God," "The APA Feature," *Evening Bee,* March 3, 1896, p. 1; "Where Angels Fear to Tread," *Monitor,* March 28, 1896, p. 4.

19 "Politics in Pulpits," *Evening Bee,* November 5, 1894, p. 1.

20 "A.P.A. State Ticket," *Evening Bee,* November 3, 1894, p. 1.

21 "The Catholic Knights," *Evening Bee,* November 26, 1894, p. 1.

22 "An Emblem of Liberty," *Evening Bee,* November 30, 1894, p. 1.

23 "Editorial Notes," *San Francisco Monitor,* June 15, 1895, p. 4.

24 "'To Arms! To Arms!' Taulbee Blows Blast Upon His APA Bugle," *Evening Bee,* July 29, 1895, p 5. McClatchy decried the speech as idiotic rot" and used his favorite invective, "it stinks and shines and shines and stinks like a rotting mackerel in the moonlight." "Rev. Taulbee's Sermon," *Evening Bee,* July 26, 1895, p. 4.

25 McDevitt, V. E., F.S.C., *The First California's Chaplain* (Fresno: Academy Library Guild, 1956), pp. 46–53. McKinnon was so taken with linking Catholicism with the essence of American patriotism that he enlisted as a chaplain of the First California in the Spanish American War.

26 "Pro Deo, Pro Patria," *Evening Bee,* August 9, 1895, p. 4.

27 "Jubilant APAs," *Evening Bee,* August 31, 1895, p. 1.

28 "The A.P.A. Is In It," *Evening Bee,* September 20, 1895, p. 1.

29 "Death Calls Former Mayor," *Saturday Bee,* December 7, 1907, p. 5.

30 "An Opportunity Lost," *Evening Bee,* September 28, 1895, p.4. McClatchy generally lashed out at the relative indifference of the city to his warnings about APA activity. One general salvo is "Cowardice of Candidate," *Evening Bee,* October 15, 1895, p. 4.

31 "The APA Ticket," *Evening Bee,* October 14, 1895, p. 8.

32 "Is Hubbard an APA?" *Evening Bee,* October 15, 1895, p. 8.

33 "The Irish Must Go," *Evening Bee,* November 4, 1895, p. 1.

34 "Mr. Sanders' Talk," *Evening Bee,* November 4, 1895, p. 5.

35 "Hubbard Slips In," *Evening Bee,* November 6, 1895, p. 1.

36 "Catholic Officers," *Evening Bee,* November 29, 1895, p. 6.

37 "No Catholics Need Apply," *Evening Bee*, February 20, 1896, p. 5.

38 "Mayor Hubbard's Candidate," *Evening Bee,* March 12, 1896, p. 2.

39 "An Un-American Mayor," *Evening Bee*, February 20, 1896, p. 3.

40 "Committee on Clean Up to Give Forth Report," *Sacramento Bee*, April 29, 1918, p 1.

41 For a solid treatment of the impact of Prohibition in Sacramento, see Kassis, A., *Prohibition in Sacramento: Moralizers, Bootleggers, and the Wettest City in the Nation* (The History Press, 2014).

42 An example of this is "Prohibition is Denounced by Rev. Guerin," *Sacramento Bee*, January 19, 1920, p. 9. Guerin was the pastor of St. Joseph's Church in Marysville and a close friend of Bishop Thomas Grace. In the sermon denouncing prohibition, the cleric "gave credit to Charles K. McClatchy ... for consistently holding the sanest view upon the liquor question and kindred topics."

43 "Rev. Redburn Calls for Stand Against Everything Catholic," *Sacramento Bee*, June 12, 1922, pp. 1 and 4.

44 "Sacramento Needs More Americanizing," *Catholic Herald*, April 30, 1921, p. 1.

45 Cooper, A. O., "A History of Westminster Presbyterian Church, Sacramento, California" (Sacramento, Westminster Presbyterian Church, 1966), p. 55.

46 For general studies of the Klan see, Chalmers, D., *Hooded Americanism: The History of the Ku Klux Klan* (Duke University Press, 1987); Gordon, L., *The Second Coming of the KKK: The Ku Klux Klan and the American Political Tradition* (W.W. Norton, 2017); and Jackson, K., *The Ku Klux Klan in the City 1915–1930* (Ivan Dee, 1992).

47 Von Brauchitsch, D. M., "The Ku Klux Klan in California, 1921–1924" (unpublished M.A. thesis, Sacramento State University, 1967), p. 126.

48 "Personal Rights Violated and Constables Attacked by Ku Klux Klan Members," *Sacramento Bee*, June 12, 1922, pp. 1 and 10.

49 "Ku Klux Klan Makes Move to Organize Here," *Sacramento Bee*, April 6, 1922, pp. 1 and 14.

50 "Six Ku Klux Klansmen Visit Local Church and Present Pastor with $50," *Sacramento Bee*, April 10, 1922, pp. 1 and 6.

51 "Police Question Organizer of Klan Here"; "Klan Ideology Exposed, Former Office of KKK Says Order Teaches Racial and Religious Hatred" *Sacramento Bee*, April 11, 1922, pp. 1 and 4.

52 "Evangelist Says Klan Force Needed," *Sacramento Bee*, April 25, 1922, p. 2.

53 "Klan is Watched While Initiating Sacramento Men," *Sacramento Bee*, April 26, 1922, pp. 1 and 27. This was held in a Masonic Hall. Later, the lodge head regretted renting the space: "Masonic Lodge Head Deplores Klan Meeting," *Sacramento Bee*, April 26, 1922, p. 1.

54 "Nine Public Officials in This City Listed as Paying K.K.K. Initiation Fees," *Sacramento Bee*, May 4, 1922, p. 1.

55 Von Brauchitsch, "The Ku Klux Klan," p. 135.

56 "Move Made to Rid City Offices of Klansmen," *Sacramento Bee*, May 6, 1922, pp. 1 and 5.

57 "Seavey to Ask Council to Oust Ten Klansmen," *Sacramento Bee*, May 18, 1922, p. 1. He was unable to do so.

58 "Kleagle's List Reveals Names of Autoists Whose Cars Were at Initiation," *Sacramento Bee*, May 18, 1922, pp. 1–2.

59 Von Brauchitsch, "The Ku Klux Klan," p. 143.

60 "Minister Defends Klan as Necessity," *Sacramento Bee*, May 15, 1922, p. 1.

61 "Council Refuses to Oust Policemen and Firemen KKK Members," *Sacramento Bee*, May 19, 1922, pp. 1 and 13.

62 Von Brauchitsch, "The Ku Klux Klan," p. 139.

63 Seavey denied Harrison's charges, branding them "too silly for reply" and noting that he was not now nor had ever been either a Catholic or a Knight of Columbus—indeed he was a member of no church. He also noted that he had never been east of Chicago—dismissing the charge that he had held membership in the Knights of Columbus in Pennsylvania. "Seavey Says Charges too 'Silly for Reply,'" *Sacramento Bee*, June 12, 1922, p. 4.

64 "Rev. Harrison Turns Tirade on all who Oppose Ku Klux Klan," *Sacramento Bee*, June 12, 1922, pp. 1 and 14.

65 "Rev. Redburn Calls for Stand Against Everything Catholic," *Sacramento Bee*, June 12, 1922, pp. 1 and 14; "Two Pastors Defend Klan From Pulpit," *Ibid.*

66 "Hughes Acts to Stop Propaganda in High School," *Sacramento Bee*, September 12, 1922, p. 1.

67 "Rev. W. E. Harrison Threatens to 'Get' Charles C. Hughes," *Sacramento Bee*, September 13, 1922, p. 1.

68 "Rev. Harrison Tells of Talk With Hughes," *Sacramento Bee*, September 14, 1922, p. 1.

69 "Veil of Secrecy Torn Off Klan Plot," *Sacramento Bee*, November 1, 1922, p. 1; "Complete Expose of Local Klan's Workings Given by Ex-Member," *Sacramento Bee*, November 2, 1922, p. 1.

70 "A Great Convention Becomes History," *Catholic Herald*, May 12, 1923, p. 1.

71 "Complete Expose of Local Klan's Workings Given by Ex-Member," *Sacramento Bee*, November 2, 1922, p. 1.

72 "Virus of Religious Prejudice Injected into Local Politics," *Catholic Herald,* July 28, 1922, p. 1.

Chapter 5

1 McGuiness, M., *Called to Serve: A History of Nuns in America* (NYU Press, 2015).

2 "Minnie Gormley, Old Sacramento Resident Dies," *Sacramento Bee*, January 2, 1934, p. 5.

3 *Cathedral Chimes*, February 9, 1889, n.p.

4 *Ibid.*

5 "Our Circumlocution Office," *Cathedral Chimes,* February 9, 1889, n.p.

6 "Ring Down the Curtain," *Cathedral Chimes,* February 9, 1889, n.p.

7 "Sacramento Cathedral Fair," *Monitor*, February 27, 1889, p.5.

8 Much information on Rooney, with the exception of her Catholic background and activity, can be found in Elaine Connolly and Dian Self, *Capital Women: An Interpretative History of Women in Sacramento, 1850–1920* (Sacramento: Capital Women's History Project, 1995), pp. 144–147, 173.

9 The others were Ella Kelly (McClatchy) and Elizabeth King. See record book St. Joseph's Academy, ASMA.

10   A brief sketch of Thomas O'Neil's life is found in Swift, D. (ed.), *Sacramento County Sheriff's Department, 1850–1877* (Sacramento, Sacramento County Sheriff, 1977), p. 54.

11   "Bishop Anxious to Make NCCW Power in Diocese of Sacramento," *Superior California Catholic Register*, April 27, 1930, p. 10.

12   "First President of N.C.C.W. Dies," *Superior California Catholic Register*, March 20, 1932, p. 10.

13   "Mary Judge is Found Dead in her Home," *Sacramento Bee*, January 25, 1945, pp. 1 and 22.

14   "A Tribute to Mary Judge," *Sacramento Bee*, January 25, 1945, p. 26.

15   "Mary Judge Estate of $140 Goes to Niece," *Sacramento Bee*, July 9, 1946, p. 4.

16   "A Good Woman Passes," *Sacramento Bee*, July 2, 1942, p. 24.

17   "Nettie M. Hopley, Teacher is Dead," *Sacramento Bee*, June 30, 1942, p. 4.

18   "Nettie Hopley Testimonial Dinner is Attended by 540," *Sacramento Bee*, May 23, 1938, p. 2.

19   Galarza, E., *Barrio Boy* (Notre Dame, University of Notre Dame Press, 1971), pp. 208–209, ff.

20   "Nettie Hopley Testimonial Dinner is Attended by 540," *Sacramento Bee*, May 23, 1938, p. 2.

21   "Community Chest Plan Benefits Numbers Says Bishop Keane," *Sacramento Bee*, February 1, 1924, p. 27. "Catholic Relief Group Performs Useful Service," *Sacramento Bee*, October 6, 1928, p. 6.

22   "Rebecca Coolot, Philanthropical Worker, Dies," *Sacramento Bee*, July 23, 1964, pp. D1–D2. "Death Claims Mrs. Coolot, Leader in Charity Work," *Catholic Herald*, July 30, 1964, p. 6.

23   Conmy, P. T., *Seventy Years of Service, 1902–1972: History of the Knights of Columbus in California* (Los Angeles: California State Council Knights of Columbus, 1972), pp. 19–20; 305.

24   "Frank E. Michel of Sacramento Buried with Requiem Mass," *Superior California Catholic Register*, November 24, 1946, p. 3.

25   "Robert T. Devlin, Leading Attorney Dies in His Home," *Sacramento Bee*, 24 February 1938, p. 1.

26   "W. F. Gormley, Undertaker, is Taken by Death," *Sacramento Bee*, July 30, 1935, pp. 1 and 5. "Funeral Service is Conducted for W.F. Gormley," *Sacramento Bee*, August 1, 1935, p. 2.

27   He served as president of the Sacramento Council in 1893 and in 1895 was international vice president of the Bookbinder's Union.

28   "Points in the Career of Wm. F. Gormley," *Sunday News,* November 2, 1902. Clipping is in Gormley family scrapbook, in possession of Barbara Gormley.

29   *Sunday Leader*, November 4, 1908, clipping in Gormley family scrapbook.

30   He had a near miss with political disaster in 1912 when he became the target of a Grand Jury investigation over the fees and charges he made to the county for jurors and witnesses summoned to inquests. Gormley racked up a comfortable $3000 in this operation until the practice was tagged by John F. Barry, expert of the Grand Jury, who discovered that the collection was contrary to the provisions of the city code. Gormley voluntarily agreed to appear before the grand jury and explained that assessing the fee of $0.25

per juror had been the practice of his two predecessors in the office (George C. McMullen and George Clarke) and even submitted the forms for each requisition to the district attorney. Gormley immediately refunded the money ($3069.25) and apart from the embarrassment of having the details of the "secret" Grand Jury probe spilled, escaped unharmed. "After Fees Collected by Former Coroners," *Sacramento Star,* April 29, 1912; "Coroner Returns Money to County," Gormley family scrap books.

31 Swift (ed.), "William Francis Gormley," p. 60.

32 "Sheriff's Fight is Tuesday's Hottest," *Sacramento Bee,* August 24, 1918, p.10.

33 "Jones Wins Sheriff Race," *Sacramento Bee,* August 28, 1918, p. 1.

34 Connelly later claimed that he graduated from Notre Dame, but a search of the records turned up no evidence of any kind of terminal degree.

35 Spalding, T., *Premier See: A History of the Archdiocese of Baltimore, 1789–1989* (Baltimore: Johns Hopkins, 1990), pp. 292–292. See also Avella, S. M., "The Catholic Press as Urban Booster: The Case of Thomas A. Connelly of Sacramento," *U.S. Catholic Historian* 25 (3) (Summer, 2007), pp. 75–86.

36 Willging, E. P. and Hatzfeld, H., *Catholic Serials of the Nineteenth Century in the United States,* Second Series, Part Eight, California (Washington, D. C.: The Catholic University of America Press, 1964), pp. 38–39.

37 John Cantwell to Thomas Connelly, July 28, 1909, Chancery Papers, AASF. Connelly paid off half the note and in August 1909, Riordan canceled the remainder of the debt. ibid. John Cantwell to Thomas Connelly, August 16, 1909, Thomas A. Connelly to Patrick Riordan, August 19, 1909, Riordan Papers, AASF.

38 Thomas Connelly to Patrick Riordan, April 2, 1907, Riordan Papers, AASF.

39 "Sacramento's Numerous and Beautiful Church Structures," *The Great West* 6 (October 5, 1907), p. 1.

40 "The Importance of the Catholic Press," *Catholic Herald,* March 14, 1908, p. 1.

41 Connelly managed to secure a steady flow of printing work from both the city and county governments.

42 "Northern California," *Catholic Herald,* November 1, 1913, p. 4.

43 Editorial, *Catholic Herald,* March 28, 1908, p. 4.

44 "For a Greater Sacramento," *Catholic Herald,* March 14, 1908, p. 4.

45 "Sacramento Did Well," *Catholic Herald,* April 12, 1913, p. 4.

46 "Capital Architect Harry Devine Dies," *Sacramento Bee,* November 21, 1963, pp. A1 and A12; Charles Dean came to Sacramento in 1908 and four years later his brother James followed, both employed by the State Architect's Office. In 1920 they departed state service and formed their own firm, participating actively in the architectural renaissance of Sacramento that took place in the 1920s. Among their prodigies were some of Sacramento's most beautiful buildings such as the new YWCA, Westminster Presbyterian, the Memorial Auditorium, Sacramento Junior College, and for the Catholic Church, the cathedral presbytery and Holy Angels School, Holy Angels School, Christian Brothers School. See Donovan, J. J., "Recent Work of Dean and Dean Architects," *The Architect and Engineer,* 90 (July 1927), pp. 39–59.

47 Devine donated plans for the following Sacramento Catholic institutions: the episcopal mansion on Fair Oaks Boulevard, St. Ignatius Church, St. Mary's

Cemetery Mausoleum Addition, All Hallows (school and convent), St. Francis convent, the former diocesan chancery, Sacred Heart (church and school), St. Lawrence Church (North Highlands), St. Mel's Church (Fair Oaks), an addition to Immaculate Conception, St. Patrick's Orphanage, and Bishop Armstrong High School. Source: Harry J. Devine to Joseph T. McGucken, n.d., Mercy Hospital File, ADS.

48 "Capital Architect Harry Devine Dies," *Sacramento Bee*, November 21, 1963, pp. A1 and A12.

49 "Clergy and Laity Mourn the Death of Msgr. Lyons, Three Funeral Masses Planned for Msgr. Michael Lyons," *Catholic Herald*, May 29, 1958, pp. 1 and 3.

50 T. A. Farrell to Robert Armstrong, n.d. 1931, Brady File, ADS.

51 "Construction of Catholic Church Started in City," *Sacramento Bee*, December 13, 1930, p. 1. "Amusement, Development, Radio Supplement; "Cornerstone for Church of Sacred Heart, Sacramento To Be Laid By Bishop Sunday," *Superior California Register*, March 15, 1931, p. 10; "Catholic Church in City Nearly Half Completed," *Sacramento Bee*, March 28, 1931, Amusement, Development, Radio Supplement, p. 1.

52 For a good overview of the history of the retreat movement in the United States see Chinnici, J., OFM, *Living Stones: The History and Structure of the Catholic Spiritual Life in the United States* (New York: MacMillan, 1989), pp. 157–171.

53 Interview with Reverend Neil Parsons C.P., Christ the King Retreat House, Citrus Heights, California, August 23, 1999.

54 Obituary, "Wilkins Raymond J.," *Sacramento Bee*, June 12, 1983, p. 19.

55 Mother Hayes to "Reverend Mother" November 23, 1953, Archives of the Sisters of the Cenacle.

56 See Bro. Kevin O'Malley, C.P., "A Brief History of the Passionists in Northern California and Western Nevada, 1852–1986," Religious Priests File, ADS.

57 "Groundbreaking for Catholic Retreat Draws More than 300," *Sacramento Bee*, April 11, 1949, p. 12.

58 "Diocese to Have Retreat House and Monastery," *Superior California Catholic Register*, January 11, 1948, p. 3.

59 "Christ the King Retreat House for Men Is Spiritual Dynamo," *Superior California Catholic Herald,* May 1, 1952, p. 3.

60 "Retreat House Festival This Sunday Will Raise Funds for New Wing," *Superior California Catholic Herald*, May 27, 1954, p. 10.

61 "Passionist Monastery Blessing This Sunday," *Superior California Catholic Herald*, October 24, 1957, p. 1.

62 In a thirty-year retrospective, an article in the Catholic press attributed the founding of the Cenacle to Monsignor Richard Dwyer, "Cenacle Marks 30th Anniversary," *Catholic Herald*, September 10, 1984, p. 9.

63 "Woman Gives up Career to Aide Lepers in the Philippines," *Sacramento Bee*, February 11, 1947, p. 3; "Capital Woman is Moving Spirit in aid to Lepers," *Sacramento Bee*, April 7, 1959, p. 11.

64 Anonymous, *Women of the Cenacle* (Milwaukee: Convent of Our Lady of the Cenacle, 1952).

65 "Outline History of the Cenacle Retreat, 1947–1964," File A11-C-218, Archives of the Cenacle Sisters, Chicago (hereafter ACS).

66 "Once an accountant at McClellan, Marie Harris Became a Peace Activist," *Sacramento Bee*, December 31, 1996, p. 19.

67 "How It All Began, Realization of a Dream, the Opening of the Cenacle in Sacramento," *Superior California Catholic Herald*, September 19, 1957, p. 7.

68 "Cenacle Nuns Purchase Site for Women's Retreat House," *Superior California Catholic Herald*, May 14, 1953, p. 1.

69 Mother Ida Barlow to "Dear Reverend Mother, February 21, 1954, ACS.

70 "Cenacle Retreat House Blessing Set for July 31st," *Superior California Catholic Herald*, July 15, 1954; p, 1; "First Weekend Retreat Set at Cenacle," *Superior California Catholic Herald*, June 24, 1954, p. 8.

71 "1425 Women at Cenacle in Opening Year," *Superior California Catholic Herald*, August 11, 1955, p. 5.

72 Capital Musical Veteran Anton Dorndorf, 64, Dies," *Sacramento Bee*, February 10, 1970, pp. 19–20; "Sacramento Catholic Schools 'Man of Music' is Dead," *Catholic Herald*, February 12, 1970, p. 1.

73 "Anton Dorndorf Will Be Honored for Service," *Superior California Catholic Herald*, November 18, 1954; Dorndorf's choir played an important role in local church music culture in Northern California, p. 8; see "St. Francis Choir to Participate in Local Mozart Festival," *Superior California Catholic Herald*, June 21, 1956, p. 5. Dorndorf also conducted a choir at Mather Airfield.

Chapter 6

1 Larkin, E., "The Devotional Revolution in Ireland, 1850–1875" *American Historical Review* 77 (June 1972), pp. 625–652.

2 *Ibid.*, p. 69.

3 Delury, J. F., "Irish Nationalism in Sacramento, 1850–1890," *Golden Notes* 36 (Sumer 1990), p. 10.

4 Delury, J. F., "Irish Nationalism in the Sacramento Region," *Eire-Ireland* 21 (Fall 1986), pp. 27–54.

5 Meagher spoke to Sacramento citizens at the largest gathering place in the city at the time, the Congregational Church, which often doubled as a public hall.

6 Delury, J. F., "Irish Nationalism in the Sacramento Region (1850–1890): Two Paths to Freedom: From Meagher of the Sword to T.P. O'Connor" (unpublished M.A. thesis, California State University, Sacramento, 1985).

7 "Italian Society Has Re-Union," *Sacramento Union*, June 8, 1908, p. 3. This was an account of the twenty-third anniversary of the Bersagliere. Luigi Caffaro gave one of the speeches of the day in Italian.

8 "High Mass for Humbert Slain," *Evening Bee*, August 6, 1900, p. 7.

9 "Italian Residents Pay Tribute to Humbert," *Evening Bee*, August 9, 1900, p. 5.

10 "Children in White Are Feature of Parade," *Evening Bee*, June 8, 1908, p. 1. The front page of the paper sported the picture of the young queen of the festa.

11 For typical accounts of these celebrations see "Our Lady of Guadalupe," *Catholic Herald*, December 21, 1929, p. 3; "Mexicans Observe Guadalupe Feast," *Superior California Catholic Register*, December 21, 1930, pp. 12 & 5.

12 "Mexicans Observe Guadalupe Feast," *ibid.*

13 "2500 Men March Through Streets of Capital in Great Profession of Faith," *Superior California Catholic Register*, January 12, 1935, p. 8.

14 "Report of Mexican Activities in Sacramento," *Superior California Catholic Register*, December 28, 1930, pp. 8 and 10.

15 "Local Mexicans Observe Annual Guadalupe Feast," *Superior California Catholic Register*, December 19, 1946, p. 3.

16 "Our Lady of Guadalupe Feast to Be Observed; Plan Special Celebration," *Superior California Catholic Herald*, December 10, 1953, p. 4; a similar account is "Local Mexican Colony Readies Elaborate Celebration of Virgin," *Superior California Catholic Herald*, December 6, 1956, p. 12.

17 The 1908 convention did cause a little dust-up between the Chamber of Commerce and local committee arrangers when promised subsidy funds for the convention were not forthcoming.

18 "Holy Name Societies to Meet Here Sunday," *Sacramento Bee*, January 8, 1930, p. 14.

19 "Holy Name Rally to be Conducted Sunday in the Capital," *Sacramento Bee*, January 1, 1932, p. 12.

20 "More than 1500 Join Holy Name Parade in City," *Sacramento Bee*, January 9, 1933, p. 1; "2,000 Will Take Part in Catholic Parade Sunday," *Sacramento Bee*, January 3, 1936, p. 14.

21 "1,500 March in Parade of Holy Name Society," *Sacramento Bee*, January 11, 1937, p. 4.

22 "Demonstration Is Set by Holy Name Society," *Sacramento Bee*, October 19, 1940, p. 14. "Memorial Rite for War Dead Will be Held by Catholic Group," *Sacramento Bee*, October 17, 1942, p. 16.

23 "Thousands to Attend Christ the King Rally," *Superior California Register*, October 6, 1946, p. 2.

24 "Catholic Rally Is Expected to Draw 10, 000," *Sacramento Bee*, April 24, 1952, p. 41.

25 "Sacramentans Give $3500 for Hungarians," *Superior California Catholic Herald*, January 3, 1957, p. 1.

26 Stanley F. Wilson, "Cleric Preached Against Reds, Dodged Bombs," *Sacramento Bee*, December 8, 1954, p. 29.

27 Virginia Ortiz to Robert Armstrong, March 9, 1949, Armstrong Papers, ADS. The building was deteriorating, and a nearby newer Catholic Church was built in the adjoining community of Bryte.

28 For an overview of the various dimensions of devotion to the Virgin Mary, see Marina Warner's *Alone of Her Sex: The Myth and Cult of the Virgin Mary* (New York: Alfred A. Knopf, 1976).

29 "Fatima Crusade Gains Stronger Parish Support," *Superior California Catholic Herald*, July 2, 1953, p. 8.

30 "Children to Portray Principal Roles in Fatima Drama Here," *Superior California Catholic Herald*, June 27, 1951, p. 1.

31 "Record Breaking Crowd Pays Honor to Mary Immaculate," *Superior California Catholic Herald*, May 7, 1959, p. 1.

32 "L.A. Bishop to Address Local Rally," *Superior California Catholic Herald*, April 20, 1951, p. 1; "Choir of 2,000 Will Sing at Holy Name Rally," *Sacramento Bee*, April 24, 1951. "Holy Name Rally Expected to Draw Large Crowd on Sunday; Impressive Musical Program Will Be Presented," *Superior California Catholic Herald*, April 27, 1951, p. 1.

33 "Bishop Says America Will Remain Free Only so Long as Citizens Revere, Worship God," *Sacramento Bee*, April 30, 1951, p. 1.

34 "Bishop Armstrong Blessed Chapel of New Orphanage," *Superior California Catholic Register*, October 2, 1932. Harry S. Devine was the chapel's architect, p. 10.

35 "Stations of Cross by Dunbar Beck Installed in St. Rose Chapel," *Sacramento Bee*, 15 January 15, 1934, p. 4; "New Stations to Be Blessed Sunday in St. Patrick's Home," *Superior California Catholic Register*, January 14, 1934, p. 6; "Art is Where You Find It Not Just in Galleries," *Sacramento Bee*, August 14, 1937, p. 18. Beck did the work in the St. Rose Chapel in memory of the late Carlos McClatchy.

36 *Sacramento Guidebook* (Sacramento: Sacramento Bee, 1939), pp. 117–118.

Bibliography

"$25,000 Campaign Underway for New Church," *Superior California Catholic Register*, June 22, 1930

"'To Arms! To Arms!' Taulbee Blows Blast Upon His APA Bugle," *Evening Bee*, July 29, 1895

"1,500 March in Parade of Holy Name Society," *Sacramento Bee*, January 11, 1937

"1425 Women at Cenacle in Opening Year," *Superior California Catholic Herald*, August 11, 1955

"2,000 Will Take Part in Catholic Parade Sunday," *Sacramento Bee*, January 3, 1936

"2500 Men March Through Streets of Capital in Great Profession of Faith," *Superior California Catholic Register*, January 12, 1935

"A Brave Repudiation of the APA Conspiracy," October 14, 1893

"A Catholic Fair," *Daily Bee*, March 26, 1857

"A Good Woman Passes," *Sacramento Bee*, July 2, 1942

"A Great Convention Becomes History," *Catholic Herald*, May 12, 1923

"A New Catholic Church," *Daily Bee,* March 16, 1871

"A Royal Bishop's Work," *Monitor*, July 27, 1907

"A Temperance Sermon," *Evening Bee*, March 6, 1895

"A Tribute to Mary Judge," *Sacramento Bee*, January 25, 1945

"A.P.A. State Ticket," *Evening Bee,* November 3, 1894

"After Fees Collected by Former Coroners," *Sacramento Star,* April 29, 1912

"Against the Nuns," *Evening Bee,* March 26, 1894

"Amusement, Development, Radio Supplement;" "Cornerstone for Church of Sacred Heart, Sacramento To Be Laid By Bishop Sunday," *Superior California Register*, March 15, 1931

"An Emblem of Liberty," *Evening Bee,* November 30, 1894

"An Opportunity Lost," *Evening Bee*, September 28, 1895

"An Un-American Mayor," *Evening Bee*, February 20, 1896

"Another New Church," *Sacramento Daily Union*, September 13, 1854

"Anthony Coolot Left No Will," *Evening* Bee, December 4, 1900

"Anton Dorndorf Will Be Honored for Service," *Superior California Catholic Herald*, November 18, 1954

"Art is Where You Find It Not Just in Galleries," *Sacramento Bee*, August 14, 1937

"Attended Church," *Daily Bee*, August 8, 1859

"Augustine E. Coolot," Sacramento County Biographies, Rootsweb.Ancestry.Com.

"Bigotry Now and Forty Years Ago," November 4, 1893

"Bishop Anxious to Make NCCW Power in Diocese of Sacramento," *Superior California Catholic Register*, April 27, 1930

"Bishop Armstrong Blessed Chapel of New Orphanage," *Superior California Catholic Register*, October 2, 1932

"Bishop DaSilva Goes Back to San Francisco," *Sacramento Bee*, March 10, 1909

"Bishop DaSilva," *Cathedral Monthly Tidings*, August 1908

"Bishop Keane Will Officiate in Local Catholic Church," undated clipping from *Yolo Independent* relates the celebration of 1923. ADS

"Bishop Manogue Dead," *Evening Bee*, February 27, 1895

"Bishop Manogue Returns," *Monitor*, January 21, 1891

"Bishop Says America Will Remain Free Only so Long as Citizens Revere, Worship God," *Sacramento Bee*, April 30, 1951

"British Volunteers, Orangemen and the APA," *Monitor*, November 25, 1893

"California Correspondence, August 31, 1854," *Freeman's Journal,* October 7, 1854

"California Correspondence, December 13, 1850," *Freeman's Journal*, February 22, 1851

"California Correspondence, January 31, 1851," *Freeman's Journal*, March 15, 1851

"California Correspondence, October 15, 1853," *Freeman's Journal*, November 19, 1853

"California Correspondence, October 20, 1850," *Freeman's Journal*, December 14, 1850

"California Protestant Churches," *Daily Union*, August 21, 1858

"Capital Architect Harry Devine Dies," *Sacramento Bee*, November 21, 1963

"Capital Musical Veteran Anton Dorndorf, 64, Dies," *Sacramento Bee*, February 10, 1970

"Capital Woman is Moving Spirit in aid to Lepers," *Sacramento Bee*, April 7, 1959

"Catholic Church in City Nearly Half Completed," *Sacramento Bee*, March 28, 1931

"Catholic Church," *Daily Union*, March 10, 1857

"Catholic Officers," *Evening Bee,* November 29, 1895

"Catholic Rally Is Expected to Draw 10, 000," *Sacramento Bee*, April 24, 1952

"Catholic Relief Group Performs Useful Service," *Sacramento Bee*, October 6, 1928

"Catholicity in California—Dedication of a Church in Sacramento—Hospitality of the City to Mgr. Alemany," *Freeman's Journal*, April 12, 1851

"Catholics Meet Today," *Sacramento Union*, September 8, 1907

"Cenacle Marks 30th Anniversary," *Catholic Herald*, September 10, 1984

"Cenacle Nuns Purchase Site for Women's Retreat House," *Superior California Catholic Herald*, May 14, 1953

"Cenacle Retreat House Blessing Set for July 31st," *Superior California Catholic Herald*, July 15, 1954

"Children in White Are Feature of Parade," *Evening Bee*, June 8, 1908

"Children to Portray Principal Roles in Fatima Drama Here," *Superior California Catholic Herald*, June 27, 1951

"Choir of 2,000 Will Sing at Holy Name Rally," *Sacramento Bee*, April 24, 1951

"Christ the King Retreat House for Men Is Spiritual Dynamo," *Superior California Catholic Herald,* May 1, 1952

"Church Edifice Finished," *Evening Bee*, May 26, 1907

"Church Festival Will be in Tent Pavilion," *Sacramento Bee*, October 19, 191-

"Church Improvements," *Daily Bee*, September 30, 1857

"Churches and the APA," *Evening Bee,* October 6, 1894

"City and Coast," *Monitor,* April 28, 1900

"City Intelligence," *Sacramento Daily Union*, March 8, 1862

"Clergy and Laity Mourn the Death of Msgr. Lyons," "Three Funeral Masses Planned for Msgr. Michael Lyons," *Catholic Herald*, May 29, 1958

"Col. M'Nassar Dead," *Evening Bee*, May 22, 1896

"Colonel McNasser Dead," *San Francisco Call*, May 23, 1896

"Committee on Clean Up to Give Forth Report," *Sacramento Bee*, April 29, 1918

"Community Chest Plan Benefits Numbers Says Bishop Keane," *Sacramento Bee*, February 1, 1924

"Complete Expose of Local Klan's Workings Given by Ex-Member," *Sacramento Bee*, November 2, 1922

"Construction of Catholic Church Started in City," *Sacramento Bee*, December 13, 1930

"Coroner Returns Money to County," Gormley family scrap books

"Council Refuses to Oust Policemen and Firemen KKK Members," *Sacramento Bee*, May 19, 1922

"Cowardice of Candidate," *Evening Bee,* October 15, 1895

"Death Calls Former Mayor," *Saturday Bee,* December 7, 1907

"Death Claims Mrs. Coolot, Leader in Charity Work," *Catholic Herald*, July 30, 1964

"Death of a Good Citizen," *Sacramento Daily Record-Union*, May 23, 1896

"Death of an Eminent Prelate," *Sacramento Record-Union*, February 28, 1895

"Death of James Bithell," *Sacramento Daily Union,* July 3, 1896

"Death of Mrs. Fair," *San Francisco Chronicle*, September 14, 1891

"Death of Mrs. Theresa Fair," *San Francisco Examiner*, September 14, 1891

"Dedicated! Sacramento's Grand Cathedral," *Monitor*, July 3, 1889

"Dedication of New St. Mary's Church," *Sacramento Union*, June 8, 1907

"Demonstration Is Set by Holy Name Society," *Sacramento Bee*, October 19, 1940

"Diocese to Have Retreat House and Monastery," *Superior California Catholic Register*, January 11, 1948

"Editorial Notes," *San Francisco Monitor,* June 15, 1895

"Ellen Bowden Active in Catholic Church, Dies," *Sacramento Bee*, October 30, 1926

"Evangelist Says Klan Force Needed," *Sacramento Bee*, April 25, 1922

"Ex-priest Slattery," *Sacramento Daily Record-Union,* March 26, 1894

"Faith of Mexico is Seen at Impressive Dedication Rites," *Superior California Register*, April 15, 1945

"Father Augustine Anderson—City's First Martyr," *Superior California Catholic Herald*, April 26, 1950

"Father Augustine McClory, OFM, 1847–1907," Chronology of Sacred Heart Province and History of St. Francis and St. Boniface Churches, AOFMSB

"Father Gualco and the Church He built," *Catholic Herald*, January 29, 1921

"Father Mela Called," *Catholic Herald,* November 2, 1918

"Father Taverna Silver Jubilee," *Catholic Herald*, January 2, 1926

"Fatima Crusade Gains Stronger Parish Support," *Superior California Catholic Herald*, July 2, 1953

"Feeling High with the Portuguese," *Sacramento Bee*, April 20, 1909

"Festival of Santa Maria Church Draws Large First Night Crowd," *Sacramento Bee*, October 20, 1910

"First President of N.C.C.W. Dies," *Superior California Catholic Register*, March 20, 1932

"First Weekend Retreat Set at Cenacle," *Superior California Catholic Herald*, June 24, 1954

"For a Greater Sacramento," *Catholic Herald*, March 14, 1908

"Frank E. Michel of Sacramento Buried with Requiem Mass," *Superior California Catholic Register*, November 24, 1946

"Funeral Service is Conducted for W.F. Gormley," *Sacramento Bee*, August 1, 1935

"German Catholic Mission," *Daily Bee*, May 23, 1871

"German Catholics in Convention," *Sacramento Union*, September 9, 1907

"Greatest of All Grand Councils," *Catholic Herald*, August 22, 1908

"Groundbreaking for Catholic Retreat Draws More than 300," *Sacramento Bee*, April 11, 1949

"Henrique Jose Reed DaSilva" in Weber, F. J., *Encyclopedia of California's Catholic Heritage* (Mission Hills and Spokane: St. Francis Mission Society and the Arthur H. Clark Company, 2000)

"High Mass for Humbert Slain," *Evening Bee*, August 6, 1900

"Holy Name Rally Expected to Draw Large Crowd on Sunday; Impressive Musical Program Will Be Presented," *Superior California Catholic Herald*, April 27, 1951

"Holy Name Rally to be Conducted Sunday in the Capital," *Sacramento Bee*, January 1, 1932

"Holy Name Societies to Meet Here Sunday," *Sacramento Bee*, January 8, 1930

"How It All Began, Realization of a Dream, the Opening of the Cenacle in Sacramento," *Superior California Catholic Herald*, September 19, 1957

"Hubbard Slips In," *Evening Bee,* November 6, 1895

"Hughes Acts to Stop Propaganda in High School," *Sacramento Bee*, September 12, 1922

"Illustrated Lecture," *Leader*, July 4, 1908

"Impressive Ceremonies at Cathedral Attend Visit of the Apostolic Delegate," *Evening Bee*, May 18, 1903

"Is Hubbard an APA?" *Evening Bee,* October 15, 1895

"Italian Residents Pay Tribute to Humbert," *Evening Bee*, August 9, 1900

"Italian Society Has Re-Union," *Sacramento Union*, June 8, 1908

"Italians Plan Grand Benefit," *Sacramento Union*, March 12, 1909

"Italians Want Language Taught in High School," *Sacramento Bee*, June 8, 1916

"Jones Wins Sheriff Race," *Sacramento Bee,* August 28, 1918

"Jubilant APAs," *Evening Bee,* August 31, 1895

"Klan is Watched While Initiating Sacramento Men," *Sacramento Bee*, April 26, 1922

"Kleagle's List Reveals Names of Autoists Whose Cars Were at Initiation," *Sacramento Bee*, May 18, 1922

"Ku Klux Klan Makes Move to Organize Here," *Sacramento Bee*, April 6, 1922

"L.A. Bishop to Address Local Rally," *Superior California Catholic Herald*, April 20, 1951

"Local Mexican Colony Readies Elaborate Celebration of Virgin," *Superior California Catholic Herald*, December 6, 1956

"Local Mexicans Observe Annual Guadalupe Feast," *Superior California Catholic Register*, December 29, 1946

"M. Diepenbrock Taken By Death," *Sacramento Bee*, January 20, 1928

"Many Fainted in the Crowd," *San Francisco Examiner*, September 17, 1891

"Many Hundreds of Portuguese Join Festival of Holy Ghost," *Sacramento Bee,* May 24, 1909

"Mary Bithell," *Sacramento Star*, July 30, 1912

"Mary E. Bithell, Pioneer is Dead," *Sacramento Bee*, July 9, 1912

"Mary Judge Estate of $140 Goes to Niece," *Sacramento Bee*, July 9, 1946

"Mary Judge is Found Dead in her Home," *Sacramento Bee*, January 25, 1945

"Masonic Lodge Head Deplores Klan Meeting," *Sacramento Bee*, April 26, 1922

"Mayor Hubbard's Candidate," *Evening Bee,* March 12, 1896

"Meeting Held to Plan Erection of a Catholic Church," *Sacramento Transcript*, August 13, 1850

"Memorial Rite for War Dead Will be Held by Catholic Group," *Sacramento Bee*, October 17, 1942

"Mexicans Observe Guadalupe Feast," *Superior California Catholic Register*, December 21, 1930

"Millionaire A. Coolot Passes Quietly Away," *Saturday Bee*, December 1, 1900

"Minister Defends Klan as Necessity," *Sacramento Bee*, May 15, 1922

"Minnie Gormley, Old Sacramento Resident Dies," *Sacramento Bee*, January 2, 1934

"Miss Bowden Left Estate of $200,000," *Sacramento Bee*, November 6, 1926

"More than 1500 Join Holy Name Parade in City," *Sacramento Bee*, January 9, 1933

"Move Made to Rid City Offices of Klansmen," *Sacramento Bee*, May 6, 1922

"Mr. Sanders' Talk," *Evening Bee,* November 4, 1895

"Mrs. Ellen Dwyer Answers the Call," *Evening Bee*, April 30, 1906

"Mrs. Fair's Will," *San Francisco* Chronicle, September 18, 1891

"Mrs. J.W, Mackay's Handsome Donation," *Nevada State Journal*, February 6, 1906

"Names of Members of Sacramento Lodges," *Monitor,* November 3, 1894

"Nettie Hopley Testimonial Dinner is Attended by 540," *Sacramento Bee*, May 23, 1938

"Nettie M. Hopley, Teacher is Dead," *Sacramento Be*e, June 30, 1942

"New Church of New Methodist Episcopal Church," *Daily Bee*, March 8, 185

"New Church of Our Lady of Guadalupe Will be Dedicated," *Superior California Register*, April 8, 1945

"New Stations to Be Blessed Sunday in St. Patrick's Home," *Superior California Catholic Register*, January 14, 1934

"Nine Public Officials in This City Listed as Paying K.K.K. Initiation Fees," *Sacramento Bee*, May 4, 1922

"No Catholics Need Apply," *Evening Bee*, February 20, 1896

"Northern California," *Catholic Herald*, November 1, 1913

"Obsequies of Bishop Manogue," *Sacramento Daily Record-Union*, March 6, 1895

"On European Trip," *Sacramento Star*, July 2, 1907

"Once an accountant at McClellan, Marie Harris Became a Peace Activist," *Sacramento Bee*, December 31, 1996

"Our California Correspondence, July 14, 1854," *Freeman's Journal*, August 19, 1854

"Our Circumlocution Office," *Cathedral Chimes,* February 9, 1889

"Our Country and Our Church," *Daily Record-Union*, February 24, 1891

"Our Lady of Guadalupe Feast to Be Observed; Plan Special Celebration," *Superior California Catholic Herald*, December 10, 1953

"Our Lady of Guadalupe Festival Next Sunday in Catholic Church," undated clipping, c. 1920, from *Yolo Independent*

"Our Lady of Guadalupe," *Catholic Herald*, December 21, 1929

"Outline History of the Cenacle Retreat, 1947–1964," File A11-C-218, Archives of the Cenacle Sisters, Chicago (hereafter ACS)

"Passionist Monastery Blessing This Sunday," *Superior California Catholic Herald*, October 24, 1957

"Pastors' Union," *Daily Record-Union*, October 28, 1890, p. 3

"Personal Rights Violated and Constables Attacked by Ku Klux Klan Members," *Sacramento Bee*, June 12, 1922

"Philos," *Freeman's Journal*, August 29, 1850

"Pioneer Doctor Passes Away," *Sacramento Bee*, November 7, 1902

"Points in the Career of Wm. F. Gormley," *Sunday News,* November 2, 1902

"Police Question Organizer of Klan Here"; "Klan Ideology Exposed, Former Office of KKK Says Order Teaches Racial and Religious Hatred" *Sacramento Bee*, April 11, 1922

"Politics in Pulpits," *Evening Bee*, November 5, 1894

"Portuguese Church Will be Dedicated," *Sacramento Bee*, February 1, 1913

"Portuguese Make a Reply," *Sacramento Bee,* April 22, 1909

"Portuguese Members Strike Against Priest," *Sacramento Union*, April 20, 1909

"Priest Fears Anarchists," *Evening Bee*, April 22, 1907

"Pro Deo, Pro Patria," *Evening Bee,* August 9, 1895

"Prohibition is Denounced by Rev. Guerin," *Sacramento Bee*, January 19, 1920

"Rebecca Coolot, Philanthropical Worker, Dies, *Sacramento Bee*, July 23, 1964

"Record Breaking Crowd Pays Honor to Mary Immaculate," *Superior California Catholic Herald*, May 7, 1959

"Report of Mexican Activities in Sacramento," *Superior California Catholic Register*, December 28, 1930

"Retreat House Festival This Sunday Will Raise Funds for New Wing," *Superior California Catholic Herald*, May 27, 1954

"Rev. Harrison Tells of Talk With Hughes," *Sacramento Bee*, September 14, 1922

"Rev. Harrison Turns Tirade on all who Oppose Ku Klux Klan," *Sacramento Bee*, June 12, 1922

"Rev. Koehne's Sermon: He Preaches the Fifth of His Series Last Night," *Sacramento Daily Record-Union*, May 14, 1894

"Rev. Redburn Calls for Stand Against Everything Catholic," *Sacramento Bee*, June 12, 1922

"Rev. Taulbee's Sermon, *Evening Bee*, July 26, 1895

"Rev. W. E. Harrison Threatens to 'Get' Charles C. Hughes," *Sacramento Bee*, September 13, 1922

"Reverend Brady, Noted Priest to be Laid to Rest," *Sacramento Bee*, October 7, 1929

"Ring Down the Curtain," *Cathedral Chimes,* February 9, 1889

"Robert T. Devlin, Leading Attorney Dies in His Home," *Sacramento Bee*, February 24, 1938

"Sacramentans Give $3500 for Hungarians," *Superior California Catholic Herald*, January 3, 1957

"Sacramento Cathedral Fair," *Monitor*, February 27, 1889

"Sacramento Cathedral," *Monitor,* December 5, 1888

"Sacramento Catholic Schools 'Man of Music' is Dead," *Catholic Herald*, February 12, 1970

"Sacramento Church Erected," *Alta*, September 29, 1852

"Sacramento Did Well," *Catholic Herald*, April 12, 1913

"Sacramento Needs More Americanizing," *Catholic Herald*, April 30, 1921

"Sacramento's Numerous and Beautiful Church Structures," *The Great West* 6 (October 5, 1907)

"Seavey Says Charges too 'Silly for Reply,'" *Sacramento Bee*, June 12, 1922

"Seavey to Ask Council to Oust Ten Klansmen," *Sacramento Bee*, May 18, 1922

"Sheriff's Fight is Tuesday's Hottest," *Sacramento Bee*, August 24, 1918

"Six Ku Klux Klansmen Visit Local Church and Present Pastor with $50," *Sacramento Bee*, April 10, 1922

"Sixty Good Reasons," *Evening Bee*, September 29, 1894

"Solemn Diocesan Eucharistic Congress, Centenary of the First Mass in Sacramento, 185–1950," copy in the Archives of the Diocese of Sacramento

"Spirit of the Time," *Monitor*, April 15, 1893

"St. Francis Choir to Participate in Local Mozart Festival," *Superior California Catholic Herald*, June 21, 1956

"St. Stephen's Story: Hard to Top," *Catholic Herald*, November 11, 1976

"Stations of Cross by Dunbar Beck Installed in St. Rose Chapel," *Sacramento Bee*, January 15, 1934

"The A.P.A. Is In It," *Evening Bee,* September 20, 1895

"The A.P.A. Not Official," *Evening Bee,* October 8, 1894

"The APA Intriguing Against a House of God," "The APA Feature," *Evening Bee,* March 3, 1896

"The APA Ticket," *Evening Bee*, October 14, 1895

"The Catholic Knights," *Evening Bee,* November 26, 1894

"The First Priest to Work in Sacramento," *Superior California Catholic Register*, October 22, 1939

"The German Catholics," *Monitor*, September 21, 1907

"The German Celebration," *Sacramento Union*, February 2, 1871

"The Importance of the Catholic Press," *Catholic Herald*, March 14, 1908

"The Irish Must Go," *Evening Bee,* November 4, 1895

"The Late A. Coolot," *Sacramento Record-Union*, December 2, 1900

"The Late Elections," November 18, 1893

"The New Cathedral in Sacramento," *Monitor*, January 9, 1889

"The Priest and the Flag," *Evening Bee*, May 14, 1894

"Thousands to Attend Christ the King Rally," *Superior California Register*, October 6, 1946

"Topics of the Times," *Monitor*, 27 January 1894, p. 1

"Tremendous Conflagration," *Sacramento Daily Union*, July 14, 1854

"Two Pastors Defend Klan From Pulpit," *Sacramento Bee*, June 12, 1922

"Veil of Secrecy Torn Off Klan Plot," *Sacramento Bee*, November 1, 1922

"Virus of Religious Prejudice Injected into Local Politics," *Catholic Herald*, July 28, 1922

"W. F. Gormley, Undertaker, is Taken by Death," *Sacramento Bee*, July 30, 1935

"Westminster Chimes Will Tell the Hours, *Evening Bee*, December 23, 1901

"Where Angels Fear to Tread," *Monitor*, March 28, 1896

"Woman Gives up Career to Aide Lepers in the Philippines," *Sacramento Bee*, February 11, 1947

"Working Up the APA," *Evening Bee*, March 26, 1894

Amusement, Development, Radio Supplement

Anonymous, *Women of the Cenacle* (Milwaukee: Convent of Our Lady of the Cenacle, 1952)

Archives of the Dominican Friars at St. Albert's Priory, Oakland, California

Archives of the Franciscan Order, Santa Barbara (hereafter AOFMSB)

Augustine McClory to Michael Richardt, November 8, 1894, "St. Francis-Sacramento File," AOFMSB

Avella, S. M., "The Catholic Press as Urban Booster: The Case of Thomas A. Connelly of Sacramento," *U.S. Catholic Historian* 25 (3) (Summer 2007)

Avella, S., *Sacramento: Indomitable City* (Charleston: Arcadia Press, 2003)

Balderrama, F. E. and Rodriguez, R., *Decade of Betrayal: Mexican Repatriation in the 1930s* (Albuquerque: University of New Mexico Press, 1995)

Baptismal Registers, Cathedral of the Blessed Sacrament, Sacramento, California

Bithell Probate, Wills and Probate, CSH

Bowden, E. M., Wills and Probate, CSH

Brother Eugenius to Fr. Provincial, July 12, 1896, "St. Francis-Sacramento File," AOFMSB

Bucchanieri, V. A., "Nevada's Bonanza Church, Saint Mary's in the Mountains" pamphlet (Gold Hill: Gold Hill Publishing Co., 1997)

Burns, J. F. (ed.), *Sacramento: Gold Rush Legacy, Metropolitan Destiny* (Carlsbad: Heritage Media Corporation, 1999)

Cathedral Chimes, February 9, 1889

Catholic Ladies Relief Society, No. 1, Report of the Works in General, October 1, 1926 to October 1, 1927, History Book, 1927–1931, ADS

Chalmers, D., *Hooded Americanism: The History of the Ku Klux Klan* (Duke University Press, 1987)

Chinnici, J., OFM, *Living Stones: The History and Structure of the Catholic Spiritual Life in the United States* (New York: MacMillan, 1989)

Circular of Father Humilis Weise OFM to the parish, December 7, 1919. AOFM SB. St. Francis File

Clementine Deymann to Michael Richardt, November 3, 1894, "St. Francis-Sacramento File," AOFMSB

Clementine Deymann to Michael Richardt, October 19, 1894, "St. Francis-Sacramento File, AOFMSB

Clementine Deymann to Michael Richardt, October 19, 1894, St. Francis File, Archives of the Friars Minor, Santa Barbara Province, California

Clementine Deymann to Michael Richardt, September 28, 1894, "St. Francis-Sacramento File," AOFMSB

Conmy, P. T., *Seventy Years of Service, 1902–1972: History of the Knights of Columbus in California* (Los Angeles: California State Council Knights of Columbus, 1972)

Connolly, E., and Self, D., *Capital Women: An Interpretative History of Women in Sacramento, 1850–1920* (Sacramento: Capital Women's History Project, 1995)

Cooper, A. O., "A History of Westminster Presbyterian Church, Sacramento, California" (Sacramento, Westminster Presbyterian Church, 1966)

Crouch, G., *The Bonanza King John Mackay and the Battle Over the Greatest Riches in the American West* (New York: Scribner, 2018)

Davis, W. J., *An Illustrated History of Sacramento County, California* (Chicago: Lewis Publishing Co., 1890)

Delury, J. F., "Irish Nationalism in Sacramento, 1850–1890," *Golden Notes* 36 (Summer 1990)

Delury, J. F., "Irish Nationalism in the Sacramento Region (1850–1890): Two Paths to Freedom: From Meagher of the Sword to T.P. O'Connor" (unpublished M.A. thesis, California State University, Sacramento, 1985)

Delury, J. F., "Irish Nationalism in the Sacramento Region," *Eire-Ireland* 21 (Fall 1986)

Donovan, J. J., "Recent Work of Dean and Dean Architects," *The Architect and Engineer,* 90 (July 1927)

Doyle, E., "Building the Cathedral," *Catholic Herald,* September 30, 1976

Doyle, E., "The bishop builds his cathedral," *Catholic Herald,* September 16, 1976

Dwyer, J., "Michael Gualco, pioneer priest of Chico," *Catholic Herald,* October 14, 1976

Editorial, *Catholic Herald,* March 28, 1908

Eifler, M., *Gold Rush Capitalists: Greed and Gold in Sacramento* (University of New Mexico Press, 2002)

Eugene Mela to Diomede Falconio, May 6, 1906, Apostolic Delegation Files, IX Diocesi Sacramento, AVA

Eugene Mela to Patrick Riordan, July 23, 1907, Riordan Papers, AASF

Father Leo to Father Prior, May 6, 1894, "St. Francis, Sacramento File," AOFMSB

Father Leo to Michael Richardt, May 6, 1894, AOFMSB

Fragment of a Diary of Doctor J.G. Phelan of Sacramento City, 1850 Biography File, California State Library, Sacramento

Gaffey, J. P., *Citizen of No Mean City: Archbishop Patrick Riordan of San Francisco, 1891–1914* (Consortium Books, 1976)

Gaffey, J., "A critical look at Bishop Manogue," *Catholic Herald,* September 23, 1976

Galarza, E., *Barrio Boy* (Notre Dame, University of Notre Dame Press, 1971)

Godfrey Hoelters to Fr. Commissarius, March 4, 1901, "St. Francis-Sacramento File," AOFMSB

Godfrey Hoelters to Fr. Commissarius, November 15, 1900, "St. Francis-Sacramento File," AOFMSB

Godfrey Hoelters, OFM to Bishop Thomas Grace, February 10, 1909, AOFMSB

Gonzales, M., *Mexicanos* (Indiana University Press, 2019, 3rd ed.)

Gordon, L., *The Second Coming of the KKK: The Ku Klux Klan and the American Political Tradition* (W.W. Norton, 2017)

Gudde, E. G., *German Pioneers in Early California,* Historical Bulletin No. 6 (Hoboken: Concord Society, 1927)

Habig, M., *Heralds of the King: The Franciscans of the St. Louis-Chicago Province* (Franciscan Herald Press, 1958)

Hardwick, S. W., "Ethnic Residential and Commercial Patterns in Sacramento with Special Reference to Russian-American Experience" (unpublished Ph.D. diss., University of California, Davis, 1986)

Harry J. Devine to Joseph T. McGucken, n.d., Mercy Hospital File, ADS

Holmes, L. and D'Alessandro, J., *Portuguese Pioneers in the Sacramento Area* (Sacramento: Portuguese Historical and Cultural Society, 1990)

Hurt, P., "The Rise and Fall of 'Know Nothings' in California, *California Historical Quarterly* Vol. 9 (March 1930)

Interview with Reverend Neil Parsons C.P., Christ the King Retreat House, Citrus Heights, California, August 23, 1999

Jackson, K., *The Ku Klux Klan in the City 1915–1930* (Ivan Dee, 1992)

John Cantwell to Thomas Connelly, August 16, 1909, Thomas A. Connelly to Patrick Riordan, August 19, 1909, Riordan Papers, AASF

John Cantwell to Thomas Connelly, July 28, 1909, Chancery Papers, AASF

Kassis, A., *Prohibition in Sacramento: Moralizers, Bootleggers, and the Wettest City in the Nation* (The History Press, 2014)

Kinzer, D. K., *Episode in Anti-Catholicism: The American Protective Association* (University of Washington Press, 1964)

Kline, C. R., "Patrick Manogue: Priest, Pastor, Bishop, 1831–1895" (unpublished MA thesis, University of California, Berkeley, 1960)

Kouba, J., S.D.S. "The Hispanic Presence in the Diocese of Sacramento," *Catholic Herald*, November 17 and 24, 1986

Larkin, E., "The Devotional Revolution in Ireland, 1850–1875" *American Historical Review* 77 (June 1972)

Lewis, O., *Silver Kings: The Lives and Times of Mackay, Fair, Flood, and O'Brien Lords of the Nevada Comstock* (Reno: University of Nevada Press, 1986)

Manogue to Richardt, August 18, 1893, "St. Francis, Sacramento File," AOFMSB.

McCoy, F. N., "A History of the First Five Years of the Sacramento, California Turnverein, 1854-1859"

McDevitt, V. E., F.S.C., *The First California's Chaplain* (Fresno: Academy Library Guild, 1956)

McGloin, J. B., S. J., "'Philos' (Gregory J. Phelan, M.D., 1822–1902) Commentator on Catholicism in California's Gold Rush Decade," *Records of the American Catholic Historical Society of Philadelphia* 67 (June 1966)

McGloin, J. B., S. J., "Anthony Langlois, Pioneer Priest in Gold Rush San Francisco," *Southern California Quarterly* XLIX (December 1967)

McGowan, J. A. and Willis, T. R., *Sacramento: Heart of the Golden State* (Woodland Hills: Windsor Publications Inc., 1983)

McGowan, J., *History of the Sacramento Valley,* 3 Vols. (New York: Lewis Historical Publishing Company, 1961)

McGuiness, M., *Called to Serve: A History of Nuns in America* (NYU Press, 2015)

Michael Gualco to Diomede Falconio, August 1, 1907, Apostolic Delegation Files, IX Diocesi, Sacramento, AVA

Michael Gualco to Diomede Falconio, June 7, 1910

Michael Gualco to Diomede Falconio, September 24, 1905, Apostolic Delegation Files, IX, Diocesi Sacramento Apostolic Vatican Archives, Rome (hereafter AVA)

Minutes of the Thirty-ninth Session of the Grand Council of the Catholic Ladies Relief Society of the Sacramento Diocese, History Book, 1927–1931, ADS

Mother Hayes to "Reverend Mother" November 23, 1953, Archives of the Sisters of the Cenacle

Mother Ida Barlow to "Dear Reverend Mother, February 21, 1954, ACS

O'Malley, Bro. K., C.P., "A Brief History of the Passionists in Northern California and Western Nevada, 1852–1986," Religious Priests File, ADS

Obituary, "Wilkins Raymond J.," *Sacramento Bee*, June 12, 1983

Obituary, *San Francisco Call*, September 14, 1891

Olson, J. S., "Pioneer Catholicism in Eastern and Southern Nevada, 1864–1931," *Nevada Historical Society Quarterly* 26 (1983): 159–171

Parmisano, F. S., O. P., *Mission West: The Western Dominican Province, 1850–1966* (Oakland: Western Dominican Province, 1995)

Patrick Manogue to Augustine Schulte, April 30, 1885, AASF

Patrick Manogue to Clementine Deymann, September 13, 1894, AOFMSB

Pierini, B., "Germans: A German History of the Sacramento Area," Sacramento Area Ethnic History Survey, 1984, CSH

Pierini, B., "Italian History and Demographics of the Greater Sacramento Area," Sacramento County Ethnic History Survey, 1984, CSH

Renwald, R., "St. Stephen's: Church with eight lives," *Catholic Herald*, November 4, 1976

Sacramento Guidebook (Sacramento: Sacramento Bee, 1939)

Schutz, O. M., "German Catholics in California: The Origins of St. Elizabeth's Parish, Oakland and the Early Move to a Multicultural Parish," *U.S. Catholic Historian* 12 (Summer 1994) (3)

Severson, T., *Sacramento: An Illustrated History: 1839 to 1874* (California Historical Society, 1973)

Spalding, T., *Premier See: A History of the Archdiocese of Baltimore, 1789–1989* (Baltimore: Johns Hopkins, 1990)

Sunday Leader, 4 November 1908, clipping in Gormley family scrapbook

Swift, D. (ed.), *Sacramento County Sheriff's Department, 1850–1877* (Sacramento, Sacramento County Sheriff, 1977)

T. A. Farrell to Robert Armstrong, n.d. 1931, Brady File, ADS

Terry, C. C., "*Die Deutschen Enwanderer* in Sacramento: German Immigrants in Sacramento, 1850–1859" (unpublished MA Thesis, University of Nevada, Las Vegas, 2000)

Terry, C. C., "*Die Deutschen Von* Marysville: The Germans of Marysville, 1850–1860," *Psi Sigma Siren* 1 (January 2003)

Thomas Connelly to Patrick Riordan, April 2, 1907, Riordan Papers, AASF

Thomas Grace to James Cantwell, March 27, 1920, Edward Hanna Papers, AASF

Thomas Grace to Patrick Riordan, April 17, 1905, Riordan Papers, AASF

Transcript of interview with Monsignor Raymond Renwald, by Olivia Wheatley, May 15, 1981, St. Thomas More Parish, Paradise, copy in St. Thomas More File, ADS

U. S. Census of Population, Sacramento, 1910, 1920, 1930, 1940

Vandenbergh, Sister M., R. C. "Attitudes and Events Leading up to the Establishment of Christian Brother's School in Sacramento, 1871–1876" (unpublished MA thesis, Sacramento State College, 1968)

Virginia Ortiz to Robert Armstrong, March 9, 1949, Armstrong Papers, ADS

von Brauchitsch, D. M., "The Ku Klux Klan in California, 1921–1924" (unpublished M.A. thesis, Sacramento State University, 1967)

Warner, M., *Alone of Her Sex: The Myth and Cult of the Virgin Mary* (New York: Alfred A. Knopf, 1976)

Weber, F. J., "Reflections of 'Manhattan'" (1) and (2), *Catholic California: Some Historical Reflections*, Archdiocese of Los Angeles, 1922

Willging, E. P. and Hatzfeld, H., *Catholic Serials of the Nineteenth Century in the United States*, Second Series, Part Eight, California (Washington, D. C.: The Catholic University of America Press, 1964)

Willis, W. E., *History of Sacramento County* (Chicago: Historical Publishing Co., 1925)

Wilson, S. F., "Cleric Preached Against Reds, Dodged Bombs," *Sacramento Bee*, December 8, 1954